WILLIAM MORROW

AN IMPRINT OF HARPERCOLLINSPUBLISHERS

TRAVIS

can i

say

BARKER

WITH GAVIN EDWARDS

LIVING LARGE, CHEATING DEATH, AND DRUMS, DRUMS, DRUMS

AUTHOR'S NOTE:

Sometimes when I'm playing, I scrape my knuckles raw and bleed all over my drum kit. This blood-splatter design is based on my own DNA, scanned by Jayson Fox.

Unless otherwise indicated, all photographs are courtesy of Travis Barker.

FIRST EDITION

Designed by James Iacobelli

Blood-splatter design by Jayson Fox

Title page photograph by Willie Toledo

Chapter title tattoo art by Franco Vescovi

Additional art by Mark Vaillancourt

Library of Congress Cataloging-in-Publication Data has been applied for.

ISBN 978-0-06-231942-5

15 16 17 18 19 OV/RRD 10 9 8 7 6 5 4 3 2 1

DEDICATION

For my family—you made me who I am today.
I'm not proud of everything in this book—
some of it makes my skin crawl with
shame—but it's the truth.
I love you.

CONTENTS

COURTESY OF WILLIE TOLEDO

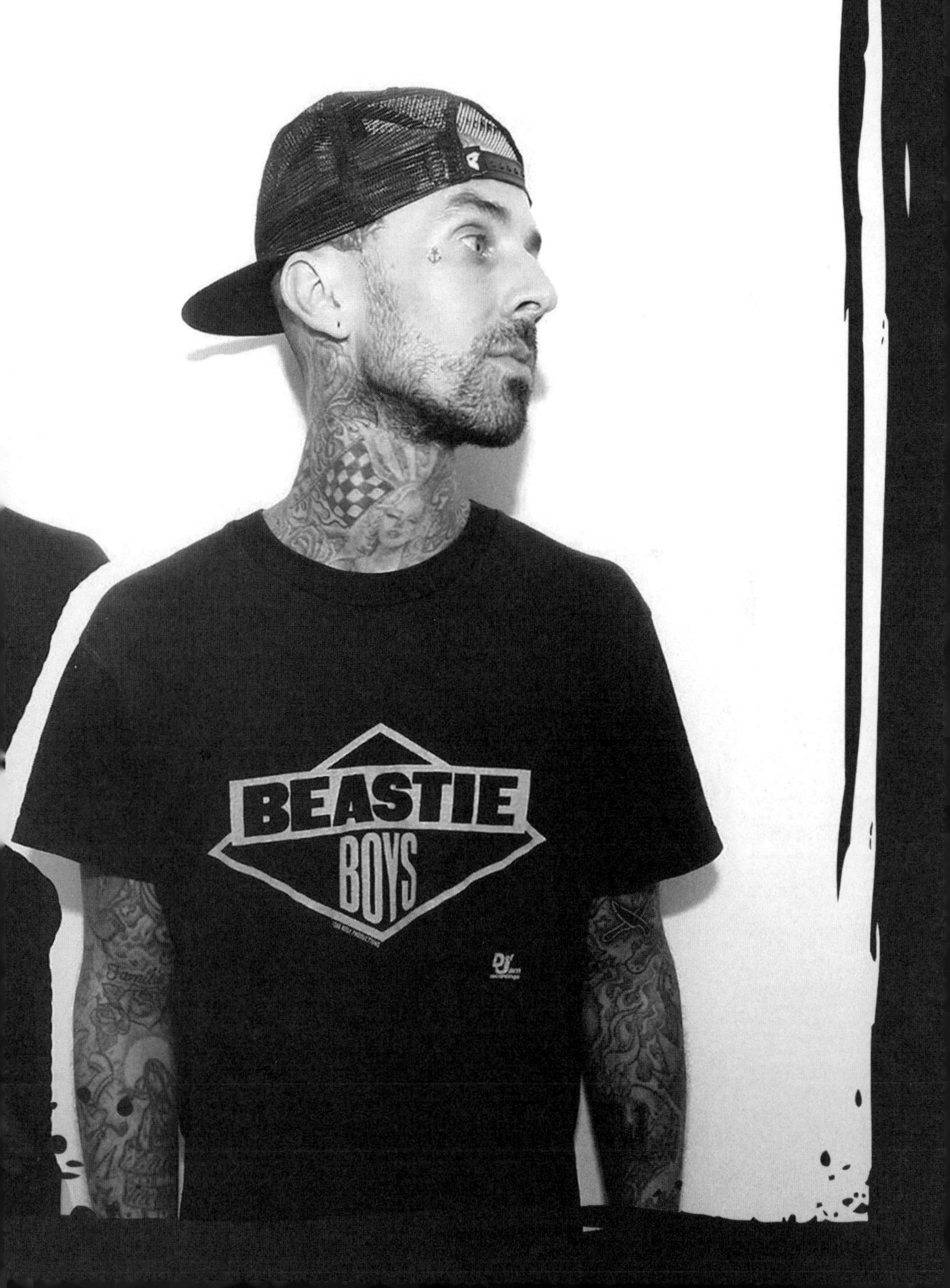

Prologue

I am on fire.

I am running as fast as I can, and I am on fire. The night is dark, but I can see my way, because of the light from my own burning flesh. I have never felt this much pain in my life: it feels like everything inside of my body is boiling and trying to burst through my skin. I am stripping off my clothes as I run across a grassy field, but I am still on fire.

Behind me, I can sense death: a burning airplane that contains the bodies of two pilots and two good friends. Less than a minute from now, it will explode. In front of me, there is a highway. Nothing that is happening feels real, or even possible. If I make it to the highway, I think that maybe I can stay alive. I hear people screaming at me, but I don't know what they're saying. All I care about is trying to survive. I want to see my children, my wife, my father, my sisters. In the final seconds of my life, anything that isn't important goes up in flames. With every step I'm taking, everything in my life is burning away, except for my family. I'm running faster than I knew was possible. I'm running toward the road that will keep me alive. I'm running for love, I'm running for my future, I'm running for my life.

LOVING DRUMS FROM A YOUNG AGE

1

Almost Famous

Animal. He was pure primitive orange insanity, and he was my hero. He would go buck wild, play an awesome drum solo, and then eat his cymbals. The first time I saw Animal on *The Muppet Show*, I wanted to eat my cymbals. I wanted to be a drummer. I was four years old.

My mother and father made sure I got drum lessons, and took me to every single one. My dad drove us, and my mom always sat in the room and taped the lesson. She learned how to read music and hold the drumsticks right; if I didn't understand something, I could always go to her. She was learning as fast as me—when I was a kid, Mom was just as good on drums as I was. But she didn't walk around copying Animal by sticking cymbals in her mouth, the way I did.

Her name was Gloria Marie Rose McCarty, but her friends called her Cookie. She was born September 10, 1947, in Chicago. She had some Osage Indian ancestry. Her half sister was an actress, Mary McCarty, who starred in the original version of *Chicago* on Broadway.*

---

* Mary McCarty played Mama Morton in *Chicago*—the part Queen Latifah played in the movie. And she was nominated for a Tony for a 1977 production of Eugene O'Neill's *Anna Christie*. She was also on the TV show *Trapper John, M.D.*, but she died after the first season.

Cookie met my father, Randall Leonard Barker (born March 12, 1942), in Fontana, east of Los Angeles; they got married and settled down together. They had two girls, Randalai and Tamara, and then, on November 14, 1975, I was born: Travis Landon Barker. I was an accident—Tamara is five years older than me and Randalai is seven years older. I don't know how my mom picked the name Travis, but the Landon was because of Michael Landon, star of *Little House on the Prairie*. She was a huge fan of him (and the Beatles, Elvis Presley, and the Police). If it had been up to her, she probably would have named me Michael Landon Barker. I was a massively obese baby: by the time I was twelve months old, I already weighed thirty-five pounds. My mom would try to give me baths in the sink, but she couldn't even squeeze me in. As I grew up, I got skinnier.

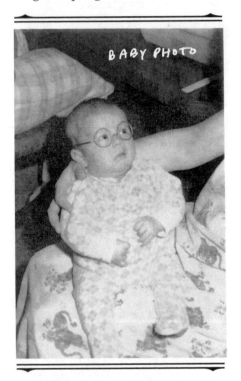

I grew up lower middle-class, but I never knew it. Both Mom and Pops came from nothing. Pops had built our house himself, with a close family friend—he didn't want to have a house payment. He bought some land and said, "I'm going to build this house with my own two hands." When we first moved in, it was like camping out: there were no drapes, no carpet, not even bathrooms or running water. We slept on the floor in sleeping bags. Mom heated water in a coffeepot to wash us.

I was just a toddler when Pops was building it. When I was fifteen months old, I was playing around his construction supplies and a pile of boards fell on my hand, breaking the middle finger on my left hand. My parents had to decide whether to set it straight or crooked. Luckily for

me, they set it crooked—if it had been set straight, I wouldn't be able to play drums effectively and I would have constantly been flipping people off. It's crooked to this day.

I had my own room; there was a TV room and a living room and a kitchen. Pops had been in the army for two years, and served in Vietnam. When he came home, he worked at Kaiser Steel—the steel mill was the main industry in Fontana. And then he was a machinist at different warehouses and factories. He was blue-collar, doing hard labor forty to sixty hours a week. He never stopped working: when he came home, he was doing yard work, fixing the car, or working on the house. And he would never run the air conditioner or the heater, no matter how hot or cold it was.

Pops has always dressed like a greaser. He wouldn't wash his hair for weeks at a time: "Your hair needs natural grease," he'd tell us. He always carried a comb and he was always dressed sharp: an extra-clean white T-shirt and creased jeans. He hung up his jeans on special hangers to keep that crease. He wore black motorcycle boots, and he rode a Harley. If he took me to Sears, I'd ride on the back of his motorcycle, holding on for dear life—but I loved every minute of it.

RANDY BARKER (FATHER)

I grew up in a steel-mill town called Elizabeth, just outside of Pittsburgh. When I was eighteen, my family moved from Pennsylvania to California—we had relatives that lived in Fontana. I was drafted into the army around 1973, and I spent two years in the military: one year in the States and one year in Vietnam. They trained me as a radio teletype operator, but when I went there, they handed me the keys to a jeep and said, "You're a jeep driver." The jeeps were supposed to have radios in them, but they took them out because they said it was unsafe—somebody in the backseat might hit his head on it. So that's pretty much what I did the whole time I was there, driving around. I

DAD AND ME

went over with an engineering outfit and then, about two
months later, I got sent to the Korean Artillery Division
with a liaison team. I wasn't crazy about being in the
armed forces at first, but it's probably an experience that
every kid should go through. Not the war—being with all
kinds of different people from all over the United States
and our territories.

When I got home, all I wanted to do was run around and
have a good time. The first two weeks I was back, I had
five speeding tickets. I had a highway patrolman chase
me to a red light. He said, "I don't know how fast you
were going, but I know damn well you wasn't going the
speed limit. I'm going to write you up for seventy-five."
I took it, because I was going somewhere between ninety
and a hundred miles an hour.

A friend of mine used to have a restaurant in Fontana
called the Red Devil—it served pizza and different
Italian dishes. He sold it, but I still went in there.
I liked a waitress, Cookie—she was a very pretty girl,
and petite. She weighed only ninety-seven pounds. I just
took a liking to her and nobody could change my mind.
Cookie's mother and her uncle were the new owners of the
Red Devil, but she and her mother didn't get along too
well. One night, Cookie just up and left. I asked her
mother, "Where's Cookie at?"

"She left."

So I went out and caught her on her way home, and picked
her up. We drove around for about four hours that night,
just talking, getting acquainted. From that time on, it
developed into a romance. We dated for maybe four or six
months before we got married. I was loafing around, but
before we decided to get married, I thought I'd better find
a job. So I went to work at Kaiser Steel—I started out as
a helper in the machine shop and I moved up from there. I
was always mechanically inclined—I don't know how many
times I was underneath my uncle's car, rebuilding the
engine. I wanted to be a machinist—that was what my dad
was, and he was my hero. (He died when he was sixty-two,
when Travis was about three years old. He had cirrhosis
of the liver: he got hepatitis C from a blood transfusion.)

Cookie told me that when I first started going into the
restaurant, her mother used to say, "Why don't you get
with a nice guy like that?" Of course, after we got
together, she couldn't do nothing but run me down. But
after a while, she knew I was in love with her daughter.

Cookie had a half sister, Mary McCarty, who was an
actress. She had been in the profession since she was a

kid—but we never, ever met her. Cookie didn't want to impose on anybody: "I don't want her to think that we're trying to get friendly with her to help the kids."

During this time I was working at Kaiser, I laid carpet on the side, and I was going to a night college to study air-conditioning. When I came home from work, she would meet me at the door with the kids and say, "This is your dad—he's going to come in, eat dinner, and change clothes, and then he's going off to school. He'll be home sometime after you've gone to bed." It got to the point where she said something had to go. I gave up the school and the laying carpet, although I took a job once in a while.

FIRST DRUM SET

TRAVIS BARKER
can i say

For Travis's first Christmas, we bought him a tin drum. One day, he was sitting on the floor, just beating the daylights out of this drum. My wife looked at him and said, "You know what, I think he's going to be a drummer." So on his fourth birthday, we bought him a full set of drums. We took him to drum lessons: Cookie wasn't crazy about driving, so I was the chauffeur and she would tape the lesson. Then for the rest of the week, she would practice with him with that tape recorder. When he gave her a hard time, I would tell him that he had to listen to her. I was just the driver and the enforcer.

I didn't allow my girls off the block, but I let Travis run the streets. I thought that someday he was going to have to earn a living and support a family, where my girls were supposed to rely on a husband. So he had to be a little more streetwise than they were.

When I was growing up, my mom was very loving, and she was there for me all the time. One of my first memories is falling asleep while she rubbed my head. Mom was a hard, hard worker. She ran a daycare at our house, so every day there were seven to twelve kids there. I loved my sisters and played with them a lot, but there were a couple of times when they dressed me up like a girl. It was cool for me to have some boys around at daycare. We would go outside and ride bikes, play cowboys and Indians, or get on our skateboards.

I knew where my dad kept all his army medals. When I wanted to play cops and robbers, I would go into his closet and put the medals on. I was really stoked to wear his pins, but I lost them all running around. He didn't find out right away—but I knew what had happened, and I felt guilty. He also had a box of pictures from Vietnam: when I asked him about the war, he wouldn't tell me much. But because of the war, he would never keep a gun in the house.

I watched boxing on TV with my dad, but wrestling was my favorite: it was like a soap opera for boys. I loved the Iron Sheik, "Rowdy" Roddy Piper, and George "The Animal" Steele. Junkyard Dog was one of my favorites: he would wear a big chain around his neck and howl when he got into the ring. One time, Pops surprised me and took me to a WWF wrestling event in San Bernardino. It was the highlight of my summer. Junkyard Dog was wrestling that night, and I reached out and touched him after he won his match, getting some of his sweat on my hand.

Basically, I was a boy. I was into skateboarding and BMX. I liked to ride my go-kart all around the neighborhood and drive it into chain-link fences. I was into throwing rocks. I would start fights with my sisters, I would get into trouble, I would talk back to my dad and get whooped. Whenever my dad thought I was getting out of hand, he'd put me in line. I could get away with murder with my mom, but Pops was in charge of discipline.

I never accepted anybody's authority: when Mom would try to get me to do something, a lot of the time I would just argue with her and generally talk back. Then she started secretly recording me with a miniature tape recorder she kept in a drawer in the kitchen. When Pops came home, she wouldn't just be saying I was out of line, she had documentary proof. I learned to fear the tape recorder.

TAMARA BARKER (SISTER)

When Travis graduated from kindergarten, he kept standing up and bowing, even when it wasn't his name being called. He was very comical.

He was also a brat. He would probably deny it, but I remember one time when he was throwing rocks at me in the backyard. When I went inside the house to tell our mom, he denied ever doing it. Another time, he jumped off the fireplace mantel and fell onto the ground—and then he said that I had pushed him.

TRAVIS BARKER
can i say

TAMARA AND ME

More than anything, I loved drumming. Every year in grade school, I would fill out a journal where I would have to say what I wanted to be when I grew up, and I always said I was going to be a drummer in a rock band. There was never a year where I wanted to be a football player or a superhero: there was nothing cooler to me than being a drummer. I had all the other kids around me convinced that I was going to drum in a rock band.

From the moment I first picked up drumsticks, my mom told me I was going to be a rock star. I don't know if she ever had aspirations to be a musician herself, or if she was just trying to encourage me, but she kept telling me that I would be her drummer boy. One Christmas, she made me learn "The Little Drummer Boy" and play it all the time. She would play that song on repeat, hoping it would have some long-lasting effect on me. She played it even when it wasn't Christmastime.

I would have spent every waking hour drumming and skateboarding if I could have, but Mom kept me busy. Once I got home from school, I had to do my homework. Then I had to do what she called "studies," which was extra homework that she fabricated for me to get ahead, or at least stay up to par if I was falling behind in school. (Nothing in class excited me as much as drumming and skateboarding.) She always tried to keep me sharp.

My other extra homework was in catechism class—that was Sunday school, where they taught me about God and the Catholic Church. When I was seven, I had my first Holy Communion. They put the wafer in my mouth and it tasted nasty, so I spat it out. Then they put the wine punch in my mouth. I had been really curious about how that would taste. The answer is that it was disgusting—I spit out the wine too. So I did the Holy Communion, but I was rejecting the body and the blood of Christ. Mom was embarrassed and Pops was furious.

Around that time, I figured out that death was a real thing. I don't know if I saw a movie, or I overheard people talking about someone who died. But I realized that my parents could die, and I freaked out. I just lay on the floor of my bedroom, sobbing hysterically—all I could

think about was that they might die any minute. Mom and Pops tried to reassure me, telling me that nothing was going to happen. But I couldn't shake that feeling.

The first fistfight I ever got into was when I was in third grade—this kid Brandon said that there was no Santa Claus, so I walked up to him and punched him. What made it worse was that later that year, my parents told me that maybe Santa Claus would bring me a real drum set for Christmas. I had been banging on my Muppets toy drum kit, or on pots, pans, and anything else I could find: I was always tapping, tapping, tapping. On Christmas Eve, I stayed up late, and I creeped out to the living room and spied on my parents setting up the drum kit. The next morning, they said, "Look what Santa brought you!"

I said, "You guys are lying to me—I saw you setting that up last night." They were speechless. And then I realized: I socked that kid for nothing! Santa Claus was a hoax!

RANDAL AL AND ME

RANDALAI BARKER (SISTER)

We lived right next to the elementary school. When my brother went to school there, he felt that because he lived two doors down, he could leave whenever he wanted. So he would walk out of school and go home to use the restroom: he liked to use it at home, not at school. My mom would say, "What are you doing home?" and have to walk him back to school. He did this all the time.

When he had sleepovers at friends' houses, maybe they lived across the street or a block or two away. He'd get his stuff together, we'd drop him off, and he'd go spend the night. Around midnight or one in the morning, we would get the call: "Mom, can you come get me? I really just want to come home." Every time. He never spent the night at a friend's house. When I was old enough to drive, I would go out and get him to save my mom and dad the trip. I don't even know why my parents let him go on sleepovers: we knew he was going to be coming home. He just had this thing about sleeping in his bed. If he had friends over for a sleepover, my brother would be in his bed and his friends would be on the floor.

My best friend in elementary school was named Ruben: we both played drums and we started hanging out. We were obsessed with any movie about breakdancing, especially *Breakin'*—we believed we were the real-life versions of the main characters, Ozone and Turbo. I would spend hours in front of the mirror, practicing. We would put on breakdancing shows. He could pop and lock, and I was a good breaker. We'd walk down the street with a ghetto blaster and a cardboard box, and we'd do performances on the side of the streets. We weren't really looking for a crowd, but sometimes cars would honk at us, and that was awesome—that was as much excitement as you could get in my neighborhood.

TRAVIS BARKER
can i say

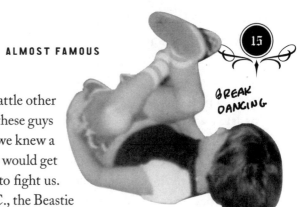

BREAK DANCING

Sometimes we would battle other breakdancers, particularly these guys who lived on our street. If we knew a move that they didn't, they would get really pissed off and want to fight us.

I loved rap: Run-D.M.C., the Beastie Boys, Doug E. Fresh, Slick Rick. I was a huge Whodini fan—I can still recite lyrics from all their songs. But I was also incredibly into metal. I used to put Slayer and King Diamond posters on my bedroom wall, and Mom would tear them off because she thought they were satanic. Sometimes I would buy a poster from Sound City, the local record store, and it wouldn't even make it twenty-four hours on my wall.

There wasn't a lot to do in Fontana. In my neighborhood, there were some houses to the left and some apartment buildings to the right—there was always trouble happening at the apartments. Up the street, there was a car wash and a place called the Golden Ox Burger. It was a tough city: there were shootings and stabbings at the Golden Ox. Behind us, there was an old house where a bunch of bikers and Hell's Angels lived. They were cool, though.*

There always seemed to be construction crews putting up more apartment buildings in my neighborhood. I would go onto the construction sites after hours and steal wood so we could build launch ramps for our skateboards and BMX bikes. There were almost always big mounds of dirt on those sites, so we would turn them into bike tracks. One time, I climbed the fence at a construction site and jumped off it, right onto a board with a nail sticking out of it. The nail went completely through my foot and was sticking out of my shoe on the top side. The board was attached to me. I freaked out and walked home with the wood stuck to me. Pops yanked it off, but then I had to go to the hospital to get a tetanus shot.

---

* The Hell's Angels actually were founded in Fontana. And Al Capone used to have a house in Fontana, with a big *C* on the chimney—there were rumors that it had underground tunnels in case he ever needed to make a getaway.

When Ruben and I were bored, we would skate down to the local 7-Eleven, which also had a gas station, plus a nook where they had two or three arcade games. There was a machine with a high-pressure air hose so people could inflate their tires for a quarter; we discovered that its latch wasn't working. So we would grab all the quarters from this machine and buy Slurpees and candy and play video games. Then we escalated: if there weren't quarters and we wanted some, we'd wait until somebody went inside the 7-Eleven, and then we'd hustle over to their car and deflate as many of their tires as we could before they came back. Whenever a customer came into that 7-Eleven, they got at least one flat tire. If we had money left over, we'd buy magazines—our favorites were *Circus*, *BMX Plus!* and *Thrasher*—or go to Rick's Bicycle City where we could buy stickers for our bikes. This scam worked for about two weeks—and then one day there was a new lock on the machine and it was over.

I had a crazy streak, and I was infatuated with fire. Fireworks, pyrotechnics, seeing explosions on TV. I had a friend named Richie whose family had money—they owned a hot-rod shop one town over from Fontana. So he had the nicest house of anybody I knew. I was over at his place one afternoon, and we started playing with hair spray and a lighter, doing one of those homemade flamethrowers. And we managed to light the living room drapes on fire. Smoke alarms were going off, and his family's maid was freaking out in Spanish. Richie and I pretended we didn't have anything to do with it, and somehow we got away with it.

Around that same time, Mom took us kids on a trip to Chicago to visit her family. Pops had to work, so he stayed home. That was the first time I was ever on an airplane, and I found out Mom was terrified of flying. She was crying, almost frantic, and because I could see she was afraid, I got scared too. That was the beginning of my fear of flying.

Once we got to Chicago, I started running wild with my cousins. The first thing I did was toilet-paper the entire neighborhood. Then I wanted to light something on fire—and there was a church next door to the house where we were staying. I got some hair spray, just like the time I burned the drapes at Richie's. I also found a can of gasoline—I was looking for anything flammable—and I went over to the church property with my cousins. They were telling me not to do it, but I started a fire. I didn't pick that church for any religious (or anti-religious) reason: it was just that it was big and convenient. Nobody was around the church at night, so I started burning some grass and weeds that were right next to it. I used a little hair spray to get it started, but the grass was pretty dry. Pretty quickly, the church caught fire—it went from me thinking "Fire, fire, fire" to "Shit, it's on fire." I bolted. The church didn't burn down to the ground, but it was seriously damaged; the fire department came and had to put it out. Neighbors came over to see what was going on, and I acted like I didn't know anything about it.

Before I left Chicago, I cut the electricity to my cousins' house. Twice. I denied everything, but they knew it was me—none of that stuff was happening before I showed up. Without Pops around, I was running wild, and I just wanted to find out how much I could get away with. How far could I take it? I think Mom knew I was making trouble, but she never told Pops because she knew the repercussions would be insane.

Mom cooked really good Italian food like gnocchi and manicotti. And if I was good all week, she'd reward me with tapioca pudding—a favorite for me and my dad. But starting around the age of ten, I didn't like to eat meat. It wasn't a big ethical thing for me—I don't think I really understood at that age that I was eating a cow, or eating a pig. I just didn't like the texture. But I never wanted to hurt her feelings, and I couldn't leave the dinner table until my plate was clean, so I would hide most of the meat from my plate in my pockets and throw it away later. Sometimes I would forget it was there and put the clothes in the laundry. Then she'd get so bummed: "What is this meat doing in the washing machine?"

We ate dinner every night at five o'clock: the kids would be home from school, Pops would get home from work, and we'd sit down together. But one time Pops didn't make it home. My mom waited for a while, worrying, and then she started calling the hospitals: "Is there a Randy Barker there?" We were afraid that he'd had an accident on his Harley, because he drove that thing like a wild man (at least when I wasn't on it). And sure enough, he had taken a spill, but he was so tough he didn't want to call home to let us know he was in the hospital.

FIRST SKATEBOARD

My mom hated that motorcycle: she was scared to death Pops would kill himself on it. Sometimes she'd push it out into the front yard and put a FOR SALE sign on it. Pops would say, "Goddamnit, what are you doing? That's my bike. You're not selling it." No doubt about it, he loved his Harley-Davidson.

Another time, Pops was late for dinner, but the hospital called us: "We have your husband, Randy Barker, here. He had a heart attack. Do you want to come down to the hospital?" But Pops didn't want us to come down: he insisted he was fine and refused to see a heart specialist. Pops was always tough as nails.

When I was in fifth grade, there was a kid in my neighborhood who had an ill half-pipe in his backyard. I wanted to skate on it, and he gave me a challenge: I had to learn to play *Master of Puppets* by Metallica front to back, or I couldn't come skate with him and his friends. It took me a week and a half to get Lars Ulrich's parts down—and then I had a pass into that backyard.

I started skateboarding with my sisters' hand-me-downs: little orange plastic skateboards. Then my parents got me a Kamikaze skateboard at Price Club, which was fatter and wider. I started learning to do tricks on that board, but it was such a generic board, real skaters would make fun of you if you showed up with it at the skate park. Our local skate park was called Upland Pipeline, which was about half an hour away by car; sometimes Pops would drive me over. There were always pros skating there. My first true skateboard was a Brand X, but I kept upgrading. After that I got a Vision Psycho Stick, and I was obsessed with Powell Peralta. I liked skateboarding so much, I started selling drums and cymbals from my drum kit to get money for new skateboard parts. At the time, none of my friends were playing musical instruments, so I didn't know anybody to start a band with.

We explored every neighborhood near us, trying to find cool places to skate and good curbs to rail-slide on. Around this time, my friend Matt and I started smoking: we'd pick up cigarette butts that weren't burnt all the way down and smoke them for a quick head rush. We thought we were so cool, sitting around after we finished skateboarding for the day, talking about who had pulled off what trick, smoking used cigarettes.

There was a Pic 'N' Save warehouse right by our house—a distribution center for the discount store—and the property had a ditch that we would skate sometimes. It was a really popular skate spot, but it was fenced off, so you had to push open a gate or break the bolts to the gate. Every couple of weeks, Pops would drive me and my friends over to the warehouse, which was awesome—he was so supportive of me skateboarding, he turned a blind eye to the trespassing. We'd load up our '79 Buick with six or seven of my friends, with all of our boards in the trunk. When we got there, there'd usually be twenty to thirty people skating in the ditch. Sometimes the cops would show up—they'd arrest people if they didn't clear out fast enough. Pops wouldn't be cutting the chain-link fence for us, but he was cool about making a quick getaway.

Skateboarding was awesome—it always seemed like skateboarders had the best taste in everything. I watched the movie *The Search for Animal Chin* over and over. I had skateboard posters on my walls, I listened to skate rock 24/7*: basically, I wanted total skateboarding immersion. I didn't want to wear anything but skateboarding clothes: the fashion then was longer shorts where the bottom half would be a different fabric. But they were hella expensive, so Mom made me a lot of them herself. We'd buy fabric from the store and then Mom would make them with her friend Twyla, who was a seamstress. My mother never drank or smoked her entire life, but Twyla smoked constantly. So if I came home from school and smelled cigarettes in the house, that meant Twyla was over and I'd be getting a ton of new shorts.

I would write messages like SKATE OR DIE or SKATE AND CREATE or band names like FACTION on my sneakers, which were usually Vision Street Wear. I didn't usually have nice shoes, but one time, Mom and Pops got me the new Air Jordans. (They were always cool like that: they'd spend their last penny on me.) One afternoon, I was at a local burrito place called Baker's—for $1.07, you could get a burrito, fries, and a drink. These eight cholos came in and stole my Jordans. I rode my bike home barefoot. And I never wanted Jordans again.

* Suicidal Tendencies, Agent Orange, DRI, JFA, TSOL.

My parents wanted me to do as much musically as I could. I sang in a madrigal choir at school for three or four years, just like my sisters had, and that was pretty fun. I took piano lessons for a while, the only instrument I ever studied aside from drums: I had to practice every day. So I'd be out skateboarding in the street, and Mom would call, "Travis, get home, you have piano lessons."

I was really embarrassed: playing drums was so much cooler than playing piano. The piano wasn't as masculine. When I was drumming, I was hitting shit. I'd pretend I didn't hear Mom, and I'd tell my friends, "She's not talking to me, she must mean my sister."* One time, my sister Randalai came out in the street to tell me it was time for piano lessons. I was so mad, I shot my skateboard off the launch ramp—right into Randalai's shin. And then I felt guilty—it wasn't her fault I hated piano.

As far back as I can remember, I was girl crazy. I had a girlfriend named Toni: we both loved metal, from Slayer to Guns N' Roses. I carved her name into my leg with a razor blade, and she did the same with my name. It wasn't a suicidal move—it was just a way of marking myself up before I started getting tattoos.

When I was eleven, I went to a party at Ruben's house—his sister was older, and she liked Jane's Addiction and listened to KROQ, which was the cool radio station. At this party, I was trying to mack on one of his sister's friends, who was about five years older than me. I was trying to impress her, so I was drinking beer and smoking weed. And I couldn't handle it—I turned green. It was terrible. Mom and Pops had to come get me from the party, and when they asked why I was sick, I told them I had too much soda and potato chips.

The first live show I ever went to was at a nearby church: they used to host Christian metal bands like Stryper. My sisters took me along, and it blew my mind. I loved seeing a drummer play live, no matter what kind

---

* Now when I'm producing tracks, I kick myself and wish that I had practiced piano more—I can play just enough to lay down chord progressions, but I'm nowhere as fluent on the piano as I am on the drums. It's never too late to improve, though. And I can't sing as well as I did when I was young, but I could still probably hold down vocals in a punk-rock band.

of music. Not long after that I went to see Stacey Q, who had a hit with "Two of Hearts"—I had a big crush on her. I also was in love with Belinda Carlisle. Soon I was going to a nearby club called Spanky's Café—it was basically a punk-rock venue, and I got to see the Minutemen and 411 there.

When I got to junior high, Ruben and I were still homies. We started spending more time with this other kid, Dick. He was cool, and he had a lot of older friends. When we were thirteen, one friend of his, Chucky, was a badass metal dude: long hair, denim jacket with Metallica, Ozzy, and Slayer patches on it. Sometimes we would go riding BMX bikes with him. Somebody would look at Chucky wrong, and Chucky would fight him right then and there. He didn't care if he won or lost, but most of the time he won. I thought he was really brave: if you picked fights like that, you could never be sure of how good the other guy could fight or what weapon he might be carrying.

After school, I would go over to Dick's house—his uncle would be hanging out, listening to Ozzy Osbourne and smoking weed. We'd get his pipe and he'd let us smoke with him. I don't even know if I was inhaling properly, but I know I smoked weed every day in sixth and seventh grade.

By age thirteen, I was staying out all night sometimes. Me and Dick and Ruben and our friend Ozzy (not Osbourne) would pull the classic trick: we'd each tell our parents that we were staying at another friend's house, and then we'd go out hitchhiking and causing trouble. We were just assholes sometimes, throwing rocks at cars. One time, we saw a bright yellow Corvette and we spray-painted it black.*

A couple of times, I stayed out all night and got caught—the sun would come up around the time I was riding home on my skateboard. My dad would be out and about at seven A.M., and he'd spot me five miles from our house. "Get over here!" he'd tell me. "I've been looking for you all night! Why aren't you at your friend's house?"

---

* I believe in karma. Everything you do comes back during your life—for me, usually not in the same way I acted out, but it comes back. The moments that change your life may seem random at the time, but I don't think they really are.

TRAVIS BARKER
can i say

"I was just there, Dad—I was heading home." When I was young I thought I could outsmart any adult.

He wouldn't buy it. "Get in the car!" And then *bam!* He put the whooping on me in the car on the way home. There were many times when the side of my face hit the passenger window while he was smacking me for staying out all night—and I would keep talking back, lying about what I had been doing all night. I deserved every bit of it.

I was the prince of the seventh grade. Ha, ha—no, really. That's not just a metaphor: there was a vote where seventh graders elected the prince and princess for the homecoming dance, and the winners were me and my soon-to-be girlfriend Amber. I was crazy about Amber—she was super hot, with amazing green eyes, and she had already developed breasts. We quickly became boyfriend and girlfriend, but we weren't together that long. We had a very sweet relationship, just kissing and making goo-goo eyes at each other. I was on top of the world: I had a good girlfriend, I was spending a lot of time drumming and skateboarding with my ninth-grade friends who dressed like pirates (they looked like they were part of the Alva team), and life seemed super cool.

In junior high, I did marching band—at that age, it's usually pretty lightweight, compared to high school. We had gotten wind of how seriously they took marching band in high school, so we decided to start preparing early. Our drum line was really badass: we went for blood. Whenever there was a competition or a drum battle, we won it.

I also had my first rock band in junior high. It was called Necromancy: me and my friend Steve played metal covers, mostly King Diamond.* We'd plan all week—*let's play on Saturday*—and then we'd set up our equipment in my backyard and play really loud. We had a couple of original songs, but usually we were covering Metallica, Slayer, Megadeth, anything like that. Most of the time there wouldn't be anybody listening to us, but we didn't care.

---

* King Diamond is a Danish metal singer who started an excellent band (named after himself) in the mid-eighties.

I did some gigs with a punk-rock band that didn't have a name. From the first time I heard punk rock on my skate-rock compilations, I loved it—and then, one day after school, three skinheads came up to me. They were ninth graders, a couple of years older than me. They knew I played drums, and they asked, "Can you play this beat?" Just the most basic boom-chick-boom-boom-chick rhythm. Yeah, I can play that beat. "Can you play it fast?" Oh, yeah. "Will you join our band?" Okay, sure. They had the full skinhead uniform: twenty-hole Doc Martens and braces.* We had one rehearsal before our first gig, which was at some block party. I didn't own Docs or braces, so they told me to wear jeans and a white T-shirt. I showed up at the gig thinking, I hope these guys are sharps—skinheads against racial prejudice—and not racist skinheads, because when they're singing, I can't understand what the fuck they're saying. But they turned out to be cool. I did only a couple of shows with them, but it was really fun.

If you wanted me to play drums in your band, all you had to do was ask. That was how I ended up playing in Jynx, a bad metal band whose primary influences were Poison and Dokken. We played at a battle of the bands at Spanky's—as usual, we spent weeks before the show handing out flyers. The winner that night was an unsigned band called No Doubt. I was totally in love with Gwen Stefani, putting me about eight years ahead of the rest of the USA. That night, I was standing outside Spanky's and she asked me for a lighter.

I wished so badly I had one so I could make conversation with her, but I had to say, "I don't smoke."

"Me either," Gwen said.

I was still singing in the madrigal choir, and it had mixed grades—I was in seventh grade, but there were ninth graders in there. One of them was this superfine cheerleader named Lorelei. I would be staring at her during rehearsals, and she was always telling friends of mine, "Travis is cute" or "I have a thing for Travis." Even though she couldn't have been clearer, I thought she was just building up my confidence. I could tell she was out of my league. But we started writing each other letters,

---

* Suspenders.

and she told me that I should come over to her house one night when her parents would be gone. Around two in the morning, I rolled over on my skateboard with Dick, Ruben, and Ozzy. Lorelei's parents were home, but the family had a trailer parked in the backyard, so she snuck out of the house and we went in the trailer—the other guys just kept skateboarding in the street.

Lorelei and I made out forever, and then I had sex for the first time. I had no idea what I was doing. She basically had to tell me, "No, put it in here." I made a mental note: a vagina felt like hot jelly. It was over in five minutes. I remember being amazed—I was crazy about this girl. She was this hot older chick, and I couldn't believe she was into me, let alone that I'd be losing my virginity to her.

I walked home with Dick, Ruben, and Ozzy, not even skateboarding, carrying our skateboards, talking and laughing the whole way, me giving my friends all the dirty details. I remember thinking, "I fucking did it. I had sex! It's not a big deal—I don't care if I ever do it again." That last part was a lie, obviously. I got home around five or six in the morning, as the sun was coming up. There was no way I was sleeping after what had happened. I lay in bed, staring at the ceiling, wide awake. The whole world felt different, except it looked the same.

And then a few weeks later, I did Lorelei dirty. I basically never spoke to her again. I don't even know why, but I wasn't hot for her anymore. I wasn't staring at her; I just didn't care about her. I was on to the next girl. I just snubbed her. She got back at me, though—she wrote me a letter telling me that she was pregnant, that it was fucked up that I hadn't spoken to her, and that I had better get in touch with her. She really had me shook: I thought I was about to be a thirteen-year-old father. But it was an evil joke for being an asshole. I totally deserved it.

I would say that she set me straight, except I didn't learn my lesson. That became my pattern: I wanted to get the girl, have sex with her, and then be over it and go on to the next one. I don't know why I did that—maybe I just liked the challenge? Maybe it was like Pringles, where I couldn't stop after one taste? I had a lot of girls that went from being absolutely in love with me to thinking I was an asshole. I thought I was the shit because I was blowing through all these girls.

There were a couple of girls, Tawny and Miranda, that both Dick and I liked. Tawny was talking to both Dick and me, but she didn't consider either of us to be her boyfriend. At night, I would sneak out of my house and go over to Tawny's house. She'd come outside, and then we'd make out. One day, I got a call from her during the daytime, which never happened: "Yo, come on over." I thought there was something weird about the situation, but I got on my bike and rode over.

Once I got to Tawny's house, I got jumped by Chucky and a bunch of Chucky's older friends. Somebody blindsided me and knocked me down. I was getting kicked around, and then somebody picked me up and mashed my face into a chain-link fence. Dick was just standing there, watching all of this, which pissed me off even more than if he had been beating me up himself. I should have told him what was going on with Tawny and me, but I didn't think she was his girl. Obviously, he disagreed. And she was willing to set me up, which shocked me. I never spoke to Dick, Tawny, or Chucky again. When I was on the wrong end of a Chucky beating, he seemed more like a psychopath than a badass. The main thing I learned from the whole experience was that I needed to watch who I trusted. Or maybe that I couldn't trust anybody.

My biggest problem at that time was that I was getting picked on by jocks. One kid was like fourteen years old, but he was already six foot four with a full mustache. He would walk up behind me, smack my head as hard as he could, and then just keep walking. I went to my dad and told him that I was being bullied; he said, "Hit him back," but I didn't even know how to fight. I wrote JOCKS on my skateboard and then put a big X through it to show that I hated them.

Some of my skateboarder friends started to hang out with the jocks that were always bullying me. I got invited to a party that had a lot of that crowd. I felt defeated by the whole situation: well, since half my friends are going, and they seem to be turning into football players, whatever, I'll go and hang out. Fuck it, what's the worst that can happen? At the party, we were all swimming in the pool, and three of these jocks jumped me and almost drowned me. I guess they thought I needed to be initiated in order to hang out with them. They were beating the shit out of me and holding me down—I fought back and got my head above the water again. That was my wakeup call. From that point on, besides Ruben, those so-called friends of mine that I grew up skateboarding with—I told them to fuck off.

The summer before I started high school, Mom figured out that Pops was having an affair. She hired a private investigator who followed him around and confirmed it, and then everything went to hell. All my life, it had felt like everything was perfect in our house, but now late at night, I could hear my parents arguing through my bedroom walls. I stayed up all night, listening. It was surreal—I couldn't believe this was my life now. The whole thing made me sad, angry, and confused.

I had a lot of anger toward Pops. I was only thirteen, but I tried to tell him that he couldn't live in our house: "You're not allowed here no more."

Soon after that bombshell, Mom got sick. She thought she just had a sore neck, so she was putting a heating pad on it. But she wasn't getting better: she was tired all the time, and her mouth was so dry, it was hard for her to talk. It turned out she had Sjögren's syndrome, which is a disease where your immune system attacks your own body. When they finally figured it out, she went into the hospital. Mom didn't want people outside the immediate family to know she was hospitalized: she didn't want people visiting her and just feeling sorry for her.

Pops was always at work or visiting Mom in the hospital at this point. But our white '79 Buick was sitting in the driveway, and I knew where the car keys were. I drove it around the block, just barely able to work the pedals and see over the dashboard. Nothing bad happened, so the next day I drove it down to the 7-Eleven and I bought a Slurpee. I kept going farther away from home until after a week, I was crossing a two-lane highway.

I crept out into traffic, and the cars on the highway slammed on their brakes. I drove across the highway, and behind me I could smell smoke and burning rubber and hear cars crashing into each other. There was a major pileup, and it was my fault. I drove home as fast as I could and never went joyriding again. I was rebelling and abusing my newfound freedom—I wouldn't have done it if I hadn't been pissed off and heartbroken. I had never been away from Mom that long in my life.

I thought Mom would be coming home from the hospital quickly. Every day, I waited for the door to open and for her to walk in and say everything was okay. But she went downhill incredibly fast—she had been misdiagnosed for a while, and her body had basically destroyed its own glands.

All that summer I went to the hospital with my family every day to see my mom. It hurt so bad to see her so weak and helpless. I wanted to help her but there was nothing I could do. She became unresponsive, and when I visited her, I would sit there, watching her fade in and out of consciousness, just lying there. The day before school started, my family was driving over to visit her, but I wanted to ride my bike. I got on my Schwinn beach cruiser and arrived about an hour after everybody else. When I walked into the hospital room, everyone was crying hysterically—I knew what had happened before anybody could say anything. She had passed, and I had just missed her. My mom was dead.

It was an open-casket funeral. I wasn't ready to see Mom lying there, ice cold, with an unfamiliar formaldehyde smell. I walked up to the casket feeling a weight in my stomach and an emptiness in my heart I had never felt before. I gave her a last kiss good-bye and touched her hand. Her body was cold. The whole day of the funeral, I felt like I wanted to kill somebody, or maybe die myself. I regretted every argument the two of us had ever had. I was trying to block out everything that happened. I felt like I was trapped in a bad movie—I couldn't imagine life without her.

Everyone in my family was weeping, even Pops, who I had never seen cry before. That broke my heart. I was trying to be tough the whole day, but when my aunt Nan came over to me, she said, "I'm sorry, Travis"—and then I busted out crying too.

One of the last things Mom told me was, "No matter what, play the drums. Keep doing it, no matter what anybody else says. Don't stop playing the drums, Travis. Follow your dreams."

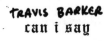
TRAVIS BARKER
can i say

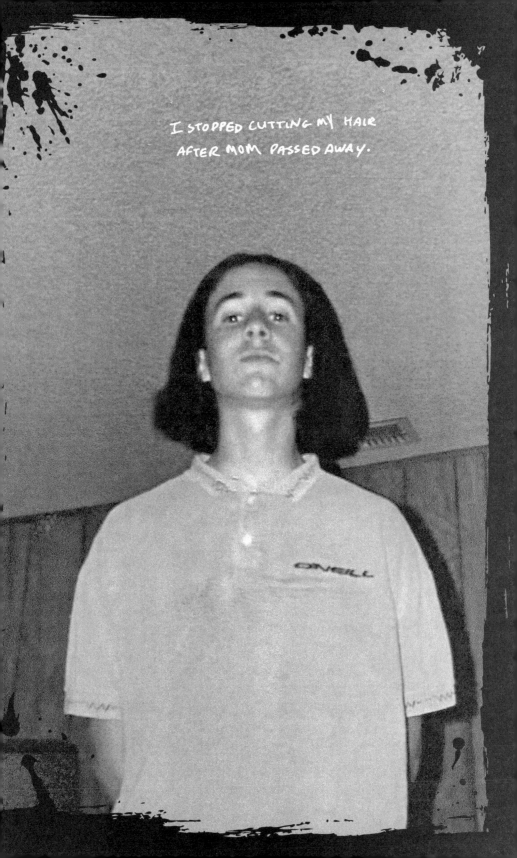

I STOPPED CUTTING MY HAIR
AFTER MOM PASSED AWAY.

OFFICIAL DRUMLINE PHOTO

2

What's my age again

Mom died the day before high school started. I missed the first day of school and showed up on the second day, extremely depressed, walking around the hallways in a daze.

I had been planning on joining drum line, the army of drummers in the school marching band. If you wanted to do that, you were supposed to go to practices all summer long. They were very strict about that: they told you that if you didn't participate in summer rehearsals, you wouldn't be allowed to try out for drum line. But with my mom being so sick, I had never showed up for a single practice and I had never even gotten the sheet music. After my first day of school, I went to the band room. I told them I had spent all summer being with my mom in the hospital, and asked if I could please try out anyway. They were decent about it and let me audition. I hadn't played drums all summer long, and I had never learned the exercises that everybody else had been working on, but my mom's words were resonating in my head: *Play the drums, don't stop, follow your dreams.*

The next day, they announced who was playing what: I had gotten second snare, which meant that I had beaten out everyone except for one senior. All the other kids in band were pissed at me, but I didn't care.

Around then, I started to take pride in being a loner. I didn't give a fuck what anybody around me said or thought. It was me and my drums. Even though I was blind with grief, I could see how all the kids around me were joining up in cliques. In high school, nobody seemed to be skateboarding: football players and other jocks ruled the school. And if you weren't a jock, then you were a gangster—but I didn't belong to either group.

I was barely passing my classes—I got lousy grades. The only reason I didn't fail was because my teachers knew I was at an all-time low after my mom passed away. I was drowning, but the drums gave me something to hang on to. My attitude to everyone around me was "Fuck you, I'm playing music." Kids could try to bully me, teachers could try to get me to care about their classes, and none of it mattered to me. I almost had a death wish. It was a relief to have only one thing in the world that I cared about, and to know that there was no way it would ever go away. That was my love for drumming.

When you love playing music, you have to sacrifice being cool. You have to sacrifice having a dope car in high school, or a stereo system, or new clothes. You have to be willing to show up at practice wearing the same clothes you wore for the last two years, and to be fine with it, and make it work. When you're passionate about something, you don't even care about all the other stuff—it just goes away.

During games and competitions, the whole marching band would play together, but during the week, we had separate practices for groups of instruments. That meant the twelve of us on the drum line spent a lot of time together—just us and a couple of great instructors.

One of the instructors was my cousin Scott—we weren't super close because he was so much older than me, but we had played drums together on holidays when we had the family over.* Some of my relatives didn't bother to hide their contempt for me. Not long after Mom died, my

---

* I still see him when the family gets together and we talk about the old times. He loves playing drums as much as I do.

family went to dinner at an uncle's house, and one of my relatives was just talking trash about me. "Did you see what Travis and his friends did? There's writing all over the wall on Alder Boulevard."

I laughed—just because there was graffiti, what made him think it was me and my friends? "Well, I just assumed it was those idiots you hang out with." He'd make fun of the way I dressed and always assume we were up to no good. It was like he was determined to teach me that I was better off not hanging out with my own family.

The drummers were my people. Drummers are the troublemakers in just about any situation, and we were all together, having a blast. Drumline practice was intense: some days we'd be hammering away for four hours. Then afterward I'd go into this tiny band room with my best drumline friends: Kevin, Richard, Brian, and Jay. We'd put our snares away, start blasting something heavy like Slayer or King Diamond, turn off the lights, and then just start moshing in this little room. We'd be slamming into each other, fucking each other up. We thought we were so cool.

I didn't realize how much I depended on my mother until she was gone. I was a mama's boy, and I knew I leaned on her emotionally—but I didn't think about all the things she did for me. Then a couple of days after her funeral, I woke up and there was no breakfast on the table. I had to make it for myself. My mom had always done my laundry, helped me with my homework, made my bed for me—now I had to make my bed, and Pops would inspect it. He had military standards—he wanted to be able to bounce a quarter off the bed. He was slowly turning me into a man.

Pops and I have called each other "pal" as long as I can remember—unless he was pissed at me. When we talked, there wasn't a lot of "How you doing, Trav? How's school? Love you, pal." It was more like, "Did you do your homework?" And then he'd walk away. Once I challenged him: "Can't you ever just say something without telling me what to do? One time, could you ask me 'What's up?' or 'How was your day?' or just 'How you doing?' Whenever you talk to me, you're yelling at me." I knew

Pops loved me—acting like that was just the way he was. He wasn't much of a talker—but then again, I wasn't much of a listener.

I went to church and asked a priest why God would take my mom. I didn't understand why it would happen, or what I was supposed to do: "If you guys have all these answers written down in the Bible, why do I have no answer now?" He didn't really answer my question, not that he could have. I still believed in God, but after that, I only went to church if someone passed away or got married.

RANDALAI BARKER (SISTER)

Our mother was one of those mellow, easy-going people. I remember her on the phone with her siblings—she was always laughing when she talked to them. It was a happy, feel-good kind of laughing. Unlike my dad, who has this laugh where you laugh because you're almost embarrassed. It's hilarious: Dad, don't be laughing out in public.

We watched musicals all the time in our house, and Elvis Presley movies. And we got stuck watching Lawrence Welk with my parents. We were big on shows with music, like *The Monkees* and *The Partridge Family*. And *Star Search*.

After our mother passed away, Travis and I didn't get along at all for a while. I think the two of us hated each other. For myself, being the oldest, it was hard knowing that I needed to be that mother figure, even though I was twenty-two.

My sisters always looked out for me after Mom passed away, and even took me to my drum lessons. It took me a long time to think about what the rest of my family was going through after Mom died—at thirteen, all I knew was my own pain, but I wasn't the only one suffering. I heard that somebody had spotted Pops standing on a freeway overpass. I don't know if he was thinking about jumping, but he was definitely going through some issues. Understandably. But the last thing I wanted was to lose him too.

Not long after Mom died, Pops moved his girlfriend, Mary, in with us. That hurt so bad—it was like proof that Mom was gone. Soon after Mary moved in, she and Pops were looking through my mom's closet, figuring out which of those clothes she wanted to keep. I freaked out. I was so afraid she would end up wearing my mom's outfits, I took an armful of clothes out of the closet, snuck them out of the house, and threw them into a trash can at the nearby elementary school. Then I lit them on fire.

I wasn't even angry at Mary—I was being protective of Mom's memory. But money was tight and the situation was just rotten. My sisters and I never conspired against Mary, or even sat around talking shit about her, but I wasn't ready to have her—or anybody else—in the house yet.

Then Pops lost his job. He and Mary had been working at the same place, and people there figured out they were dating. There was a policy against coworkers having a relationship, so he got the chop. One night, he announced we might be moving to New Mexico: there was supposed to be work there. I had to drive all the way to New Mexico with him and

HANGING WITH MY SISTERS

Mary to check it out. That was the first time I spent an extended amount of time with Mary, seventeen hours in the car together. It turned out that she was a nice woman. It was good that we were getting to know each other better, but I hated New Mexico, and I let Pops know it.

"Dad, if you move here, I'm moving in with Aunt Nan. No one plays music out here. All I want to do is play the drums, and this isn't the place to do it. There's no way I can live here." Pops explained that he had what potentially looked like a good job offer, and if the family didn't have some money coming in soon, we'd all be living in the street, me and my drum kit included. We stayed two days at a little hotel while he interviewed for the job. The landscape was all desert and cactus, which made the whole city look extra tough.

The New Mexico job didn't pan out, so we went back to California. Sometimes Mary lived with us; then she got an apartment around the corner, but she'd still be over at our house a lot. One night, Mary made dinner for all of us. I got home and I saw that it was meat. I said, "Dad, I'm not eating meat. I'm going to eat somewhere else." He was livid, because I had said it right in front of Mary and I was hurting her feelings, so he hit me upside the head, sending all one hundred pounds of me into the wall.

A month into my freshman year, I got a serious girlfriend, Michelle. I was crazy about her: she was super hot, and she was my connection to humanity. At a point when I didn't want to hang out with anybody else at my school, she changed my rhythm. That was the first time I really fell in love. We spent all our time together and we even looked like each other: people used to say we looked like brother and sister. I always had Tony Hawk skater hair with bangs in my face, but after my mom died, I never cut my hair. I let it grow out until I looked like a metalhead, what we called a hessian.

In high school, I was fully into metal: Metallica, Slayer, Sepultura. But I still loved hip-hop: I had discovered KRS-One, House of Pain, the Pharcyde, N.W.A, and Cypress Hill. Then around my junior year, I discovered everything that was happening up in Seattle, and I loved that music: Soundgarden, Alice in Chains, Screaming Trees, Mother Love

Bone, Mudhoney. Michelle and I were always passing all those tapes back and forth to each other.

I was living in a broken home, feeling the pain of my mom being gone. The music was a way for me to rebel, whether it was hip-hop or punk rock. (The drumming and the skating helped too.) All that music has a rebellious energy to it, where you feel like you're tearing down everything around you. I was blaring Descendents, Face to Face, and Rage Against the Machine. With my life the way it was, I didn't feel like throwing on some Billy Joel.

All my musical tastes came together as I grew up with the Beastie Boys, because they rapped but they were also punk: sometimes they played their own instruments, and they had covered a Minor Threat song. When I was a kid, I loved "(You Gotta) Fight for Your Right (to Party!)," but as my musical taste evolved, the band matured right along with me. Right around the time of *Check Your Head* (one of the best albums ever), I met Jim, who became a very good friend.

Jim and I swore we were the Beastie Boys. We dressed like them, we learned all their music, we studied all the bands that they covered and talked about in interviews. We went to see them live whenever we could—I was lucky enough to see them ten times. They changed my life: the way I dress, the music I listen to, my outlook on the world. I shaved a part into my head, the way Ad-Rock did. To this day, if I grow out my hair, there will be a line there—my hair grows a part because of how I used to try to look like Adam Horovitz.

Listening to the Beastie Boys made everything in life more fun. Jim and I would put on one of their albums and just rap along. I liked doing Mike D's parts, and he'd always do Ad-Rock. And then as I got older, Yauch became my favorite. They also made my drumming better, as I tried to replicate their programmed parts: Jim would challenge me to play a song like "Hey Ladies"—it had a lot of busy fills, but yeah, I could play that.

Michelle and I stayed together for about two years, on and off, but around junior year, we drifted apart. I guess that's the nice way of saying it. Actually, I was a dick: I cheated on her. A lot. I started sleeping with her best friend, which was cold. All three of us would be at Michelle's house. I had given Michelle the impression that I couldn't stand her friend, and her friend had made her think she hated me. But when Michelle fell asleep, we would go downstairs and make out, and that turned into having sex. Eventually, Michelle figured it out, and that was the end of our relationship. She moved away for college and found a guy who treated her better. I couldn't stop chasing girls; by the time I graduated from high school, I had easily slept with fifteen girls.

Fontana was a racist place in a lot of ways. Historically, it was an extremely white working-class town. But the Hispanic population kept growing over the years, and some of the white people freaked out and got militant. Whenever I shaved my head when I was growing up, skinheads would give me fucked-up white-power literature. Every year when I was a kid, there was a big Fontana Day parade through the center of town, and the Ku Klux Klan would openly march down the street in their hoods. It made me sick to my stomach.*

In school, it felt like more of a blend: there were Chicanos, there were white kids, there were black kids. The social groups included gangsters, stoners, and goths. I loved my Mexican friends just as much as my black friends and I loved hip-hop just as much as I loved punk rock. I didn't have a big group of friends in high school, but I could float from one crowd to the next and be cool with all of them. There was lots of fighting at my school, but it never felt like it was a race war, just kids being kids.

My crowd was musicians. I was drum tech for a hair band called Voyce: they were the biggest rock stars in the world to me, because they played shows, people knew their songs, and they had a demo tape. I was too young to get into the clubs where they were playing, so I would set up the drums, then wait outside while they played. I did it for free—I just wanted to see how things worked.

I kept joining and starting rock bands. I was in one band called Poor Mouth that was awesome. We sounded like early Soundgarden—a little Alice in Chains, but mostly Soundgarden. At live shows, my friend Dorian

---

* Fontana is majority Latino now—take *that*, Ku Klux Klan.

TRAVIS BARKER
can i say

used to put a paper bag on his head and come onstage to dance with us. We did pretty well, but broke up after a couple of years. I wanted to find more musicians to play with, but I didn't understand the hustle at first. I would put up flyers at local music stores and place ads in papers like the *Recycler*, which was a free local paper with lots of classified ads. My sisters would give me money, or I'd just swipe some from my dad's wallet. Then the phone would start ringing at our house. Everyone else in the family would be asking, "How did our number get out?" I'd tell them that I put an ad in the *Recycler* because I was starting a band. "Thanks, Trav."

I made some cool friends through those *Recycler* ads: one of them was a ripping guitar player from LA named Mario—he was in his late twenties, but he'd come over and we'd play metal songs together. I was also jamming with a bassist named Randy Stewart. He was about four years older than me, but we ended up playing in a bunch of different bands together. Sometimes on weekends we'd drive around in Randy's Mustang, listening to Jane's Addiction and Danzig, throwing eggs and rocks at any targets we could find. One time, we were driving by the mayor's house. Randy said, "Watch this." He drove onto the mayor's yard and did a bunch of doughnuts before he peeled out and hit the road again. Ten minutes later, we were pulled over by the cops and arrested. That was the first time I ended up in a holding tank. Luckily, the cops that arrested me had gone to high school with my sister Tamara, so they called her to pick me up instead of my father. Pops caught wind of my arrest, though—and when he did, he was not happy.

I got my first tattoo when I was sixteen. It had my nickname, Bones: people called me that because I was so skinny. My second tattoo came just a week later: the symbol for Dag Nasty, which was a hardcore band from Washington, DC, that I loved. My dad didn't want me to get tattoos, especially if it was anywhere that people might see it. "Nobody's going to hire you with the way you look," he told me. "Tattoos are job stoppers. You'll have nothing to fall back on."

That resonated so hard with me. When he said that, I thought: *Exactly.* I didn't *want* anything to fall back on. The more tattoos I had, the less there was to fall back on. My ideal situation was that I wouldn't be able to get a normal job anywhere and I would be forced to play the drums.

Never give yourself an out.

When I went in for meetings with my guidance counselor, she'd always ask me about my plans after high school.

"I'm going to be a drummer," I'd tell her.

"No, Mr. Barker, that's not realistic. Have you considered community college?"

"I'm not going to do that. My family doesn't have the money for that. Besides, I'm just going to play the drums." I wasn't counting being on a rock star: I just wanted to earn enough money playing drums to live and eat. The counselor was so frustrated with me. It didn't help that I was on the verge of failing all my classes. I was doing just enough to get by, and that was all they got from me.

Pops wanted to make sure I had a plan B in case music didn't work out. So I did everything I could to make sure that there was absolutely no plan B. I wanted my back to the wall, with no turning back.

The end of my senior year, I spent a lot of time with my friend John Sanchez, the guy who gave me my first tattoo. I'd hang around the Empire Tattoo shop every day, sometimes eight hours a day, listening to him crack hilarious jokes, waiting for an opening in his schedule. I was a shop rat: I'd just be killing time, listening to music, maybe talking to girls, absorbing everything that happened at a tattoo shop. And the minute somebody didn't come in, I'd hop into the chair and get tattooed. I always had an idea for what I wanted my next tattoo to be.

Two things blow my mind about tattoos today: that you can get them removed, and that you can apply a cream to make the tattoo process painless. That makes me sad: I miss the old days when you had to be an outlaw or a real brave soul to get a tattoo.

Pops used to tell me, "Your mom would be so pissed at you right now." And when it came to the tattoos, he was absolutely right—she would not have approved of me getting ink on my body at all. If she saw how many tattoos I had, she would have killed me. If she was alive, I don't think I would have gotten tattooed in the same way.

The tattoo that upset Pops the most was the one on my forearm, because it was the most visible. But once he saw it was a tribute to Mom, there was no denying it was beautiful. He loved it.

RANDY BARKER (FATHER)

Travis wasn't too fond of high school. It was tough to get him up in the morning. I was the same way when I was in high school: as far as I was concerned, it was boring. One day, I was in a mechanical drawing class. I wrote myself a note out, signed my dad's name to it, and gave it to the teacher. I left and never came back.

THIS IS ME PLAYING WITH POOR MOUTH, ANOTHER HIGH SCHOOL BAND. OUR FRIEND DORIAN WORE A BAG OVER HIS HEAD.

I always told Travis, "If you come home with a tattoo, you're going to have to go to the hospital to have my foot dug out of your backside."

One day, my youngest daughter and I were sitting in a room, watching TV, and she said, "Dad, you know Travis has a tattoo."

"No, I didn't know," I said. "Who got it for him?"

"I did."

"You know how I feel about the tattoo situation." I wasn't crazy about it, and I told him, "One of these days you're going to be sorry." He had been wearing long pants to cover up the tattoo—once he knew I knew, he went back to wearing shorts. I was okay with the tattoos where he could cover them up, but when he came home with one on his neck, I screamed and hollered at him: "That's some gangster shit right there."

Around the time I was hanging out with John Sanchez, his brother Chris was active in a gang. One time I showed up at their house and it was all shot up—every window was gone, and there were holes in the walls. Just minutes earlier, someone had done a drive-by. A week later, I was at John's house when another drive-by happened: suddenly, glass was shattering everywhere. Some of us hit the floor; some of us went out and shot back.

JOHN SANCHEZ (FRIEND)

My house had been shot at before, so we knew what it was right away. The house was on a cul-de-sac, and we lived right at the end, so we were able to see anybody driving in and out of that street. By the time we heard gunshots,

we were already outside, shooting back. It turned out
that most of our bullets ended up in a house down the
street. My roommate had a high-powered rifle, so I guess
the bullets went right through the car as they were
driving away and hit the car at the end of the street.
It was gnarly. The whole house was riddled with holes.

Chris was cool as fuck, and when he was with us, he was a normal, happy guy: he'd come to barbecues and punk-rock shows. We always had a good time together in the short time I knew him. Unfortunately, two weeks after the drive-by, he was murdered one block from his home.

That stuff was happening a lot. A couple of my buddies were active in gangs, and a lot of my buddies were carrying guns. I'd be out at clubs with friends, having a good time—and then somebody would get shot in the parking lot. So many nights ended with us hiding under cars because people were shooting.

I know most people don't see it this way, but I think it was somewhat enlightening to be in that environment. I was fortunate enough not to be around when really bad shit happened, or to be in harm's way—but after people around me died, I realized how badly I didn't want to die myself. (But I knew that if I did die, at least I'd be reunited with my mom.) As much as I cared about my friends, it was obvious that I wouldn't be missing out on anything if I left town.

I always say that I didn't go to my high school graduation. The real story is that I went, but I didn't put on a cap and gown and get my diploma like my classmates. I showed up with my skateboard and hung around outside the fence, watching everyone else walk on the field up to the podium. At that point, I was thinking about other things. I always knew the world was a much bigger place than Fontana.

WASHING MY DAD'S TRUCK

3

Other peoples trucks

When I graduated from high school—class of '93—it felt like everyone else in my class was moving away to go to college. I was seventeen years old. I spent my time listening to music, playing drums for hours every day, and dreaming about being in a band. I kept putting ads in the *Recycler*—sometimes I had three ads going at the same time with different names and different influences. "Drummer available for a band influenced by King Diamond," "Drummer available for a band influenced by Minor Threat," "Drummer available for a band influenced by the Descendents." Guitar players would drive out from LA and we would jam. I just wanted to play music.

I was in a band called Psycho Butterfly with some high school friends. Dennis was on vocals, John played guitar, Jason was on guitar and vocals, and Marcos played bass. It was straight-up rock 'n' roll: we covered Led Zeppelin and "Train Kept A-Rollin'." We were listening to a lot of grunge: we sounded a lot like Soundgarden and Alice in Chains and Mother Love Bone. The other guys were really talented musicians, and we played a lot of local gigs—anywhere in the Inland Empire that would have us.

A few months after graduation, we broke up: just the usual personality differences. I didn't mind, because it meant I could start fresh. Whenever I was in a band that broke up, I'd start a new band with whoever the most talented guy in it was.

Around that time, a friend and I started printing bootleg T-shirts. His dad had a T-shirt printing business in his garage, and while he was sleeping, we'd print up shirts for whatever band was playing at the Blockbuster Pavilion—like the Spin Doctors, of all people. We'd go up to the venue with boxes and bags full of T-shirts and sell as many as we could before the police confiscated our shirts or kicked us out.

I had a job at Wherehouse, which was a music chain store.* I was pulling down $4.25 an hour, working in the video department. Wherehouse sold videocassettes—DVDs hadn't been invented yet—and also had a video-rental business. I met a lot of interesting women in the video department: sometimes older ladies would come in to rent adult films, flirt with me, and end up giving me their phone numbers. I hooked up with one woman who was married, but it was too crazy. Her husband came in to return a video—I thought he was there to kick my ass, since twenty-four hours earlier, I had been in his house, having sex with his wife—but he had no idea what had happened. It was screwed up.

My sister Tamara bought me a moped so I could get to work. It was an AMF moped: basically a bicycle with a motor. If you pedaled while you were running the engine, you could get it up to fifteen or twenty miles an hour. It wasn't registered, so I had to stay off main streets to avoid the police, which meant going through some sketchy neighborhoods. One night I was pedaling down a side street and I passed by an open garage full of hoodlums, drinking and partying. They thought there was nothing funnier than this white boy on a moped. They ran after me, throwing bottles and shouting, "Fuck you, Pee-wee Herman! Give me my bike back!"

I actually learned a lot about music working at Wherehouse. We had to play all kinds of music to make the customers happy, so I listened to a lot of stuff that I wouldn't have normally heard. Once or twice a week, we had to refile all the CDs and make sure everything was in alphabetical

---

* They're out of business now, like most record stores.

order. I learned to appreciate all styles of music. Sometimes I'd have to do a big window display: Aerosmith would have an album coming out, and I'd take a big pile of posters and make the window look dope.

Wherehouse was a weird place, but we had this cool community of people. We were all united by hating our manager, who was this forty-two-year-old dude who was obsessed with Disneyland. He was so weird—he ate, slept, and breathed Disney. It was like he wanted to be Mickey Mouse. At the end of the day, if the manager wasn't around, my friend Jim and I would bust out some cardboard boxes, turn up the radio, and take turns breakdancing, basically battling each other. We would bust out old-school moves like back spins, knee spins, and flares—closing time was the best part of the day.

There were always fights in the parking lot and we used to get robbed all the time. Anytime somebody came in to rob us, we were supposed to just give them whatever they asked for. But one time, some guys came in with bandanas over their faces—they pulled out guns and asked for all the money. An assistant manager, Little Sean, cleaned out the cash register for them. Little Sean was really dope—he was a cool dude who went on to be a cop. After he gave them the money and they left, the whole experience wasn't sitting right with him. He couldn't let it rest—he walked out and confronted them. They very easily could have killed him—he was lucky they just took off.

Pops taught me how to drive. He was strict about it, but for a good reason: he wanted to teach me right, and that's why I'm a dope driver today. I learned in his big blue full-size extended-cab GMC truck, just a year or two old. Our family always drove GM cars: Chevys most of the time, and Cadillacs if we could afford them. I aced my test—100 percent. I couldn't afford to buy a new car with my Wherehouse money, so Pops helped me get a used square-body Chevy truck for three grand. It had a small-block 350 engine and it sucked down gasoline, but it was badass. Pops and I worked on it together, priming it and painting it.

Soon after I got the truck, I had it in the shop—I think I was getting the brakes fixed. I wanted to go to Circuit City to look at car stereos: I

dreamed of bumping Nas or Tha Alkaholiks in my truck. For the first time ever, Pops told me I could drive his truck. After all those tense lessons, it was good to know that he approved of my driving. I drove over to San Bernardino, about twenty minutes down Route 66. I knew the town pretty well: I had a girlfriend over there.

There was a Guitar Center across the street from Circuit City, so first I checked out some drum equipment I couldn't afford. Then I went to Circuit City and looked at the auto speakers. I couldn't afford them either, so I was pretty much window-shopping, but I was having a good day anyway. It was fun to be driving around in my dad's truck instead of tooling around on my moped.

I left the store, unlocked the car, and got in. As I was shutting my door, a guy opened the passenger door, got in, slammed it shut, and put a pistol to my head. "Drive, motherfucker," he told me.

He was an older dude, reeking of alcohol. I was scared out of my mind, but I stayed cool. "You want the truck?" I said. "Just take the truck."

"Drive, motherfucker. I don't want your truck," he snapped.

He told me to get on the 215 freeway. I stepped on the gas and headed north. He wasn't saying anything. If I tried to talk to him, or if I even tried turning in his direction, he'd smack me in the head with his gun. "Don't look at me, motherfucker," he said. He wasn't quite pistol-whipping me, but

TRAVIS BARKER
can i say

he was nudging me with the barrel of the gun to keep me looking forward and just driving where he told me.

We drove for about twenty minutes before he told me to get off the freeway. For all I knew, he was going to take me to an empty field and shoot me. But he directed me to this sketchy apartment complex and told me to park the car. He said, "Don't you dare fucking move. I'm going to go in here for one minute. If you leave, I swear to God, I'm going to shoot your fucking brains out."

"I'm not going anywhere."

He poked me in the cheek with his gun. "I'll be able to see you. And I'm watching you. So if you try to leave, I'll kill you."

"I got it, man," I told him.

He scooted sideways across the seat, keeping the gun pointed at me so I wouldn't look at him. As soon as he got out of the truck, I smashed out of there so fast, tires squealing. I didn't even care if he shot at the truck. I was in survival mode, and all I knew was that I no longer had a gun pressed up against my head.

My heart beating double-time, I headed straight home, and it was the most awesome drive I've ever had in my life, just being glad that I had made it out alive. I replayed the whole thing in my mind, trying to figure out if I had made a mistake, but there really wasn't any point at which I could see how I might have done something differently. I hadn't even seen this guy coming toward the truck. I got home and I told my dad and my sisters, and then I got freaked out after the fact: somehow talking about it made it seem more real. After that, I tried to be really conscious about what I did and where I went, so I wouldn't put myself in a situation like that again.

My truck needed money for gas, so I got a weekend job at Pizza Hut. I showed up on my first day, thinking they were going to teach me to make pizzas. Nope, I was on delivery duty. After paying for gas, it was barely a money-making situation with my big Chevy truck. My first few deliveries went fine, and then there was an order in a bad part of Fontana. I was trying to stay away from sketchy areas, but pizza had its own agenda. I was heading into this apartment building when I got robbed by seven dudes with knives: they wanted the pizza. If I had given them any trouble, they totally would have shanked me and not lost any sleep about it. I gave them the pizza, went back to my truck, drove back to the Pizza Hut, and quit.

I also quit the job at Wherehouse. The pay was lousy, and the Mickey Mouse boss seemed weirder every single day. Once I knew I had two weeks left, I started stealing CDs like crazy, grabbing anything I liked. Afterward, I felt hella bad. Jim, my best friend at Wherehouse, was also stealing CDs. I told Jim that I hoped we didn't get caught, but either way karma meant that we were due for a lot of bad luck.

I had a big CD case with about three hundred CDs in it—the ones I had been stealing, and the ones I had been buying with my own money since junior high school. Soon after I left Wherehouse, I put this huge CD case down on my truck; I had a lid over the rear cargo area and I left the CDs there. I forgot that I had put down the CD case and I drove off, which meant that I lost not only all the CDs I stole, but all the ones in my personal collection. That's karma: things always come full circle, although not usually so quickly.

I started taking oddball jobs through a temp agency. They would give me an address: I never knew exactly what the work was going to be until I got there. I would, say, show up at a warehouse and get told, "Okay, unload these two trucks." That was how companies looked for permanent employees: they wanted guys who were hungry and unloading those trucks like crazy. I'm strong for my size, but I'm pretty small, so hauling all these boxes was hard work. For eight hours straight, I'd be busting my ass. But it was cool: jobs like that meant that I still had some money to buy CDs and drumsticks.

Dreams don't work unless you do.

Sometimes I'd get night-shift jobs and be working from two A.M. until ten in the morning. If I got on that schedule, then on my days off,

I wouldn't be able to sleep at night. On one of my days off, I told Pops, "I'm going out tonight, and I'll be gone all night."

To my surprise, he told me, "You know what? You're young—go do it. I used to go out and have a good time all night—sometimes I wouldn't sleep for two days." He would have moments like that where he was more relaxed about what I was doing: I think part of it was just that I was getting older, and part of it was that he could see I was working hard, and he respected that.

After he said that, I started going out more. There's no handbook for life: you just have to figure it out. It had been four years since my mom died, and I felt ready to explore the world. I was meeting people and screwing around. Sometimes my friends and I would pile into a car and drive around town for a while. Sometimes we'd end up at a late-night street race.

In Fontana, these street races were always dangerous—the people who were running them were just kids, so they weren't big on safety precautions. People got accidentally run over; people got shot. These races would usually be for pink slips, but sometimes the loser would say, "Fuck you, I'm not giving you my pink slip"—and then people would be fighting or pulling out their guns.

One night, I drove down to Newport Beach with Jim. Being able to go all the way to the Pacific Ocean was one of the advantages of having a car. When I was a kid, I was constantly begging Pops to take me to the beach. He took me once in a while, but if I had it my way, I would have been bodyboarding and surfing every weekend.

We cruised around town and met a couple of local girls: they thought we were cool just because we were from out of town. We hung out with them, and the girls wanted to get some alcohol. We said, "Okay, no problem, we got it," and the girls drove us to a liquor store. It was just talk on our end—being underage and not even having a fake ID, we didn't think anybody would sell us anything—but the girls really wanted the booze. We figured we'd bluff our way through it.

We got lucky, because there was a dude waiting out by the front of the store, clearly over twenty-one. I asked him, "Hey, man, will you buy us

ME AND BIGHEAD JIM

some alcohol? I'll give you an extra twenty—I just need a twelve-pack of beer." He was cool about it: he took the money and came back with the beer. As we were walking away, a whole bunch of cops jumped out of the bushes. We weren't so lucky after all: that guy was an undercover cop, and apparently he was staking out the store because they had been selling a lot to underage people. It was a setup.

We got arrested. Jim had some speed on him, but he stayed cool and kicked it away before the police searched him. The girls were waiting in their car for us, but when they saw what was happening, they took off. It was humiliating. I tried to explain to the cops that we weren't even planning on drinking the beer—it was for the girls. They said it didn't matter: we had bought beer from an undercover cop. They took us to the police station and threw us in a holding cell. It was awful—the only comfort was knowing that if they had found Jim's speed, we would have really been screwed.

I was old enough that they didn't call my dad to tell him that he needed to pick me up. I just had to stay in jail until they were ready to release me the next day. Part of the condition of my release was that I had to go to AA meetings every day for a couple of weeks. That was eye-opening: I was in trouble just because I was trying to get these girls some liquor so we could have some fun. But these people had real problems. Before the meeting started, some of them would drink and then throw up in the bathroom. I resolved to be smarter, and never to ask an undercover cop to buy me alcohol again.

Another time, Jim and I drove across the Mexican border, going down to Tijuana to see Tool play. That was my first time in Mexico, and it was a crazy show. The band was playing in the dark except for some weird blue lights onstage. The crowd was a mix of locals and people from San Diego. Security looked badass and you had to watch your step. A couple of drunk American guys got into a fight and I remember thinking, *Those guys are ending up in a Mexican jail tonight and it's not going to be fun.*

During the show, we met these American girls and they invited us to crash at their place in San Diego. So we hung out with them, drinking and talking about how great the show had been. I said something about how Maynard—Tool's lead singer—got so into it onstage, he looked like he was having a seizure. One of the girls got offended: she said she suffered from seizures herself. I apologized, but I figured she was exaggerating. Then she actually started having a full-on seizure. Her friend knew how to take care of her episodes, so she was okay, but it put a damper on the evening. I felt awful. Even as this girl was flailing around, she was looking right at me, like she was trying to say, "Great fucking timing, man."

I was totally girl crazy. I never had any trouble convincing the ladies to go home with me—my problem was that because I couldn't keep my dick in my pants, I would make bad decisions. My friends called me Dumpster Dick. One time, I went to a party with John Sanchez, my tattoo-artist friend. The party was kind of lame—the beer had run out by the time we got there, and there were hardly any girls. I was hanging out with John and my buddies Ricardo and Wilmer, smoking cigarettes, figuring out what to do next. Then I heard this girl talking to the guy who brought her to the party, telling him, "I need a ride home."

"I can't drive," he told her. "I'm drunk."

"I can drive her home," I said. I figured that driving a cute chick home was a better time than what was going on at this party. "But I came here with my friend John, so I don't have a ride."

"You want to drive my truck?"

"Yeah, I'll drive. I'll be good in your truck—just let me bring my CDs."

We didn't really know each other—he was a friend of a friend, and he decided I was okay. "Alright, bro, take her home," he said. I didn't know exactly what their relationship was.

Halfway to her place, we stopped at a red light and she started making out with me. Then things were cracking. Fifteen minutes later, we were having sex in the truck. For two hours, we made out and had sex. About an hour in, the dude started blowing up my pager, sending lots of messages with his phone number.

I dropped her off and called John to figure out what I should do. "This girl was on me from the moment we left," I told him.

"Dude, are you serious?" he said laughing. "He's really pissed off. He thinks you're driving around in his truck."

"I wasn't, I swear to God! Tell him I was having sex with this chick."

I came back to the party, and my friends were like, "Oh, my God, you are fucked." I walked up to the guy and gave him his keys back. "Dude, here's the condom," I said, and I showed him my used condom. I was dead serious—I didn't want him to be bummed at me, and I figured he would be less mad about the girl if I could prove I wasn't fucking around in his truck. Everybody at the party was tripping, laughing, but he was a good sport about it. If she had been his chick, she wasn't anymore. "Ah, fuck that bitch," he said. Stuff like that was always happening to me.

I started bringing girls back to the house more flagrantly, not trying to conceal them from Pops. I'd be in my room, getting fresh with some girl, and he'd be banging on the wall, trying to get me to keep it down. There was this one super-hot girl who was just a total freak—she was basically a sex addict, and she turned me into one too. Any time of night, if I called her, she'd find a ride and come over. I'd sneak her into the house, and pretty soon we'd be going at it—and Pops would be banging on the wall again.

One day, Pops laid down the law. "You can't keep bringing girls here like this," he told me. I thought he was pissed because I was being too rowdy late at night when he was trying to sleep, but it was deeper than that. He said, "Pal, you're going to get one of these girls pregnant. And then your ass is going to be in trouble. You don't have a good job, you don't have no fucking money, you're too young to have a kid. You need to slow down, pal."

He was looking out for me. It was good advice, but I didn't pay a lot of attention. I figured I had always been using condoms, anyway. My attitude was that I was nineteen and I had a dick. I dated this skinhead girl for a while—one night, when my dad was out, we were hanging out at my house, along with Jim and her best friend. We talked about playing strip poker, but that seemed like too much work, so we did strip coin-flipping instead. If it was tails, the skinhead girl was supposed to take off a piece of clothing. If it was heads, I was supposed to. So Jim and I started flipping a coin—and every time, no matter how it came up, we told her it was tails. We convinced her that the coin came up tails eight times in a row, so pretty soon she was buck naked in my living room. And not long after that, we were both buck naked in my bedroom.

Pops and Mary were getting married, but I didn't want to go to the wedding. My aunt Nan sat me down for a talk—after my mom died, she was one of three people in the family who I would listen to. (The other two were my sisters.) Aunt Nan said, "Your mom is gone. It's terrible, but you have to accept it. Now you need to support your father and what makes him happy."

I said, "Okay, I accept it, but I'm just not ready for it. I'm cool with it—Mary never did anything wrong to me—but I can't be there. It's too hard for me."

So I stayed home, hanging out with my friend Jim. I had invited a girl over. She was a white girl who loved hip-hop—we had met at a punk-rock show down in San Bernardino. By this time, I had a group of girls that were down with coming over to my place to have fun, and not worry about whether we were boyfriend and girlfriend. I thought maybe she'd bring a friend, but she didn't. Jim was cool about being solo—he gave us some privacy. I turned on Snoop Dogg—the *Doggystyle* album had just come out, and that was my idea of a romantic jam.

I was fucking this girl in my room, and while we were doing it, I looked out the window. Our backyard didn't have a pool or landscaping: it was all weeds and dirt. But Jim had gotten bored and driven his Volkswagen bus into the backyard, and he was doing doughnuts. He saw me looking out the window and he gave me a thumbs-up. I started laughing and I gave him a thumbs-up back. While we're still having sex, this girl said, "What are you doing?"

"Just giving Jim a thumbs-up, letting him know everything's okay in here."

All this time, I was in a bunch of bands. One of them, we printed up flyers for our first show—but we broke up before we ever played the show. Some of the bands never even made it that far: it was just me and my buddies playing in somebody's garage. I had a punk-rock band called Doyt with my friends Shane Gallagher and Anthony Celestino. Shane played guitar and Anthony played bass; the band was influenced by Hüsker Dü, Minor Threat, Operation Ivy, and especially the Descendents. Never did I connect with any band the way I did with the Descendents (and their offshoot All), musically and lyrically. I loved punk rock, and they sang about everything I was going through, from girl problems to being called a loser. Once I discovered them, I never turned back.

Doyt was kind of experimental, and if we had ever found a singer, the band would have been awesome. We would be practicing in my garage, and then in the middle of a song the door would open: Pops was home. He'd roll in on his Harley and knock over Shane's amp. Nobody would say anything about it. Pops terrified all of my friends.

I was operating on the theory that it wasn't possible to be in too many bands simultaneously, so when my friend Randy (the one who did doughnuts on the mayor's front yard) told me that his band needed a drummer, I joined. The band was called Feeble, named after the skateboarding trick "feeble grind": it was a great punk-rock band based in Laguna Beach, about an hour away, and all the members were formerly from Fontana.

I had been out of high school for around two years when Pops gave me an ultimatum. "Your sisters can live here," he told me. "They don't even need to pay rent." (They actually did help him out with the rent, though, just because they were cool.) "But you're a man now, so the rules are different. You either have to get a real job, where you work sixty hours a week, and pay me some rent, or you've got to take your drums and move out."

I thought about joining the army. My whole life I had dreamed of playing music, but it didn't feel like it was happening. I started to think that Pops was right—being in a band was just a fairy tale. He had always said that the military would make a man out of me: "You've got to grow up and be a man. You can't be a little boy in a man's world." Fontana had recruiting offices in strip malls, right next to the ninety-nine-cent stores. I went in to get a pamphlet, but the minute I stepped into that office, I knew it wasn't right for me. I had a lot of respect for Pops and what he did, but I wanted to keep pushing forward.

I still didn't have anywhere to go, so I hustled around looking for a steady job and got a position at Target Warehouse. It was about sixty-five hours a week, for decent money. But I wasn't going to have time for the drumming. I told Noel Paris, the lead singer of Feeble, what was up: I had to get a job or I wouldn't have a place to live, and that meant I was going to have to stop playing the drums, at least for the time being.

Noel said, "Man, I feel like you're making a big mistake. You're too talented not to give this a shot. Why don't you come stay on my couch? If it don't work out, you can turn around a couple of years from now and get that stupid job again. But who knows if you're going to get the opportunity to play the drums like this again? You don't want to look back five or six years from now and regret it, realizing that you should have been a drummer."

He was right. I said, "Pops, you're calling me out, I'm out." I packed my drums in my truck and moved to Laguna Beach.

You are what you choose to become. Be who they say you cannot be.

FIRST FEEBLE DEMO—ART BY NOEL PARIS

4

Best friend for a night

I moved into Noel's place with a drum kit and a sleeping bag. He was nice enough to let me sleep on his couch—or the floor, depending on whether anyone else was crashing there that night. In the morning, I'd roll the sleeping bag up and put it away in the corner. We were living in a studio apartment on Route 1, the Pacific Coast Highway, right next to the Royal Thai restaurant.

Noel got me a job working for the city of Laguna Beach as a trashman. It was actually a cool job—the uniform was basically a Dickies button-up shirt and Dickies pants. Which was pretty much what I wore anyway, so I felt right at home. My first week on the job, I found a hundred-dollar bill on the top of a trash can outside of a bar. Somebody must have thought it was a piece of paper crumpled up in his pocket and thrown it away—I was stoked.

The entire sanitation department was cool. Everyone in Feeble had a job working as trashmen, so we had a lot of fun. We were terrors. We

figured out how to rig one of the big trucks so the windshield-wiper fluid would go out in a big spray on the truck's right. Then we'd drive next to the beach and squirt people who were walking on the sand. We spent our days meeting up or talking on the phone, figuring out our next move. Sometimes we'd go to Kinko's while we were on the clock for the city so we could make flyers for our next gig. We used to play gigs at the local bars—Hennessey's and the Sandpiper—wearing our trashmen uniforms. We took pride in being city trash workers, and we were local stars—among our friends, anyway.

NOEL PARIS (LEAD SINGER, FEEBLE)

I grew up in Fontana, and the only thing I wanted to do in life was get the hell out of Fontana. Right after high school, I went to art school in Laguna and got a job with the city. It was my goal to get all my friends from Fontana jobs with the city so they could move out.

I was focused on painting at the time, so the band was more of a fun thing. But Travis brought a sense of us being a real band. He raised the level of all of us, and we felt more comfortable playing shows just because we actually sounded good. It was a drastic change.

Drummers would come to our shows just to watch Travis. They could care less about the band—they would just sit there and watch him play. There were a lot of times when I just wanted to turn around and watch him play as well—he was relentless.

And girls loved him. We were all like, "What the hell?" Here's this skinny-ass little kid, but beautiful girls would just crumble over him. It was insane—there were girls knocking on the window of our tiny studio on PCH in the middle of the night, or sitting in their cars in

the parking lot, just hoping he'd wake up. I've never seen anything like it since.

RANDY STEWART (BASSIST, FEEBLE)

Once Travis joined the band, our style changed. He obviously is a talented drummer, but he's so good at arranging songs. He'd have complete ideas for songs: the guitar is going to accent right here, Randy is going to be playing something right here. And he kind of taught me how to play bass. I'd played guitar before, but it's completely different. We'd practice every day and play shows three or four times a week. For a band that wasn't signed, we worked pretty hard.

One night we played a club in Riverside, and we had a rough crowd. One of our friends got in a fight with one of the bouncers, and they started macing him. And then a full-on brawl broke out: tables were getting thrown, people were hitting each other with chairs, and people were getting thrown out. I looked over at Travis, and he was throwing drumsticks at the bouncers—while he was playing. He'd throw one, then grab another from the little pouch on the side of his kit, and he kept playing the whole time.

One night at Hennessey's, we played a good show. It was fast, melodic punk rock, but we sounded clean, and I had a chance to do some cool drumming. There was one chick in the audience who couldn't stop staring at me. She looked like she was in a state of shock, and I couldn't help but notice her. After a while, I realized it was actually a dude. When we finished our set, he came up to me and said, "Dude, you're a really great drummer. You're gonna do things." I was like, Thanks, man, or Thanks, babe. I wasn't 100 percent sure. But it turned out to be Taylor

PLAYING WITH FEEBLE

Hawkins, who went on to be the drummer for the Foo Fighters. He was from Laguna Beach, and he was already playing music professionally—at the time, he was touring with Alanis Morissette. I was used to drummers being competitive with each other, not giving each other compliments, so him saying that gave me a lot of motivation.

I was as girl crazy as ever. I was nuts for one girl who worked at Hennessey's, and one night after a Feeble show, I took her home. Feeble ended up writing a song about her called "Best Friend for a Night." The girls in Laguna Beach seemed like they were in a different league than some of the girls I had grown up with—and now that I was out of school, I was meeting a lot of older women.

During the day, my route included the office of a law firm. I saw one of the secretaries for this attorney parking her car, a vintage Impala. I'm always stoked about old Chevys, so we started talking about her car and we hit it off. Pretty soon, we were taking long breaks from work to hang out together during the day. I'd park my trash truck in her garage so nobody could find me—we'd be making out for hours, having crazy sex. Then I would come back to sanitation headquarters and make up some story about where I had been: "I was out on Laguna Canyon Road, litter-picking." Eventually, I got caught. They took away my truck and busted me down to downtown duty. I had to pick up cigarette butts and clean out the ashtrays on top of trash cans—but it was worth it.

It was a really cool time. The guys in Feeble were like the big brothers I never had. They taught me to surf and to skim-board. One of their buddies was a pro beach volleyball player—if he had a big win, we'd always end up at his place for a barbecue. Nobody had a lot of money, but we were young and having a great time. All I wanted out of life was some money to buy records and to eat lunch at Wahoo's Fish Tacos every day. I became friends with the guys who worked there. I would always tell the owner, Wing, "If I ever get money, Wing, I'm going to open a Wahoo's Fish Taco."

"Sure you are, Trav."*

---

* Six years later, I opened two Wahoo's Fish Tacos with Wing in the Inland Empire. I'm a 49 percent owner, and he runs them. One of them has an old drum kit of mine hanging from the ceiling. It's a dream come true—I love Wahoo's to this day.

Everyone in Feeble cut their own hair. I learned how to do it from Noel, not that there was much technique: I would just grab a pair of scissors and start cutting. Most of the time, the hair would be all different lengths, and I would have a really fucked-up punk haircut. The best you could say for it was that it was shorter than it was before. I did that for a while until I bought my own electric razor and used it to shave my head. Once I had that razor, I would shave my head every three weeks and then dye whatever hair was left.

There is nothing wrong with looking one way while the world looks another. Imagine if this whole time, we've been looking at it wrong.

I told Jim, my best friend from Fontana, how excellent life was in Laguna, and he moved down too. We went to the beach every day. Noel's apartment was a couple of miles away from the water, so we would all walk to the beach or ride our skateboards down. On weekends, sometimes we would go back and forth between the apartment and the beach four or five times a day.

One day, we went surfing and there were monster waves: not as big as you would get in Hawaii, but four to six feet high. Jim and I were stoked, but there was a really bad riptide. Once we got out there, the undertow was so strong, it kept pulling us out farther—we couldn't make anything out on land. Houses had turned into tiny dots. It was the scariest shit ever. We were both tripping, but eventually we realized we had no choice except to start paddling. It took about an hour to make it back to the shore—by the time we got there, all our friends were gone, and Jim and

I just lay on the sand, exhausted but glad to be alive. You could tell we were out-of-towners.

Laguna Beach has a large gay community. I don't have anything against gay people, but when I was growing up, I didn't know a lot of them, so that was new for me. (Or maybe I did know gay people, and they were just quiet about it.) There weren't any gay clubs in Fontana, and Laguna had a really popular, big nightclub called the Boom Boom Room. When I was making my trashman rounds, I had to pick up used condoms that had been left outside the Boom Boom Room: *that* was nasty.

Jim got a job at a café by the beach, but he was the only straight guy on staff. Whenever he bent over to pick something up, one of the other waiters would stand behind him and pretend that he was freaking him. I would see it happen when I skated by the café—Jim got so pissed, but it was hilarious.

Jim and I got tickets to Epitaph Summer Nationals—this was a three-day festival of pretty much all the bands on the Epitaph label. It was the coolest show: this was the epitome of everything that was going on right then, all the dopest bands that were just starting to pop. We saw Total Chaos, we saw SNFU, we saw Rich Kids on LSD. That was the first time I ever saw Rancid live—I was in the front row. Tim Armstrong sometimes spits when he sings, and he ended up spitting on me. I didn't care—the whole weekend was the best.

Being in the front row of that show, it was like I was standing right next to my dream. In some ways it was closer than ever—but I still had no idea of how to make it happen. Sometimes I drove back inland to see shows at the Barn, which was a small club on the UC Riverside campus. One night outside the Barn, I spotted a drummer I knew—they were playing that night. He wasn't my favorite drummer, but I was excited to talk to *any* working drummer. I walked up to him and started hitting him with questions: "Hey, what time are you guys going on? What kind of drums are you playing?"

He basically said, "Get away from me, kid—I don't have time for you."

I was stunned—I couldn't believe he was that big a dickhead.*

I started hanging out at the Barn a lot, and got to be good friends with Bill Fold, who was the club's promoter. He was a few years older than me, and he was a cool guy. It took me an hour and a half to drive to the Barn—each way—but Bill booked the illest shows, whether it was hip-hop or metal or punk rock. And he loved the Misfits, so he made sure to book the Misfits at least once a year. Sometimes I would just hang out and watch the show; sometimes I would take tickets at the door, or whatever else Bill asked me to do.

Feeble was my main gig, but I played on the side with pretty much anybody who asked: sometimes I called myself a drum whore. For example, I was in a trio called Crawl with my friends Billy and Alex—we were very post-hardcore, with heavy influences from Quicksand and Rocket from the Crypt. We played two gigs, and then one of the guys left. We replaced him and put together another slew of songs with the same approach, and called ourselves Box Car Racer. That band also lasted two gigs.

One night after Feeble played Hennessey's, I was hanging out, feeling bummed because the girl I was hot for wasn't working that night. Two older ladies came up to me—they had just watched us play. One of them, who looked like a gypsy, said, "I don't listen to this music, but I see you making so many people happy. You're going to be playing in front of thousands of people and selling millions of records. Honey, I see things—I do this for a living." She was drunk, but there was something about her—I was really zoned in on her. She went on for hours. It got to be like two A.M., and I could hear my friends heckling me, saying that I was trying to pick up on her. But hearing her talk about how I was going to be a great drummer and how I would make people happy—it was awesome, and it reminded me of the things my mom used to tell me. I went home that night feeling full of hope.

---

* Years later, when Blink-182 were starting to make it, that same drummer got in touch with me and asked if we could get together so I could show him a few things. I wanted to tell him so bad that when I had asked him the same thing a few years before, he told me to get away. I didn't say anything, but I certainly never jammed with him. Nor did I ever treat a fan like he treated me.

Jim decided that he missed Fontana and he moved back home, although he always drove down to Laguna Beach whenever I had a show. I hardly ever went back home, but I called Pops and my sisters regularly. Things with Pops were better as soon as I left the house—even if he wasn't sure about the road that I was taking, he respected that I was trying to make it on my own. And I missed him.

Mike Ensch managed Feeble and he lived upstairs from Noel. Sometimes I would stay up at his place so Noel and his lady could have some privacy. Noel never complained about me being on the floor, but I could see he needed some space.

I had never been a big drinker, but when I turned twenty-one, I started experimenting with alcohol. One night, I came home to Mike's place totally drunk. I was feeling really emotional and I told him something I had never told anybody before.

"I'm going to die in a plane crash." I didn't know where the feeling came from—I had only ever been on a plane once, that time my mother took me to visit her family in Chicago. But I couldn't shake it. The conversation weirded Mike out a little bit—he was cool about it, but he didn't know what to say.

Eventually Noel's girlfriend moved in with him, so I moved upstairs to Mike's place. I brought girls home and had sex with them on the floor, and he never had a problem with it. He was a super-cool roommate.

For a while, Feeble played dirty punk-rock gigs at a place called the Copacetic Café. Sometimes another band called BHR would be on the bill: those initials stood for Butt Hole Rebellions. My friend Chad Larson was the bassist for BHR, and then he joined another band called the Aquabats, who were a big deal—they had recorded an album and were touring all over the country. One day the Aquabats' drummer quit. They had a show coming up, and Chad remembered me. He called me up on a Monday: "Hey, my other band, the Aquabats, is opening up for Fishbone on Friday and we need a drummer. Are you down?" I said yes, the way I always did when people asked me to drum with them. That time, saying yes would change my life.

WITH FEEBLE, COURTESY OF FRANK VELASQUEZ

MIKE ENSCH (MANAGER, FEEBLE)

If the United States is a bubble of the world, California is a bubble of the United States. And Orange County is a bubble within California, and Laguna Beach is definitely a bubble within Orange County. It's surrounded by mountains, and it's kind of sealed off. It has its own culture—it's kind of quaint, but a lot of famous surf brands have started there.

Around '94 or '95, I was living in Laguna Beach and I had some friends who were playing in a little punk band called Feeble. I had become close with the lead singer, Noel Paris, and one day at the beach, he told me, "We just found this amazing drummer—he's nineteen, and we're

going to move him out. He's going to live on my floor and
I'll see if I can get him a job with the city of Laguna."

I went to see Feeble one night, and they were amazing.
Noel had a certain presence, and Travis was ten times as
good as the last drummer they had. I had never managed
a band—I was going to UCLA at the time, commuting up a
couple of days a week—but I said, "You guys are great.
Do you have a manager?" They did, so I asked, "What does
he do for you?"

Noel said, "He takes ten percent of whatever we make,
and he doesn't do much."

I said, "Well, I'll do it for free. I'm your friend, and
we'll see if we can get this thing going." Done deal.

That night was the first time I met Travis. He was very
shy. You could tell he was out of his element, and he
didn't talk a lot, but he had a good sense of humor and
he seemed like a solid kid.

The craziest thing is that even when he was nobody, the
ladies absolutely loved him. They would just flock to him.
I couldn't figure it out: I was always asking myself,
"What does this kid have?" Some people have the knack—
they don't have to work at it like the rest of us.

After a while, Travis moved out of Noel's place and moved
in with me. When he lived with me, girls would just show
up at the door. He'd let them in, and sometimes he'd ask
them to strip for me—and they would. It was unreal. I
didn't mind, obviously. These girls didn't take much convincing: if they were knocking on our door, they were
there for one thing. This was before everybody had a cell

phone, so if they were trying to hook up with Travis, the best way to make it happen was actually to show up. The band wrote a song about Travis's sex life, called "Best Friend for a Night."

Travis was a great roommate. He wasn't messy: he'd leave for work at five in the morning, and he'd pick his stuff up and put it in a corner. He came out of his shell during that year: he told me about his mom dying, and how his dad told him that if he ever got a tattoo, he'd kick the shit out of him.

It was a great summer: we were all getting our careers going. I was working at the Surf & Sand Hotel; I was the guest services manager. But I got to write my own schedule, so I could go to Feeble shows when I needed to.

When Feeble went into a studio to record some songs, Travis always nailed it. Drums are usually the most difficult thing to lay down when you're recording, but I used to call him One Take Jake. If I had more business savvy, I would have signed him to a management contract. But it wouldn't have seemed right—those guys were my friends.

Feeble lasted maybe a year after Travis left, and then the core of Feeble, Noel and his cousin Frank, started a band called Scrimmage Heroes. I managed that band too. In 2002, Travis took Scrimmage Heroes on the Pop Disaster Tour with Blink-182 and Green Day. We played one of the side stages as the kids were walking in. It was cool for him to do that—it got us a lot of publicity—but the band eventually broke up anyway.

One thing I've noticed about people who have made it in the music industry: they don't only have the talent, they also have the drive. There are some people who are talented players, but they want to sit back and have somebody else do the actual work for them. That's not Travis. It's just like any other business—you have to have the drive to be the best you can be, or else you're not going to do it.

5

The Fury of the Aquabats

The Aquabats were an eight-man ska band whose gigs felt like a live superhero cartoon. Christian Jacobs, the lead singer, was the mastermind, and every show he came up with a new costume or a new stunt. The band had a song called "The Cat with Two Heads" and another called "Marshmallow Man"—during those songs, people dressed up as those characters and the Aquabats would battle them while playing their instruments. When I showed up for that first Aquabats gig, I didn't know they dressed up in costume. One of the horn players was part of a family that owned a wetsuit rash-guard company called Aleeda, so everyone in the band wore these rash guards that looked like bright green superhero outfits, plus swim trunks, goggles, and a helmet. Rash guards basically look like wetsuits, but they don't keep you warm in the same way—they look like something you might wear to the gym, if you had really bad fashion sense. I wasn't crazy about the costume, but I knew it was part of the gig, so I put it on without complaining. I had invited some friends to that first gig and none of them were sure it

was me onstage. They had no idea who the Aquabats were, or that they dressed up—all they knew was that they had never dreamed I would *ever* wear anything like that.

PLAYING WITH THE AQUABATS.
COURTESY OF COREY POLLOCK

We did our opening set for Fishbone and kicked ass. It was one of the biggest crowds I had ever played for, and I was totally stoked. As soon as we got offstage, the band asked me to be their drummer, and I said yes.

CHRISTIAN JACOBS
(LEAD SINGER, THE AQUABATS)

We started this ska band, the Aquabats, to make fun of the scene and make fun of ourselves at the same time. Once we started playing shows, we wanted to take it on the road and tour, but our drummer had a serious job—I think he was working for ESPN. He could play on Friday and Saturday nights, and that was it.

We started feeling around and someone said, "There's this kid Travis who's nineteen, but he's the best drummer you'll ever hear." So we called him up—he drove down in his orange lowered truck. At the time, I was working at a skateboard company and I lived at the office: I had a futon downstairs where they stored the boards. We had band practice in my office after hours.

Travis had baggy skater shorts and a couple of tattoos. He set up his drums, and he said, "Well, I've heard of you, but I've never heard your band. Could you play a song, and then I'll play it with you?"

I said, "I may not know a lot, but you're going to have to listen to it more than once."

"No, I can listen to it one time."

So we played him the first song on our CD, and then he went right into it—he played it much better than it was played on the CD. We played some more songs, and at the end, I said, "Hey, dude, do you want to be in this band?"

He said, "Okay, sure, I got the songs down."

Travis's first show, I handed him a little bag and said, "This is your costume."

He said, "What do you mean, my costume?" The look on his face was so funny. It was definitely messing with his mojo. He eventually warmed to it a little bit, because he saw we were being ironic. We weren't just total supernerds— although we are supernerds.

Because we'd only practiced a couple of times, I told Travis, "Hey, if you mess up, don't worry about it." I was trying to be encouraging, but it was totally insulting to him. He didn't say anything that night, but later on, we talked about it. He told me, "I can't believe you ever said that to me." He's very focused and he didn't make a mistake. The band had never sounded so good.

In the Southern California ska-punk scene, there was no other band like the Aquabats, and that really benefited us. We had shows every weekend: we built a great buzz in Orange County, and did more and more touring across the States. We'd be crammed into a ten-person passenger van, doing our own driving, and head all over the country.

We had a bunch of different Aquabats uniforms in rotation—a white set, a powder-blue set, a silver set—but if some of them got ripped or went missing, then we might end up wearing the bright green ones for

ONSTAGE WITH THE AQUABATS

six shows in a row. There wasn't any easy way to wash them on the road, so that van developed a really interesting stench.

I had told Feeble that I would keep drumming for them when I wasn't busy with the Aquabats, but pretty quickly, we figured out that I was going to be busy with the Aquabats most of the time. I did a couple of final shows with Feeble, and then I had to quit. The other guys understood it was a great opportunity—but I could feel they were still really bummed. I knew I would never have the chance to play with the Aquabats if Noel hadn't encouraged me to come to Laguna Beach and stay on his couch, and I was really grateful to him—but I couldn't figure out how to tell him that when I was quitting his band. It was hard to leave Feeble, especially because they were all like brothers to me. I cherished my friendship with Noel, Randy, and Frank. I learned so much from those guys—starting with the lesson that it was possible to leave Fontana.

Everyone in the Aquabats had stage names. Christian called himself the Bat Commander, Chad Larson was Crash McLarson, guitarist Charles Gray was Ultra Kyu, saxophonist James Briggs was Jimmy the Robot, trumpeter Adam Deibert was Prince Adam, trumpeter Boyd Terry was Catboy, and guitarist Courtney Pollock was Chainsaw the Prince of Karate. Christian gave me my Aquabat name, which was like getting initiated into a secret club or becoming a Knight of the Round Table. Or maybe the Superfriends. Oddly enough, the name he chose was the Baron von Tito—which was a variation on the Red Baron, the famous World War I German pilot that Snoopy always used to fight in Peanuts. With my heavy visions of dying in a plane crash, I was tripping: Was this dude really naming me after an airplane pilot? I didn't say anything about it to Christian, but that name haunted me from day one in the band.

The Aquabats were an awesome bunch of guys. I had no idea when I joined the band that most of them were Mormon. They didn't smoke. They didn't drink alcohol. They didn't even drink Coca-Cola. They didn't curse, especially not in their music. Whereas I was basically like Satan standing next to them. I drank, I smoked, I had tattoos all over my body. Christian gave me a hard time about my smoking—it became a running joke that if I had a cigarette in my mouth, he might knock it out. He was a positive influence on me; even though I was so different from the other Aquabats, they were always incredibly cool to me and treated me with love. I had a blast playing with them.

Even though we were so different religiously, we had a lot in common. We all grew up skateboarding. We all loved punk rock and grew up on Southern California punk-rock bands like Agent Orange and the Descendents. I'd never met a Mormon my whole life, and now I was getting a crash course in Mormonism. I even went to church with them a couple of times. I've always been open to whatever anyone has to tell me, whether it be Mormonism, Buddhism, anything. It's cool knowing that there are so many different ways to believe in God. The more faith you can absorb, the more hope you can have.

In a lot of ways, the Aquabats were just as punk rock as most of the bands I've ever played in. Christian was totally crazy. Backstage, he'd black out his teeth with magic marker, just to get a laugh. Sometimes he would spray lighter fluid on my drums without telling me. Then in the middle of the set, I'd count off a song and he'd ignite my drums. I would hit my cymbals, and a fireball would explode. Suddenly I'd be trying to play a song with my entire drum kit on fire—it was awesome. People at the clubs would flip out, and fire marshals would want to throw us in jail. I had so much fun playing in that band.

I spit a lot when I'm playing drums. I try to avoid hitting any of the guys I'm playing with, but it was hard sometimes in the Aquabats with at least eight guys onstage. Sometimes I'd accidentally spit on Christian—he'd turn around and spit a loogie right back at me. Then we'd end up having a full-on spitting war in the middle of a show.

CHRISTIAN JACOBS (LEAD SINGER, THE AQUABATS)

Travis might not have seemed like the poster boy for "wacky," but he was more of a merry prankster than people realize. We were on tour with Reel Big Fish and a band called Kara's Flowers, who are now called Maroon 5—they were cool kids back then. One of the first dates of the tour was Milwaukee, at a place called the Eagle Ballroom. It was rumored that Buddy Holly, Richie Valens, and the Big Bopper played their last show there before they died, and the promoter said it was haunted. After the show, we stayed across the street at the Ambassador Hotel, which was rumored to be the hotel where Jeffrey Dahmer had dismembered a couple of his victims. We were all tripping out, but Travis had a gleam in his eye.

We split up into different hotel rooms and got ready for bed. An hour went by, then—BAM BAM BAM—there was a pounding on the door, really scary. I hesitated for a second and went to the door. I looked out the peephole, and someone was in the darkened hallway with a sheet over his head. He had two eyes cut out and was going "Whooooooo!" I cracked the door open, and I could see it was Travis under the sheet. He ran away, laughing.

One time in Colorado, there was a drunk snowboarder in the audience, and I started making fun of him. So he got

upset and came onstage to grab the mic. I looked back, and Travis was jumping over the drums—with his Aquabats costume on, which made it funny—and he was going to stab the guy with a screwdriver. He had that caged-tiger look in his eye: *No one messes with my singer.* I pushed the snowboarder off the stage, and then even after the show, Travis was like, "Let's go get that guy." He literally had my back.

Travis came to my wedding with Tim Milhouse, all decked out with tattoos. People were looking at them sideways. My wife and I registered at Target: Travis got us a Nintendo 64 as our wedding gift.

Since I wasn't playing with Feeble anymore, it didn't seem right to be sleeping on Mike Ensch's floor. I briefly moved back into Pops's house, but now that I had turned twenty-one and had a taste of independence, it felt lame to be staying at home. I had something to prove—to myself, and to Pops. So I moved in with my friend Bill Fold, the promoter at the Barn. He had a three-bedroom house in Riverside, and he would rent out a room for a couple hundred bucks a month for anybody who needed a place to live for a while. It was a revolving door for musicians and kids in the scene.

That was my first time having my own space. It was just a bedroom in Bill's house, but it was still a place to call my own. I painted a big Wu-Tang Clan symbol on my closet door. I probably should have asked Bill, but I didn't: he came home one day and there was a big W on the door. I wanted to make sure nobody could look into my room from outside and I didn't have curtains, so I slapped stickers all over my window.

I couldn't hold down any normal job because my schedule was too inconsistent: the Aquabats would go on the road for a week, or sometimes three weeks, and then come home. Sometimes I worked as a paralegal with Christian: this woman Carol had a daughter who was psychotic about the Aquabats, so she got us jobs filing papers at her law firm. And Bill hooked me up with a part-time job working for his production company, 98 Posse. It was six guys crammed into a tiny office, but it was always fun to hang out with them, and I loved spending every waking moment thinking about music. Sometimes I would just stare at bands' road cases, as if I could learn something about touring by looking at them.

We got lots of demos at 98 Posse: every week, fifteen to twenty bands would send in cassettes and CDs, hoping that they could get hired to play a show at the Barn. One of my jobs for Bill was to listen to all the demos and let him know if any of them were any good. It was fun whenever I discovered a good new band, but most of those demos were horrible. I would sit in Bill's second-floor office listening to the demos, and whenever any of them sucked, I would throw them out the window onto the University Avenue sidewalk, where all the Riverside bars were. It was educational to listen to all those demos, because I learned what *not* to do: most of the bands I heard were either trying too hard or just imitating other bands.

Bill worked insane hours. He would get home from putting together four gigs in one night at different venues. Then he would stay up and work on flyers and ads for his next month of shows. He had an awe-inspiring work ethic: he reminded me of my father, but in the music world. He convinced the Aquabats that he should be their manager, and he and his partner did a great job taking care of the band's business.

For some reason, Bill's house was filled with crazy animals. In his backyard, he had a coatimundi, which is basically a South American raccoon, chained to a pole. When we had people over, if they got too drunk or too high, we'd convince them to go out in the backyard for a smoke. And then this coatimundi would start hissing and charge them. He would scare the fuck out of people—he had teeth as long as your pinkie. Usually that chain would stop him from biting people, but one time he chomped on one of our friends. We laughed it off, but that animal was vicious.

Bill also owned Elvis: that was a five-foot-long iguana who lived inside his house. I loved Elvis during the day, when he was chilling. But if I got home late at night and I had forgotten to lock my bedroom

door, Elvis would get into my room and take up residence in my bed. And there was no way of getting him out: if I even got close to him, he would get territorial, thrashing his tail around until I backed off. I'd have to go sleep in the living room, on an old couch next to Elvis's lair. And then halfway through the night, he'd come back into the living room and kick me off the couch.

Bill had a beautiful old Cadillac, a 1968 model, candy green, with hydraulics, restored from the ground up. It made me hungry to have a Cadillac of my own, so when I had five hundred bucks, I bought a used Caddy from Ron Yerman, a pro skater pal of mine. He tried to talk me out of it: "Dude, I know you want a Caddy, but don't buy it. This isn't the one." I wouldn't listen to him: I basically forced my money on him. I spent hours working on the car in Bill's driveway, with blocks under the tires so it wouldn't roll into the street. It was a 1963 four-door Coupe de Ville. The whole car was dented and pitted, the interior was thrashed, and the hood had cancer holes—but I loved that car. I would be waxing the car and Bill would cruise past me in his beautiful Caddy. He'd say, "Bro, what are you waxing? It's primer everywhere." The whole thing made me feel like my dad—when I was growing up, he always had a broken-down blue Cadillac in the backyard. Pops never actually got that car running—and I got only forty or fifty miles on mine before it caught fire while I was driving it on the highway.

Riverside was a lot closer to Fontana than Laguna Beach had been, so I was seeing my family and friends more often, especially Jim. He came to a lot of Aquabats shows—whenever he was there, they'd get him to dress up in costume and come onstage as the Magic Chicken.

One time, Jim even rode to Las Vegas with us in the Aquabats van. We played a great show—the Magic Chicken made a cameo—and that night, I met a girl. We hooked up and she stayed for the night in the hotel room I was sharing with Jim. She wanted to ride to the next city with us—and that was always a bad sign. It's not fair to your bandmates to bring tagalongs on a crowded van. And usually I wasn't trying to hang out with the same girl two nights in a row, being the jerk that I was. So I decided I'd leave before she woke up—but somehow, *Jim* got stuck in the room with her. I think he felt guilty. I was paging Jim from the van: "Get out here, man, we're all waiting for you. You can't hold up the van." When she got distracted, he bolted for the door and jumped into the van. We peeled out of the parking lot.

I wasn't the only guy in the Aquabats interested in the opposite sex: some of the guys knew girls in different cities that they'd meet up with. But they were true to Mormonism, which is a pretty serious religion. One day, I read one of their books and discovered they weren't supposed to be dirty dancing or even masturbating. I was definitely more wild than the other Aquabats, but I didn't mind letting their morals rub off on me. I think they calmed me down a bit: I started treating the ladies better. In return, I turned the Aquabats on to the Wu-Tang Clan: I would play *Enter the Wu-Tang (36 Chambers)* in the van all the time, and we would rap along. Horn players could do complete verses by Method Man and ODB. Christian the Bat Commander was our RZA, so he would take his parts. But when there was a curse word, they'd skip that lyric.

In the summer of 1997, we recorded an album, *The Fury of the Aquabats!* It was the group's second album; they had put out *The Return of the Aquabats* themselves before I joined, but it was my first time making a real album, so I was stoked. We spent two weeks in Orange County writing songs and rehearsing, and then went in the studio courtesy of Paul Tollett, who was partners with Bill at his promotion company, Goldenvoice. It was all family in the studio: there was no out-of-rhythm A&R guy tapping his foot. We did the whole thing in a couple of days—when you don't have a big budget, you need to make the most of your studio time, so you do it fast and don't get much sleep. The drum parts came first: I knocked them all out in about six hours, and then hung around to watch the rest of the creative process.

After the album came out, great things started to happen for the Aquabats. Our single "Super Rad!" was all over KROQ, which is a major radio station in LA. MTV even played the video a few times. We kept getting booked as the opening band on tours with cool British bands: the Specials, the Toy Dolls, and Madness. I wasn't making a lot of money—the band had to split everything eight ways—but I was living my dream of playing in a band and touring everywhere with best friends. I would have been content to do that for the rest of my life.

We upgraded from a van to a bus. Then we got booked on the 1998 SnoCore package tour along with Primus, the Long Beach Dub All-Stars, Tha Alkaholiks, and Blink-182. That tour took us all over the United States, all the way to New York City: I'd never seen so many buildings so high and so close together. And I couldn't believe I was in the hometown of so many of my favorite rappers.

The first day we were in New York, I was hanging out on the tour bus with Tim Milhouse, a friend who I had gotten to be my drum tech. We had left the door to the bus unlocked, not thinking about it—and then six huge dudes walked on and told us, "Motherfuckers, we're taking whatever we want on this bus." They took everything they could carry, including our CDs and merch shirts. They even opened our fridge and took drinks. We were so young and green, we didn't know what was going on—but when you're outnumbered that badly, there's not much you can do. We couldn't believe we had gotten robbed on our first day in New York. After they left, we went looking for help and I found a cop—who turned out to be a super-hot blonde woman. I had never met a hot cop before. While I was talking to her, I got so distracted, it was hard to remember that I was supposed to tell her about the theft. She was really nice about it, but she couldn't do anything for us. Meeting her almost made up for having all the CDs swiped.

TIM MILHOUSE (FRIEND)

I met Travis at the Barn, a small venue on the Riverside campus of the University of California. It held only about six hundred people, but they had shows by bands like Rage Against the Machine and No Doubt before they blew up. Travis and I clicked, and immediately we were like brothers: same background, same music, same sense of humor. He was about to go on tour with the Aquabats, so he said, "Man, you should come on tour. It's so much fun and there's so many girls. I'll teach you how to set up my drums."

So I did that for a while. We didn't have any money on tour, so I would sell our allotment of VIP passes and tickets. I could get $50 to $100 for each of those, because we were giving people backstage access. Travis would sign his drumheads, and I'd sell those for twenty-five or fifty bucks. Then we'd take the money and go to a strip club.

Sometimes I'd go out in the crowd and bring some girls backstage for Travis. I'd check their IDs to make sure they were of age and escort them onto the bus. We always had to watch out for his tour laminate: there were a couple of times when a girl would give him a blowjob in the back and then want to jack his laminate as a souvenir. I guess she wanted to prove that it was true—she really did suck his dick.

Our first trip to New York, we were staying outside the city, in New Jersey. This was before hotel phones had a direct line out. If you wanted to call somebody and you hadn't activated your phone, you had to call the front desk first. We were trying to find a girl to come over to our room to dance for us. We made about ten phone calls before I said, "This is getting too weird, calling these dudes at the front desk. I'm going to activate the phone."

I went to the front desk and the clerk said, "Hey, are you guys looking for a good time?"

I went back to the room and told Trav, "Yo, this dude thinks we're looking for a hooker."

TRAVIS BARKER
can i say

He said, "Well, fuck, see what you can do." So we ended up jumping in a car with a guy who takes us to a different New Jersey hotel. The hotel was at the top of a hill, and the check-in office was at the bottom. You went up and there was a line of cars and a line of girls, and you picked one. We picked this Puerto Rican girl and went into a hotel room with her. She got fully naked and we started conversing with her, asking her what life was like in New York.

Suddenly we heard her pimp banging on the wall, shouting, "I don't want to hear no talking in there!"

She said, "I gotta do something or I gotta leave. What do you guys want?"

I said, "This is too weird. I'm going to wait outside." So I went outside and got in the car that took us there, while Travis did his thing.

Suddenly, I saw headlights pull up all around us—there were five or six cop cars coming in. It was a bust.

Our driver hit the gas and peeled out. I said, "Dude, what the fuck are you doing? You have to stop."

"No way, man, I'm not getting in trouble."

"That's my boy in there. Stop the car!" The driver got down to the bottom of the hill and stopped there. I got out of the car to see what was happening. The hotel people tried to get rid of me: they knew they were about to get busted, and they told me I had to leave. I said, "Fuck you, I'm about to check in. I'm just calling my friend."

I picked up the pay phone outside the office and called somebody from back home, just talking shit and stalling.

Suddenly, I saw Travis running down the hill with his shirt off. He got to the car and jumped in.

The driver tried to hustle us for fifty bucks. We didn't have any money, so after he drove us around for a while, we ended up back at our hotel and woke up our tour manager so he could pay this guy off.

Chicks always wanted to be with Travis. Back home, he had two Cadillacs, a Coupe de Ville and a white convertible. We'd go to a club: I'd drive one car, he'd drive another. Neither of us would dance at the club—we'd just stand there. We'd pick out a group of girls and say, "Yo, we're going back to the house," and they'd jump in the car. And then we'd party all night. I remember one specific time when I was sleeping on the floor and Travis was in bed with a girl. He started tapping me: "Yo Tim, yo Tim, get in the mix." I was too out of it—I just rolled over and went back to sleep.

Another time, we had this girl stripping in his room. Another one of Trav's friends said, "Act like I'm your stripper pole." So she was taking off her clothes and dancing on him. Travis and I hid her clothes and kicked her out of the house. When she left the house, we sprayed her with a water hose, and I think we threw eggs at her car. We were really disrespectful assholes. But when the girl got home, she called us up: "Hey, I've got more clothes on—can I come back?"

When that tour finished, we stayed on the road with Blink-182, doing a mini-tour up the West Coast. I hadn't known a lot about Blink before I went on the road with them. When I was in Feeble, we had recorded a demo in one day. We sold it at live gigs, and a fanzine

reviewed it alongside Blink's demo (which didn't have a real name at the time, but which people later called *Cheshire Cat* after the art on the cover). *Cheshire Cat* got four pages of coverage, while we got a blurb that was no more than half a page, which bummed us out—we thought our demo was much better. But when I met the band in person, I really liked them and their music. The two main guys were Mark Hoppus, who sang and played bass, and Tom DeLonge, who sang and played guitar. Pretty quickly, I realized that these guys didn't take themselves seriously at all. I thought that was awesome—onstage, they would tell dick jokes and mess around. And offstage, they acted just the same way. They were two best friends who had started the band to have a good time, and they were having lots of fun.

I instantly became friends with Mark and Tom, who were inseparable, and spent a lot of that tour hanging out with them on their bus. Their drummer was never around—they didn't seem to be close to him. I had a lot in common with Mark and Tom. All three of us listened to the same punk-rock bands, and we all loved skateboarding: we could talk about the skaters we had grown up idolizing, like Christian Hosoi and Tony Hawk. The biggest difference was that because they were from San Diego, they had more of a surf influence, and because I was from the Inland Empire, I was into hip-hop. So they might be wearing surfer shorts and a T-shirt with a big Hurley logo on it, while I'd be in Dickies shorts and a Wu-Tang Clan T-shirt.

I got close enough to Mark and Tom that we all started fucking with each other. One time, I ran onstage during Blink's set and pantsed Mark while he was playing. He was wearing baggy shorts, and I pulled them all the way down. He covered his nuts with his bass guitar, but from behind, you could see his ass.

Then Blink-182's drummer suddenly left the tour and went home. No one really knew why he had left, but the upshot was that the band was down one man. Mark and Tom came up to me backstage and asked me to fill in. "If you don't," Mark said, "we're going to have to cancel the show. We'll have a lot of pissed-off fans."

Mark had to do some press interviews before the show, so Tom took me to a small room and taught me their set list. I had about thirty-five minutes to learn twenty songs, so we just whipped through them. Then I had to go do my opening set with the Aquabats. Right after that, I came back onstage with Mark and Tom: I was playing drums for Blink-182, having the time of my life. They paid me half of their regular drummer's fee, so I earned more money that one night than I did playing entire tours

ME WITH BLINK-182

with other bands. But I had such a good time, I would have done it for free. All three of us came offstage sweaty and totally pumped. "We've never sounded so good," Tom told me. "Damn, that was fun!"

I finished the tour playing for both the Aquabats and Blink-182—we did three or four more shows. When the tour was over, Mark and Tom asked me if I would be interested in joining Blink-182.

I told them, "I don't think it's right for me to say that when you still have somebody else in the band. But if the time comes when you need a drummer, I love you guys as people and I love playing with you—give me a call."

The Aquabats had a break after that tour, so I flew out to Detroit—I also had an invitation to play with the Suicide Machines, a cool ska-punk band that had been going for a few years. I was a huge fan of the band, and I was good friends with the two main guys, Jay Navarro (the singer) and Dan Lukacinsky (the guitar player). I stayed with Dan and we had a couple of rehearsals, while I tried to get my head around the idea of living in Detroit. Dan and I would smoke cigarettes in the snow and I would try to figure out Michigan. "Where's the mall? Where do you go skateboarding? Where are the fine girls at? Holy shit, when is it going to stop snowing?" I pretty much had the gig, but I still couldn't get my head around moving to Detroit.

While I was out there, a girl I had been dating told me that she thought she was pregnant. I told Jay and Dan that I had to leave: "Hey, guys, my old lady's pregnant—I've got to do the right thing and go home." A few days after I got back, she took a second test. Much to my relief, it came back negative—but once I was in California, it was hard to imagine going back to Detroit.

BILL FOLD (MANAGER, THE AQUABATS)

In 1994, I started promoting shows at the Barn, which is a venue on the UC Riverside campus in Riverside, California. Around 1995, I kept hearing people talk about how this guy Travis, in a band called Feeble, was a cool drummer. I don't think Feeble ever played for us at the Barn, but Travis started hanging out in our production offices.

One night at the Barn, Suicidal Tendencies were playing. Travis and his friend Tim Milhouse had gotten into a war with Samson, who was our head of security, and my right-hand man Art Marino. Samson got a water-balloon launcher and was firing water balloons in the backstage area, taking people out. This is our *head of security*. The war left the Barn and continued at my house, where they were launching eggs and flour at each other. It was impossible to clean up. Usually there was more seriousness at the Barn, because that was where we conducted business. Everywhere else, we were screwing around.

Suddenly, Travis was the drummer for the Aquabats. Art and I didn't know them, but we went to see them play at this show called Independence Day—I believe it was at Irvine Meadows in Orange County, but in the entrance area, not in the actual amphitheater. The show had one hundred bands on ten stages, and it was just a disaster. How do you find production for ten stages, let alone have it be good? The highlight, though, was the Aquabats. I remember Christian, the singer, holding up a Roman candle that fizzled out. It was a perfect metaphor for the show: *Yeah, things aren't going that well.* But Art and I fell in love with the Aquabats, and after meeting with them, I somehow convinced them that I should be their manager.

Travis moved in with me: I had a three-bedroom house in Riverside that was a revolving door for friends and kids from bands. It was sort of a crash house. In the garage, I had a Cadillac, a 1968 convertible de Ville. Travis's dream car was a Cadillac. One day he came home

with this piece-of-shit four-door Cadillac. Travis and Tim started tearing it apart in the driveway—the driveway was on a slope, and it was very steep, so they had bricks under the wheels to stop it from rolling into the street. My Cadillac was painted and somewhat nice, but at the time, it wasn't a finished restoration—they inspired me to take my car apart too, so I could redo all the chrome.

Travis was a great housemate. At first he was very shy, and cautious about what he said and who he was hanging out with. But he opened up. His concerns at the time were drumming, friends, and girls. And then he realized that Cadillacs are badass, so it became drumming, *Cadillacs*, friends, and girls.

I convinced Paul Tollett to start Goldenvoice Recordings, and to make the Aquabats album his first release. They made an incredible record, and we got some good things going. There was a song called "Super Rad!": Bobcat Goldthwait directed the video and got some cameos from famous people, and KROQ-type stations around the country started playing it.

The Aquabats wore masks made of neoprene, the stuff they make wetsuits out of. They looked like the Lone Ranger, or the Teenage Mutant Ninja Turtles. They would get five or six hundred people coming to their shows, tons of them wearing these masks and silver swimmer's caps—the band sold them as merch. The Aquabats had these crazy characters onstage, many of which ultimately made their way into *Yo Gabba Gabba!* One of the villain characters was "Powdered Milk Man": he would attack with an explosion of white powder. The Aquabats were fans of the theatrics of Gwar, but it wasn't sadistic or evil or mean: instead of shooting blood at people, it was powdered milk. There was a really good energy coming from the stage, and the songs were catchy.

Even in the early days, the way Travis played drums inspired younger kids to play a different style than the Peter Criss setup of drums pointed at you. He led a movement of kids adopting an attack style of drumming. In the early days, he really stood out—now you can find a bunch of people who look like they're playing as aggressively as he does, whether or not they're good players.

Travis never wore his mask onstage—he was the rebel of the band. So everyone knew who Travis was. On tour, he'd be looking to go find some girls and party and have fun. Everyone else in the band was goody-two-shoes, but every day, Travis was showing up with new tattoos, slowly covering himself.

We booked the Aquabats on a Blink-182 tour. Blink already had huge radio play and people were going crazy for them—but their drummer just wasn't taking it seriously. Mark and Tom, as goofy as those guys are, were very serious about the business aspect of the band. They weren't screwing around when it came to playing shows, and they weren't getting loaded every night and being assholes. The drummer, on the other hand, it was almost like he was on the outs with these guys from the very beginning of their success.

Travis filled in for a couple of shows with Blink, and right away the whole band changed. All of a sudden, they weren't just a mediocre band with some songs that a bunch of teenage girls liked. When you put a real drummer in that slot, they could be goofier and play sloppier—but they actually sounded better.

TRAVIS BARKER
can i say

Back in Bill's house, I tried to figure out my next move. Even though Bill was the Aquabats' manager, he was my friend first. So when I talked to him about all these different options, he tried to give me the best advice he could. We went into the backyard to hash it all out. The coatimundi left us alone—I think he was sleeping—but Bill's neighbor had pet emus, which look a lot like ostriches except they're a tiny bit smaller. So we were trying to have this serious conversation while a gang of emus made weird noises and stuck their heads over the fence, trying to check us out.

Both Blink-182 and Suicide Machines were doing well: they were getting radio airplay and having successful tours. I could have been happy playing with either band, but I had more fun with Blink, plus California was home. I was having a blast playing with the Aquabats; I loved everyone in the band. But I knew Christian's ultimate goal was to have a television show. He loved touring the world and playing in the band, but really, his priority was having just enough musical success that he could parlay it into his own television program. I didn't share that vision: I just wanted to be a drummer, not an actor on a TV show.

It worked out great for Christian and the Aquabats: when they finally got to make a TV show, it was *Yo Gabba Gabba!*, which is awesome and a huge hit with kids. It's very cool that Christian brought that to life: from day one, that was his vision. He was very careful: the Aquabats always made music that was targeted toward kids but that still could cross over to adults. (They also recently started a show about the adventures of the Aquabats, called *The Aquabats! Super Show!*)

Mark was calling me about once a week, saying, "I think it's going to happen this week." It felt like I was getting a new girlfriend, one who was calling to say, "I'm going to break up with my dude—I'll hit you as soon as he leaves."

Three weeks after Blink-182 and the Aquabats got off the road, I got the call from Mark and Tom, telling me I was in the band: "Hey, your first gig is tomorrow in San Diego, be there." Blink was playing a birthday party—but it was at a club and there were a thousand kids there. It was overwhelming. I couldn't believe everything that was happening in my life: even though my mom had passed away, I felt like she was upstairs, orchestrating everything.

MARK HOPPUS (BASSIST/SINGER, BLINK-182)

When we asked Travis to be in Blink, I drove up to Riverside from San Diego and picked Travis up at his house. He and I went out and grabbed some food, and then we went to a club in the Inland Empire and watched a ska band play. Travis is never rude to anybody, but he's not going to just start chopping it up with somebody that he doesn't know. Once you know Travis, he talks to you all the time—we've always been friends.

CHRISTIAN JACOBS (LEAD SINGER, THE AQUABATS)

Going on tour with Travis, it became obvious that people were not interested in the Aquabats as much as they were interested in Travis. People from record labels or television studios would come see us and say, "That was cool, but your drummer's amazing." Travis was playing stuff in our band that was far and away more difficult than anything he played later in Blink: different time signatures at light speed. I think one reason he stuck with our band so long is because it was challenging to him creatively. But being in our band was hard: we weren't cool, and we weren't making any money.

A lot of the bands that we played with tried to recruit Travis. I didn't really worry about it: I just had faith that he was down for the cause. This was the guy who had jumped over the drums with a screwdriver. As he started getting more offers, he started getting more distant—he wanted to break away, but he didn't know how.

Travis reminds me of Kobe Bryant on the Lakers. A lot of people don't understand Kobe and say he's arrogant: "I wouldn't want to play with that guy, he doesn't share the ball." And there were times with Travis when I would ask him to slow down, because if you want a song that you can dance to, you've got to groove a little bit. And he would speed up: that wasn't necessarily about what was best for the band, that was more about "I'm the king." At the time it was annoying, but in hindsight, it was fine.

On the SnoCore tour, we were playing with all these cool guys with tattoos—Primus, Blink-182, Long Beach Dub All-Stars, and Tha Alkaholiks—and we were out there saying, "Hey, brush your teeth," assuming everyone was in on the joke. Mark and Tom were so arrogant and jocky on that tour. It felt like they were into punk because it was a fashionable way to make money. But without Travis, Mark and Tom would have been, at best, a lukewarm poser pop-punk band. A couple of hot dogs wiggling around in a bucket.

When Travis did that first show with Blink, they sounded awesome, and all the guys in our band were telling me, "Dude, it's over." I was saying, "What are you talking about? This is the guy with the screwdriver." When Travis told us he was going to join Blink, I started laughing. "Are you joking? Those guys are posers, and you're the real deal." I tried to talk him out of it—but I knew I couldn't hold him back.

I asked Travis to play one last show with us in Salt Lake City—we were headlining over the Vandals, who we worshipped. He said, "That's the same night as my first show with Blink. We're playing a private party for this girl and they're going to pay us forty thousand dollars." I wasn't mad, but I was hurt. I felt betrayed. It cut deep. For years afterward, I had dreams that I would meet Travis and reconcile with him.

I had to quit the Aquabats. We were playing a grad night at Disneyland, where the park stays open all night for high school seniors on school outings. We did two or three sets, playing from midnight until five in the morning. It was a rad gig: No Doubt had booked it the year before. That night, at Disneyland, I told the Aquabats I was going to join Blink, and it was a really hard departure. The band was upset, and I felt like crying myself. Some of the Aquabats tried to talk me out of it.

I tried to explain: "I just want to play drums, and be on tour all the time, and make a living."

I had a really fun year with the Aquabats. When you're in a band like that, you become family, but I felt like Blink-182 was the next chapter of my life. The idea of being in a three-piece punk-rock band—without costumes—seemed much more like who I was.

Once I left the Aquabats, one of the band's reps made noise about how we had a contract entitling them to a percentage of my earnings for the next ten years, no matter what project I went to. I was pissed and shocked. I called the guy up and said, "This is my dream. I finally have an opportunity to make a living doing something I love and you're going to come at me with some bullshit contract I didn't even know I signed? If you do that, I won't even be in this band, because I'm not going to give you the money."

Don't trust words; trust actions.

Bill Fold had nothing to do with it, but it was time for me to leave his house—he was an awesome friend and mentor, but once again, I couldn't keep living with the manager of a band that I had just quit. It felt disrespectful. I packed up my drums and headed down to San Diego.

COURTESY OF ANGIE MELCHIADE

6

Drums Drums Drums

wouldn't be the person I am today if it weren't for the drums. Whenever anything in my life has been bad, I knew I could go to my drums—for me, the drum kit has been better than a girlfriend. Drumming has kept me focused, kept me competitive, kept me out of trouble. Except for my family, nothing in the world makes me happier than drums. I feel like drumsticks are extensions of my hands that just pop on and off.

I never forgot how much I loved Animal when I was a kid. He never played anything difficult—he was a puppet!—but he was always exciting to watch. There's nothing worse than a drummer who looks like he hates his job. When I was growing up, I never wanted to watch somebody like that, even if he was technically proficient. So when I started playing in bands, I never wanted to be one of those dudes—and I also never wanted to be a guy who was showboating but couldn't really play.

One of the first times I got behind a drum kit was in elementary school, when I played drums on Neil Diamond's "Song Sung Blue" for a talent show. I'm left-handed, but the school's kit was set up for a right-handed

player. They told me if I wanted to drum, I'd just have to deal with it. I did, and I still play with a right-handed setup: their being obstinate turned out to be a blessing, because now I'm pretty much ambidextrous.

My first drum teacher was Ed Will, followed by Alan Carter, and then Bobby Dominguez. I owe them all a lot. They were older jazz cats and they weren't really interested in teaching me rock drumming—that was something I had to figure out on my own time. They started with the basics, like different note values, which is basically how long a note lasts (although with drums, you're resting between beats rather than sustaining them). They taught me to read music, independence, and how to play with drum charts for jazz and Latin arrangements. One of the first beats I learned was the bossa nova. Soon I was kicking ass: they would put me in sight-reading contests, where you have to play a chart with just a snare drum, and I would win prizes.

My teachers would also play me Coltrane records and make me pay attention to the drums. At first, jazz all sounded the same to me, but as I listened to more and more of it, I was able to tell different drummers apart.

My all-time drum hero, second only to Animal, is Buddy Rich. Buddy was a wild man—there are crazy bootleg tapes of him yelling at his band. But he had great chops—pure technical ability—as a soloist and he also sounded great with a band. Usually, drummers are one or the other: if they sound good with a band, they can't solo worth a shit. Or if they sound great by themselves, they sound awful with a band because they're overplaying or not complementing the other musicians' parts. Buddy had the full package, and he had enough showmanship to keep you watching him, not just *listening to* him.

I loved Gene Krupa, who was a big-band superstar: he's the guy playing the toms on Benny Goodman's "Sing, Sing, Sing." Then Louie Bellson, who played with everybody from Duke Ellington to Ella Fitzgerald, and who pretty much invented the double-bass setup. And Elvin Jones, who's the drummer on John Coltrane's *A Love Supreme*: he had a really clean, tasteful style. I love jazz, and it's the foundation of a lot of my playing. I always say that when I retire, I'm going to play jazz again.

Meanwhile, I was listening to lots of different types of music—but only stuff that I liked the drums in. It wasn't until I got older that I could appreciate music that didn't have good drums in it, or really even *listen* to it. If a drummer wasn't doing anything interesting, or exploring a little bit, I'd just say, "Fuck, that band sucks."

Pops loved modern jazz like Chick Corea and rebel country music like Buck Owens, Johnny Cash, and Willie Nelson. In the car, that's all he played. I loved that rebel music, even though the drumming wasn't front and center. A lot of country drumming is about what you *don't* play. Mom loved the Police, and that was a good thing to be exposed to at a young age, because Stewart Copeland's such a tasty drummer: he's got a cool reggae-influenced style, and he's great on the high hats.

When I got to junior high school, I discovered metal, and that blew my mind. Slayer's "Angel of Death" was relentless, and Dave Lombardo kept attacking his drums. King Diamond was a huge influence on me—he always had great drummers, like Mikkey Dee and Snowy Shaw.

EARLY DRUM LESSONS

I was also listening to go-go funk and drummers like Zigaboo, also known as Ziggy Modeliste, the awesome drummer from the Meters. Playing along with Zigaboo, I appreciated how creative his parts were. In Sly and the Family Stone, the main drummer was Greg Errico, while in James Brown's band, the funky drummers included Clyde Stubblefield, John "Jabo" Starks, Clayton Fillyau, and Melvin Parker.

One band I could never handle was Rush. Neil Peart's a great drummer, but I cannot listen to Geddy Lee's vocals for more than thirty seconds. I can stomach a couple of songs, but I wish Geddy didn't sing for them, so I could appreciate Neil more.

I read *Modern Drummer* magazine religiously: they also had a series of videotapes, and I watched those. Their videos would showcase different drummers, first playing with a band, then soloing. That turned me on to a lot of the drummers I loved, but when I was watching those tapes, three guys stuck out: my hero Buddy Rich, Dennis Chambers, and Steve Gadd.

Dennis Chambers had insane speed and explosive chops. I knew from reading interviews that he couldn't read music, that all of his playing was by ear. He was one of the first guys to do crossover patterns with lightning

ME IN ELEMENTARY SCHOOL, WHEN PHIL COLLINS
WAS MY DRUM HERO

speed—where the drummer's hands cross each other on the kit—and he could do really flashy stuff. He played with lots of bands, but spent years in Parliament/Funkadelic in the seventies and eighties.

DRUMS! MAGAZINE PHOTO SHOOT. COURTESY OF NEIL ZLOZOWER

Steve Gadd played with Chick Corea and Steely Dan. He had the nastiest groove and the craziest pocket. And he would incorporate all these marching-band chops into his stuff, which really connected with me. He was never about blasting a million beats per minute—what he chose to play was so tasteful. You can gain chops by practicing and drilling, but feel comes from years of playing with other musicians. You need chops *and* feel: it's a balance. As a kid, you're attracted to the guys with monster chops, because that's physically impressive, but Steve Gadd taught me that feel is just as important.

Before I graduated from high school, I studied for a little while with a drummer named Bobby Rock. He taught out of his house in Los Angeles; my sister Tamara would drive me in to meet with him once a month. Bobby had played in a bunch of hair bands—he was the substitute drummer for Kiss. He had studied at the Berklee College of Music and he had a cool drum video called *Metalmorphosis*. He basically reassured me that I was on the right track, and reminded me that I needed to create my own color palette as a drummer. "You've been playing jazz and Latin since you were a kid," he said. "Rock drumming should come easy to you—put everything you do into a melting pot and let it create your own style."

Training will only take you so far—you can have all the technique in the world, but you don't want to sound like a robot behind the kit. The goal is to create your own style. My playing is fast and hard and wild, but it's also grounded in those hours of drum line and jazz lessons. I grew up learning Latin rhythms and Afro-Cuban rhythms, and I still find ways to apply that today.*

Your first job as a drummer is making up your parts. Your goal is to make up interesting parts that complement the song.† And you have to love playing them, so you won't get bored. And then you've got to play them, and play them good every time. But if you can pull it off, and make people want to play air drums along with the song, then you've really won.

If you need fifty takes to record something and then you can't play the part live, you should rethink the part. These days, you can be a sloppy drummer, and people will just fix it with Pro Tools software—I hate that. Every Blink album through the self-titled one (in 2003) was recorded straight to two-inch tape. There was no fixing anything—I had to play each song perfectly all the way through. But as the years go by, I've become less of a critic of other drummers. If you're not a puppet, and you're writing and playing your own music, I respect that.

---

* There were times with Blink-182 when I played a sped-up Latin beat, and Tom and Mark would say, "Dude, that's crazy—do that." They didn't know exactly what it was—it just sounded like some crazy rhythm played way too fast—but they knew that it worked. Pretty soon, we'd have a new song built around that beat.

† Sometimes when I go on tour, I have to go back and figure out the drum parts that I've played. I'll be listening to the album, saying, "What the fuck was I doing there? That's a crazy-ass part."

TRAVIS BARKER
can i say

My number-one thing with other drummers is I want them to enjoy themselves. *Dude, you're a drummer—you're the coolest one in the fucking band.* Act like you love being there and give me a reason to *watch* you.

I've always been a minimalist with my kit. I don't use a double bass. I have one rack tom, one floor tom, a snare drum, and a bass drum. (And sometimes an auxiliary snare.) In some ways, that limits my sound, but I've always wanted to do more with less: play on the smallest number of drums possible and kill it. And when I was coming up, I always had to set up my drums myself. I didn't want to haul a huge kit in and out of the club. I just wanted to put up a tiny kit, not worry about it, and rock.

DANIEL JENSEN (DRUM TECHNICIAN)

I started making drums for Travis when he was in the Aquabats, and kept working with him when he joined Blink-182. A few years later, I started coming on the road with Travis as his drum tech—I've outlasted wives, managers, and record companies. Funny but true. We've been to the four corners of the earth, but no matter where we are, the world revolves around an eight-by-eight square.

When we first met, Travis was playing really small, tight, high-pitched drums—and playing them really fast. Because of the way he played, people always thought that he would be a loud person offstage, but he is actually a quiet, somewhat private guy. He never had a microphone onstage with Blink-182. So during shows, Mark or Tom would ask the crowd, "Hey, everybody wanna hear Travis talk?"

The crowd would cheer, so one of them would hold a microphone up to Travis, who would say, "Hi." And then people would go totally nuts. They never heard him speak, so it was always a big deal.

He's a focused man. There's a certain amount of luck to anything in life, but the things he got didn't just fall into his lap. He's definitely a little piggy who made his house of bricks instead of straw. When he joined Blink, Mark and Tom used to joke, "Now we have a musician in the band!"

Travis's drums are still high-pitched—not as much as they used to be, but more than most drummers like it. It comes from that marching-corps mentality: that way, his playing cuts through the sound. He does a lot of intricate, fast playing, and with the high pitch, you can hear what he's actually doing much better than you would if the drums were downtuned, which would make it mushy and sloppy.

We have a pretty simple kit, compared to a lot of other drummers. Travis doesn't put anything out there that he's not using. For a gig with a DJ, we usually use smaller drums. And when it's a big rock gig, the sizes increase— but it's basically the same setup. Travis has no yellow light: it's stop or go, and when he's on, he's always on 100 percent.

Most drummers set up with their drums tilted toward them—it's easier to hit the drum when it's right there. But I've always set them up totally flat, probably because I got used to playing that way after all those years on drum line.* There are a few other drummers who do that: Stewart Copeland sets up almost flat. Mikkey Dee sets up flat. Mike Bordin, who played with Faith No More and Ozzy Osbourne, sets up flat. But we're a small club. As cats get older, they start tilting their drums, because they don't want to work as hard. When I play somebody else's kit, the tilted drums are incredibly comfortable—I can see why people do it.

---

* Some drummers have asked me if I set up flat so people can see me better. I tell them that's not it at all.

COURTESY OF ADAM ELMAKIAS

My cymbals are hella high—when other drummers sit in my kit, they wonder how I even hit them. The first thing they do is tilt the drums and lower the cymbals. The way I set up my kit probably makes it harder for me to play, but it's what I've always done. It feels weird if I change it, like driving a Ford instead of a Chevy.

I know I'm doing things that I'm not supposed to when I'm drumming: I flail my arms when I play, I hit the drums way too hard, and the proper technique is to keep the sticks lower than I do. I could sit behind the kit and play like the biggest technique monster you've ever seen. But it would bore you, and it would bore me. Playing the way I do makes it more challenging and more exciting and, most important, fun.

I've been drumming so long now, anytime I move my wrists, they click and pop incredibly loud. Before shows, I usually stretch a little and warm up for an hour and a half. I play for half an hour on a pad, getting loose, and then for a full hour, either on a practice-pad drum kit or on a real drum kit. I then go out and play the set, so the full regimen is three hours of drumming. Once the show starts, I'm in a different world. I zone out, and I'm not really thinking: I'm just playing the drums. If I start thinking—about the drums or something else—then I'm not in the moment, and I'm probably not having a good show.

It's not unusual for me to get offstage and find that my hands are bleeding, especially after I've been on tour for a week or two. I can start off by taping my hands, but I always have to escalate. I used to close my wounds with Krazy Glue; these days I have friends who give me surgical glue. It's just part of the job, and I don't like to complain about it. As I always say: *Nobody cares, go harder.*

That's especially true with drumming. I look forward to long bus rides on tour because I know I can play the drums without interruptions. It takes seven hours to get to San Francisco from my house? Great, that means I've got uninterrupted time with my practice pad. I'll sit there with my metronome for hours. Sometimes I just practice speed: whenever I master a tempo, I go up another five beats per minute.[*] Right now, whenever I

---

[*] Mastering a tempo is doing an exercise for a minute straight—otherwise, I don't count it.

try to do 250, I get weak about forty-five seconds in, so I won't move on until I can do it consistently. Once I max out the metronome, I'll just have to start playing the beats double-time.

That's how I develop my stamina for playing with aggressive bands like the Transplants, where a lot of our songs are at 210 or 220 beats per minute. A lot of drummers get bummed out if they have to work with a click track in the studio: that's basically a computerized metronome that you have to play along with. But I've practiced with a metronome since I was a kid, so I've always loved it. I tell other drummers they should consider the metronome to be their friend.

Growing up, I spent hours playing along with records, which is not so different from playing with a metronome. I'd learn to play with records by Van Halen, King Diamond, Run-D.M.C., or the Beastie Boys, but then my sisters might be bumping Janet Jackson or Madonna. I learned a lot from playing along with all those albums, even the ones that didn't have live drummers.

With *any* instrument, if you love it, you continue learning. I've spent hours shedding in my practice room, and that's where I come up with new stuff for future projects. I might spend hours playing in a crazy time signature I'll probably never use, just to challenge myself. Right now I'm relearning how to play everything I do where I lead with my right hand, using my left hand instead. Even if I don't use that skill all the time, there will come a time when I will break it out—and because I've been practicing, it'll be easy. If you're boxing or skateboarding, you can do more if you're not always leading with the same foot or hand. (Skaters call an opposite-foot stance "goofy-footed.") Teaching myself to be ambidextrous, or goofy-handed, might lead to something new on the drums—it's never-ending.

For anybody who loves what they do, mediocrity is not enough. You don't have to be the best in the world, but you should be the best that you can be.

PRACTICE TIPS

1.) SET SOME GOALS. WRITE DOWN SHORT + LONG-TERM GOALS OF WHERE YOU WANT TO BE PLAYING-WISE, (2 WEEKS, 3 MONTHS, 1 YEAR, ETC.) DOWN THE ROAD FROM NOW.

2.) BREAK IT UP. IF YOU'RE NOT INCLINED TO SIT DOWN FOR HOURS AT A TIME, TRY PRACTICING AT 15-30 MINUTE INTERVALS THROUGHOUT THE DAY.

3.) MIX IT UP. MAKE PRACTICING FUN. HAVE LOTS OF VARIETY. KEEP IT FRESH. PUT THE BOOKS AWAY + JUST WAIL ONE DAY, WORK ON TECHNIQUE ANOTHER, PLAY ALONG W/MUSIC ANOTHER, ETC...

4.) ALWAYS HAVE A TAPE RECORDER HANDY IN THE PRACTICE ROOM FOR WHEN YOU STUMBLE ACROSS A COOL IDEA, OR IF YOU JUST WANT TO CHECK ON HOW YOU REALLY SOUND.

5.) SCHEDULE INTERESTING ROUTINES. RENT A COUPLE OF MOVIES AND HAVE A 3-4 HR. DOUBLE-FEATURE PRACTICE PAD MARATHON ON A WEEKEND NIGHT; PLAY 1 LICK FOR 30 MINUTES WITHOUT STOPPING; PLAN A 1 HOUR DOUBLE-BASS "AEROBIC" SESSION, ETC...

6.) GET THE TECHNICAL STUFF OUT OF THE WAY 1ST, THEN PLAY AROUND.

7.) FOR THE REAL TECH-HEADS.... SET A WEEKLY QUOTA OF HOURS, TIME YOUR TOTAL HOURS OF PRACTICE DAILY ON A STOP WATCH, THEN CHART YOUR PROGRESS THROUGHOUT THE WEEK.

8.) WALK-AWAY FROM IT! IF YOU START GETTING BURNT - SPLIT!

ME DURING BLINK-182's EARLY YEARS

7

California Babylon

I wanted to show Mark and Tom I was dedicated to Blink-182. They lived in San Diego, so I decided I should live down there too. I figured being there would also save me a ton of driving: I wouldn't have to spend two hours on the road each way every time we practiced. In the spring of 1998, I found an apartment in Carlsbad, about a half hour north of the city, and moved in with my friends Brent, Adam, and Porno Pete. Carlsbad was kind of a quiet town—lots of retired people and military families—but we turned our place into a bachelor-pad paradise. Wild parties, Cadillacs everywhere, naked girls roaming around the apartment complex at four A.M., loud music; it was awesome.

That lasted about two and a half weeks—then our landlord served us with an eviction notice.

BRENT VANN (FRIEND)

Travis lit my armpit on fire. I used to sleep on the floor, on my back. And then one morning, I woke up and my armpit hair was on fire. He was sitting there laughing, and I started chasing him through the house. I got him behind a heavy steel door. He couldn't breathe, and he was screaming at me to stop, but he was laughing, so that made it worse. I kept shouting, "My armpit hair! Let me do yours!" "Nooooo!"

Getting kicked out of the Carlsbad apartment was our first real falling-out. We started blaming each other, but it was both our problems. When he was on tour, I'd invite a bunch of people over, and eventually someone wouldn't show respect. Our neighbors were big-time dickheads: they'd get pissed off because Travis washed his Cadillac, and you weren't allowed to wash cars in our apartment complex. Or I used to run around the complex naked, just to be retarded, and I'd get busted for that.

"I'm never even here—I'm on tour, so you're the reason why we got kicked out."

"No, you're the reason, because you're fucking girls with the windows open."

We got in this argument and went our separate ways for a while.

I took the eviction as a sign that although Blink-182 might be the right band for me, Carlsbad was not the right town. I moved back to the Inland Empire. It turned out that I didn't really need to be near San Diego, because Blink-182 never practiced. Ever. I just needed to be on the bus when a tour started.

TRAVIS BARKER
can i say

I moved in with my friend Gay Ray—he had a house in a residential section of Riverside, a little bit south of Fontana, where I grew up. Ray wasn't actually gay; he just got the nickname because it rhymed.* When I moved in with Ray, it felt like the Carlsbad party was continuing, except now we wouldn't get thrown out.

RAY COOMER (FORMER ROOMMATE)

When Travis moved in, he didn't have a whole lot of furniture, and he didn't buy anything new. He bought stuff from secondhand stores, and he came up with some amazing stuff. The house wasn't plain, because he liked animal-print stuff, so if we had a shelf, he'd line it with some cool-looking leopard print. It was a fun house—it was a party house.

We never cooked food. Our refrigerator was full of Red Bull and Jones sodas. Travis got shipments of Red Bull—that's why I'm addicted to it to this day. And one time, Jones Soda shipped us two pallets of soda, which was, like, fifty cases of the stuff. We didn't pay for it—I guess they wanted him to endorse it. But we weren't home, and they dropped it off at our neighbor's house. We brought it all over to our place on skateboards, one case at a time. It was way too much, and we didn't have room for it. But it came in handy, because anytime we wanted the grass mowed or anything like that, the neighbor kids would come over and do it for a few sodas.

Travis hardly drank. A lot of the shows that Blink-182 played, there'd be alcohol there, but none of those guys

---

* Later on, when he got older and his hair color changed, people started calling him Gray Ray.

would drink it, so it was free game for me. Always a good time.

When Travis moved in, a couple of people recognized him when we went to the mall: one of his favorite spots to eat was Miguel's in the Tyler Mall. But as he started getting famous, we couldn't go there anymore because crowds would follow him around. I never remember him being a prick to anybody. He was a rock star, but he didn't have the attitude.

But when he started Famous Stars and Straps and started promoting it, that was when things got crazy. He was putting on events at bars, and lots of girls would come over. He kept all his stuff locked in his room because people would take souvenirs, just so they could say they got something from Travis Barker's house.

When Travis went on the road, he would board up the garage so nobody could get into his Cadillac. He was so worried about it: he'd always tell me, "Don't bring your friends over to look at my Cadillac."

One night, he and I brought home three girls. It became obvious that the girls wanted nothing to do with me: they were only there for Travis. One of them ended up in his room, one of them slipped away into the bathroom, and one of them he put in our other roommate's room (he wasn't home.) I never saw them again, but all three of them went home happy.

Riverside was awesome: I was going back to my Inland Empire roots, but now I was an adult in a town that had a good music scene. Some of the local bands that played around that time were Voodoo Glow Skulls, Falling Sickness, and Assorted Jelly Beans. I reunited with my old friends,

TRAVIS BARKER
can i say

plus some cool new people. Soon after I moved in, I met one girl at a club. She said she wanted sex lessons, so she started coming over to the house every Tuesday at lunchtime. I had been banging her for a few weeks when Ray found out—he told me that he had been dating her just two weeks before. He wasn't thrilled, but he was cool about it. I felt horrible.

Ray and I had some crazy parties. Late one night, one girl decided to put on a show for everyone. She stripped off her clothes, and then she stood on top of our glass table, banging herself with a bottle. She was getting excited, bumping and grinding—and then the table shattered underneath her. At first we all laughed, but then we realized it was serious. She was nude, and there was broken glass everywhere. Luckily, the bottle didn't break inside her. It could have been really serious, but she was fine. After that night, we cooled everything down for a while.

I was gone a lot of the time: Blink-182 played a lot of shows. For bigger tours, we'd rent a bus—shorter trips, we had a band van. Pretty quickly, I figured out my job in the band: the guys wanted me to hold things down musically, which let Mark and Tom have fun, play songs, and tell dick jokes. The two of them reminded me of my friends from my high school drum line—they were just always saying raunchy shit, being ornery and funny, talking shit about each other's moms—but they were adults. I was having a blast. They treated me like the band's guinea pig, and I'd do whatever crazy thing they told me. The first time we went to Europe, they took me to the red light district in Amsterdam and handpicked the girl that I would have sex with. And pretty much every show, I would find a new girl to hang out with afterward. (Not always sexually—sometimes just to hang.) The next day, Mark and Tom would want to squeeze stories out of me: "Just tell me what happened!" Not that it was hard to find beautiful girls at Blink shows. Sometimes I'd be playing the drums and I'd look over to my left—standing by our monitor engineer would be four hot girls, all shirtless.

One night, I was doing my drum solo, busting ass and really concentrating. In the middle of the solo, I felt a hand grabbing my nuts—*what the fuck?* It was Tom, crouched down behind me: fondling me and laughing his ass off. Nobody could see him, and I had to keep playing.

One time, we were at a huge airport, waiting at the counter to get our tickets sorted out. Mark got me back for the time I pantsed him onstage: he and Tom teamed up, with one of them pulling down my pants and the other stepping on them so I couldn't pull them back up. It was embarrassing, but it was funny.

At that time, I had big piercings in my ears—plugs that stretched out my earlobes. They ended up smelling really bad: on tour, I sweated a lot during shows, so unless I took out the plugs and sanitized them every day, they would get disgusting. One time during a photo shoot, the three of us were all standing right next to each other and Mark said, "Dude, what's that smell?"

"That's my ear," I told him. "Want to smell it?"

He backed off. "Dude, that's gross."

"C'mon, man, don't be scared. Just smell it—it's an *ear*, bro!"

Then Mark said, "I'll make you a deal. I'll smell your ear after the next show, but I'll put my hand on my nuts and then put it a foot from your face. We can see who smells worse."

"I'm game," I told him. So the next day we did that—my ear won.

For months, we kept playing this game, and my ear would win every time. It didn't matter what Mark did. He would come up to me, feeling confident because he hadn't taken a shower, and my ear would always murder the stench that was his nuts.*

Mark and Tom were funny as hell, but sometimes I needed time to myself—on the tour bus, I would wear my headphones, just so I could listen to my music and chill out. They were worried at first that they were bumming me out, but pretty soon they figured out I just liked to vibe out and listen to music by myself and recharge.

Early on, I got into an argument with Tom: in fifteen years of knowing him, I think it might be the only argument the two of us ever had.

---

* Once I grossed out Mark even worse than that. With Blink shows lasting an hour and forty minutes, I end up spitting a lot, but I know how to time it so I don't hit Mark or Tom. There was one time when Mark ran right into my spit, and it landed right in his mouth. I felt so bad, because Mark's a germ freak. He stopped playing, went over to his bass cabinet, grabbed some hand sanitizer, and started pouring it into his mouth.

BLINK-182 ON TOUR

We were on the tour bus, and he said that metal sucked. "What are you talking about?" I said. "Dude, half the punk-rock bands you and I like have a hardcore metal influence. Metal is badass. Pantera fucking rules." At the time, all he liked was the Descendents and Propagandhi. I told him, "No, metal's dope too, Led Zeppelin's dope, Pink Floyd's dope, the Beatles are dope. There's tons of rad music out there." At the time, Tom didn't even know how many guys were in the Beatles. A couple of years later, he discovered lots of music outside punk rock and it blew his mind.

I actually understood why he loved punk rock so much. They were the same reasons *I* loved it: it challenged everything and questioned *everything*. When you listened to it, it felt like you could do whatever you wanted. It all sounded so much more dangerous than anything else you'd hear on the radio. Good rap music was like that too. But there was other great shit that I loved, from the Beach Boys to Stevie Wonder.

After a few months, it was time to record Blink's next album. The one before, *Dude Ranch*, had gone gold, so everyone in the management office and at the record label had really high expectations. We locked ourselves in a rehearsal room and wrote the album in about two weeks. Going into it, I wanted to mess around with some different tempos. I told

Mark and Tom, "It's going to be repetitive if all our songs have the same punk-rock beat all the time. Why don't we try some different tempos?" And they were really open to it.

TOM DELONGE (GUITARIST/SINGER, BLINK-182)

The first time I met Travis, he was playing drums for the Aquabats. He was wearing goggles and rash guards. I think he was dressed up like a fish. I might have said hi in passing—I didn't really meet him until our drummer had a domestic issue and had to go back home. The worst thing was that it ended up being a nonissue: his girlfriend couldn't handle that he was on tour, so she made up some big story that was a lie. Although that wasn't why we parted ways with that drummer, that was what started it. When we played with Travis for the first time, Mark and I were looking at each other out of the corners of our eyes: *the band sounds a lot better.* We couldn't believe it.

Mark and I figured out pretty early that if we could make Travis laugh, we probably had struck something pretty good.

A big moment early on was when we wrote *Enema of the State*. I had a conversation with Travis: he told me he was bummed out because the songs all had basically the same beat and the same tempo. I looked at him and said, "Dude, I just play guitar and write melodies. You own the beats. If you have an idea, that's what *you're* supposed to do." After that, he owned it—he could jump right on the steering wheel.

In Blink-182, Travis is the musician of the group. Mark is the spokesperson and the voice of reason. I'm the voice of no reason.

TRAVIS BARKER
can i say

Travis plays drums all day long. That drive must be difficult to maintain—but it's also what keeps him so great. He's very regimented with his life, which is the opposite of me. I have an extremely good work ethic, but I'm working on fifty different things at one time, and then I prioritize them by canceling some of them.

I don't think that Travis and I could be any more different, personally. We disagree a lot, but we never talk about it, really. Travis is the kind of guy who would rather let issues work themselves out, instead of throwing more gasoline on the fire. My perception of Travis is that there are no gray areas with him: it's either this or that. Which is good, because I'm totally gray area. I can find good and bad in a lot of different ways, which is philosophical, but also leaves me confused.

Some of our bigger disagreements are about the things that make Blink-182 great. I'm not into urban culture at all. It's just not in my DNA. That doesn't mean I think I'm better—in many ways, I'm a worse musician and performer than a lot of those guys. But what I like in music and art is different. That push and pull between us can lead to greatness, because there's a guy trying to play hip-hop beats on a punk-rock song. And so I can't even say if that's a disagreement at all.

The way Mark and Tom used to work, they'd each write their songs and then they'd come in and teach them to the drummer. But now we were writing together. Some songs would start out with me playing a drumbeat, and one of them would say, "Yo, I'm going to write to that." Other times one of them would have a hook, and then we'd work together to figure out how to make it work as a song.

On "All the Small Things," we were jamming, and we purposely came up with a midtempo song. Tom went away and came back with that "na-na-na" hook, and we couldn't believe how catchy it was. But we kept teasing him: since he called the song "All the Small Things," Mark and I always said it was about Tom's penis.

Mark wrote "Adam's Song" because he felt suicidal when he was lonely on tour, since he didn't have a girlfriend at home. We called it "Adam's Song" because of a sketch on *Mr. Show* about a band that writes a song with that name encouraging one particular fan to kill himself. Mark's song was a total anti-suicide song, about having those heavy feelings but finding a way out. "What's My Age Again?" was basically Mark's lyrics, about how he was a grown man but kept acting like a kid. The musical ideas for all those songs came from the three of us jamming.

Anytime you write a song, it's better to physically play it in the arrangement that you want to record it. You will always come out with better results than just piecing parts together in a studio; it will flow more. Because if you're just listening to it instead of playing it, then you're just hearing a bunch of parts squished together—it can be very hard to tell if it rocks.

MARK HOPPUS (BASSIST/SINGER, BLINK-182)

When I come up with a song idea and bring it to Travis, I'll say, "And maybe the drumbeat will go like this," and then I'll tap something out on my knees. Travis nods, and says, "Okay, okay." Then he goes in to record it and does something completely different that makes the song a thousand times better. He goes for the unexpected, but somehow it makes sense in the context of the song. He's not just looking to make a beat—he thinks about the song. When we're recording, he and I talk a lot about phrasing: how's this verse going to work going into the chorus? We make space for Trav to do his flourishes and

then we come in with the vocal. He has a good ear for what's going to fit in a song.

Tom is always trying to push things out in a song; I'm always trying to push things in. And Travis is like lightning: you never know what's going to happen.

After two weeks of songwriting, we recorded the album in three or four days. We made the whole album at the home studio of Chick Corea, the jazz pianist. Pops always used to play his music in the car, so I was excited to be in his house. I recorded all of my drum parts in one day: that took about eight hours. And then Mark and Tom did guitars and vocals. And that was it. With Blink-182, the stuff that is the most rad is the stuff that isn't too thought-out. We made the album we wanted to make, being who we were but trying a couple more things than what the band had done before.

We had an awesome producer, Jerry Finn, who was just a few years older than us. Jerry was usually wearing a Replacements T-shirt and Vans sneakers. He had worked with Green Day, Jawbreaker, and a bunch of bands on Epitaph Records, including Rancid and Pennywise. Jerry wasn't some asshole rolling up to the studio in a Bentley—he was one of us. He could be honest with us, and we would listen to him, which is really important. These days, "producer" means "I'm going to write some songs for you." He didn't do that—he was more about giving us ideas and lending an extra set of ears. He'd say, "Hey, that sounds cool—why doesn't that part at the end go a little longer?" Or "What if this song had an intro?"

Jerry hated my snare drum, because it was always tuned too high for him (like a marching snare). But what he hated most of all were vibraslaps: that's a percussion instrument with a wooden ball attached to a box with pieces of metal inside. It makes a distinctive crashing sound. You hear it in a lot of Latin music, and it's all over "Crazy Train" by Ozzy Osbourne. It became a running joke between the two of us: I would keep trying to sneak in a vibraslap, and he would get irate.

We called the album *Enema of the State*. (At the time, Tom was worried about his diet, so he was experimenting with enemas.) Soon after we handed it in to MCA, our record label, they freaked out and told us it was going to be huge: we would be going platinum and playing arenas around the world. We all laughed it off—that just seemed ludicrous. I told myself it was going to sell horribly—I figured that way, if it did well, I'd be extra stoked. The first thing we had to do after finishing the album was to film a video for "What's My Age Again?" The directors, Marcos Siega and Brandon PeQueen, had found out that sometimes we stripped down onstage. I would get hot, so I would play in my boxers. Sometimes Mark would take off all his clothes and put his bass over his junk.

So we got the word: We want you guys to do the video in the nude. A week later, we were running down Third Street in Los Angeles naked. People kept staring at us and honking their horns. This went on for about fifteen hours—between shots, we would put some clothes back on, but then we'd have to take them off again. The directors kept shouting, "Derobe!" When there were kids around, they gave us some skin-colored Speedos, but those weren't much more flattering than just being buck naked.

COVER SHOOT FOR ENEMA OF THE STATE.
COURTESY OF DAVIDGOLDMANPHOTO.COM

Soon after the release of *Enema of the State*, in early June 1999, we went on the Warped Tour. Tom and Mark warned me about Fletcher, the guitarist for Pennywise. The band had taken out Blink a few times, which was awesome, but then he would sit at the back of the venue with a pellet gun and shoot pellets at them while they were onstage. At the time, Blink were traveling in a van—but it had a little trailer attached to the back for their gear and merch. Fletcher locked them all in the trailer and then drove to the next gig: "This is the initiation, motherfuckers."

The first day of the Warped Tour, Fletcher came up to the band—I had heard all the horror stories, so I was nervous. He told us, "I'm going to be sitting behind you tonight. I don't know anything about your new drummer, but this motherfucker better wail, or I'm going to kick his ass." I played my ass off, not because I was worried he was going to hurt me, but because it was Fletcher from Pennywise. I did everything ten times faster than I usually did it, and put in as much extra as I could. When I came offstage, he gave me props, and that was huge.

The Black Eyed Peas were on that Warped Tour, back in the days when they were more of a hip-hop act than a pop act—they used to breakdance a lot during their live set. I would sit in and play them. The Warped Tour had always been nothing but punk rock—that was the first year they mixed in some hip-hop. Eminem was on that tour too; he and his partner Proof would hang out on the side of the stage, watching us play. That tour lasted over a month, with shows almost every day—and I think I saw every single set Eminem and Proof did. We didn't spend a lot of time with Em, but Proof would hang out with us almost every day.* That was the year Em blew up: he had never done any shows, never been out on tour, but he was killing it every day on this punk-rock tour. He was out of place, but it was the most beautiful displacement ever. He got bigger and bigger as the tour went on. People were responding to this white kid with bleached-blond hair who was saying the most insulting, crazy, shocking shit. He was destined to be huge.

Enema of the State kept blowing up while we were on the Warped Tour, and the response was mind-blowing. Every show was bigger than the day before, until it got to levels we couldn't even comprehend. Every day, before we even went onstage, there would be tons of kids packed in like sardines at the front of the stage.

Ice-T was also booked on that tour, which was awesome—I had grown up on his album *Power*. One day, we were hanging out in one of the band

---

* Rest in peace, Proof.

trailers, chopping it up, and he told me, "If a motherfucker disrespects me, I'll set him on fire. I'll build a damn bomb. You wanna know how to build a bomb?" And he went through the whole procedure. That night, when I watched his set, he gave the same speech onstage, giving the whole crowd step-by-step instructions on how to build a bomb.

Our album was selling more and more—but it really exploded when we released the video for "All the Small Things," where we parodied the videos of boy bands like 'N Sync, the Backstreet Boys, and 98 Degrees. It was awesome to be clowning those groups—in interviews, they tried to be cool about it, but you could tell they were really hurt. The weirdest thing about that video is that in some countries outside the United States, they genuinely thought that we were actually a new boy band.

Our videos were in heavy rotation on MTV and were played constantly on *Total Request Live,* the MTV daily countdown show hosted by Carson Daly. We became regular guests on *TRL*—one time we had a BMX bike race inside the studio. Halfway through, Mark decided he would compete better if he took off his clothes. Somehow, he won. Carson was supposed to interview the winner of the race, but he said, "I've never interviewed a naked man in my life, and I'm not going to start now."

TAMARA BARKER (SISTER)

The first time I ever saw Blink-182 play a big concert, it was at the Forum. The funniest thing was that every time they would show Travis on the video screen, these girls would start screaming. They were screaming louder for him than they were for Mark or Tom, and that was just weird. I'm not saying he's unattractive, but I never pictured him as a sex symbol.

I felt bad for Travis after he got famous—he can't go anywhere without people coming up to him, and I don't know how he does it. You want to sit and have dinner, or go to Disneyland with your kids, but every five min-

utes he has to sign autographs. All that attention just
seems weird.

That album took us all over the world, for months at a time. We were
playing awards shows with Britney Spears and Christina Aguilera when
we were used to hanging with bands like the Vandals, Unwritten Law,
and Seven Seconds. It was awesome being thrown into a whole different
world. We didn't belong there: we were the misfits. We were proud, but
we didn't understand what all the fuss was about. It was always weird
when people would ask us to sign autographs: we never felt like we were
cool enough to do that.

We won a Moon Man at the MTV Awards (Best Group Video, for
"All the Small Things"). Dr. Dre and Steven Tyler were handing out
the award, and they were two of my biggest heroes, so when we came
up onstage, I didn't even touch the Moon Man: I just went and shook
hands with both of them.

After one of the first *Enema* tours, we had a few days off at home.
I still didn't have anything dependable to drive, so I went to a local
Cadillac dealership. I stood around the lot for about forty-five minutes,
and nobody wanted to help me. I had dreadlocks, I was wearing shorts
and a sleeveless T-shirt, and they could see my tattoos: they didn't think
I was a serious buyer. Some of them thought I was homeless. Finally,
a salesman came out—to tell me that I couldn't be walking around the
cars and I would have to leave.

"Actually, I'm here to look at a car," I told him. The guy did not want
to help me—he wanted proof of funds for me to even get close to an
Escalade. He said, "You know this costs sixty-five grand?"

I said, "That's fine."

"What do you mean, 'That's fine'?"

"I mean that's fine—I have the money for it." Finally, I said, "Can
you please get a manager or something? I've stood out here for forty-five

minutes, and I'm asking you honestly for help, but you don't think I have enough money to buy this."

He went and got Woody Dutton, who owned the dealership. I told Woody I had no credit—the salesman was saying, "See? I told you!" That guy was just not on my side. But Woody listened to me. I said, "I know I just met you, but I'm not bullshitting you, man. You can turn on MTV and we have the number-one video on *TRL* right now. I have money for this. I know I don't have credit, but I want to buy this Escalade."

Woody was such a G. He got on the phone with his finance guy and said, "Turn on MTV. You watchin' it?" Luckily, our video was being played right then. "See that kid with the tattoos? He's here in my dealership, he wants to buy a Cadillac, and I want to help him out. What are you going to do for him?"

He walked me through all the financing. I got the Escalade, and that was the beginning of me having a credit history. Woody believed in me—and he told the salesman that the next time I came in, he was to help me and treat me with the utmost respect. Over the years, I've probably bought twelve cars from Woody.

WOODY DUTTON (GENERAL MANAGER, DUTTON MOTOR COMPANY)

Travis didn't have any bad credit: he had no credit at all. He was a ghost. My friend at GMAC called me back and said, "Woody, I saw the video—I'm going to take a chance on this one."

When I told Travis, he said, "I can't thank you enough for taking the chance with me. I'm coming back in another month and I'm buying one of these cars right here with cash, for my dad." And he did.

I used to get that attitude from fancy restaurants, too: I'd come in with a girl and they'd say, "I'm sorry, sir, we don't have public restrooms."

"I'm not here to use the restroom—I'd like to eat."

They would say I couldn't eat, or I'd have to go home and change, or put on a jacket they provided. After a while, I made a promise to myself: *Fuck any restaurant—or any other business, for that matter—that doesn't want me as a customer, showing up however I look.* I'm not going to wear the maroon host's jacket anymore—if I can't look the way I look, I don't want to give them my money.

I've never dressed to reveal what I'm worth. I will never not be myself just to gain something, and I will break every stereotype.

PROMOTIONAL POSTERS FOR FAMOUS

8

Famous Stars & Straps

When I started my company, Famous Stars and Straps, I had no idea what I was doing. I just had a vision: I wanted to do something that didn't exist yet, something that came out of my lifestyle. I was into skateboarding, BMX, cars, tattoos, rap, metal, punk. I didn't see any clothes that reflected that mix, and I wanted to make some clothes that anyone could wear. Your clothes are your second skin—I wanted to be responsible for that second skin, and make sure that it would represent people outside their bodies, saying who they are.*

The seed was planted when I was a teenager, making bootleg concert T-shirts with my friend Marcos and selling them at local shows. I learned then that if you had an idea, you could get the artwork together, print up shirts, and bring them straight to the people.

---

* Ironically, I own a clothing company but I'm severely colorblind. Sometimes I think I'm wearing a blue shirt but it's actually purple. I can't see the difference between greens and browns. In high school, my girlfriend helped me buy clothes. When I grew older, I learned that I really liked black T-shirts. Luckily, at Famous, I have a team of people who can guide me—and black and white still seem to be the most popular colors for T-shirts.

Famous really started, however, when I was still in the Aquabats. I would make random stickers, just experimenting with digital printers that could make one at a time. At first it was called Voltron Crew (I had been listening to too much Wu-Tang Clan/Method Man) to represent the whole crowd that I was hanging out with at Bill Fold's house: me, Brent Vann, and Tim Milhouse. But the name didn't feel right, so I started messing around with other ideas. Then I came up with Famous Stars and Straps, and I loved everything it meant. It's obviously a play on "stars and stripes," but "straps" has a lot of associations, from guitars to guns. And everybody wants to be famous.

I got passionate about Famous: whenever I had some extra money, I'd print up shirts and stickers. Then I'd walk for miles, plastering the stickers everywhere. When I joined Blink, my first check from the band was for $3,000, which seemed like an enormous amount of money. I told my Pops I had just gotten three grand, and he said, "You better save every penny of that, because you're probably never getting paid that much money again."

I took his advice halfway: I saved fifteen hundred and I used the other fifteen hundred to print up stickers that said I LOVE ORGASMS. It was a funny slogan, but it also totally fit me: I was a bit of a sex addict, just a horny young man in a band. I also made a couple of T-shirts, found some fonts that I wanted to use,* and came up with a logo. I sold the shirts and the stickers at Blink shows, and they did really well; I put all the money right back into printing up more. When I wasn't making stickers, me and my friends would photocopy our genitals at Kinko's and paste those up too. Somewhere in Cali, next to an old Famous sticker, there is also a wheatpasted photo of my junk.

I had a lot of friends in the fashion industry: Bob Hurley from Billabong, Jack from Black Flys, Luke from Silver Star, and Kelly from Third Rail were always visiting Blink backstage when we were touring. I talked with them about their businesses and figured if they could sell shirts, I could too. I said, "Yo, I'm going to open a store back home. It's

---

* Especially the Steelworks typeface, which made everything look like a Slayer album.

going to be called Famous Stars and Straps. I'm going to carry you guys, I'm going to carry Hurley, Tribal Gear, Zero, and Alien Workshop. I'm going to carry all these cool brands and I'm going to carry my own shit there too."

So I got this guy in Riverside to lease me an abandoned building. I didn't have a business license, I didn't have any paperwork, I hadn't applied for any copyrights or trademarks. I built out some of the ground floor into a retail space in about three weeks: me and my friends did the construction ourselves. Sometimes we took Ritalin, chain-smoked, and stayed up for three days at a time. Then we got a couple of friends to come in and spray-paint murals onto the walls.

I asked Tom and Mark if we could play a free show for the grand opening of Famous Stars and Straps, and they said, fuck yeah, we'll come do it. We played outside, and a huge crowd showed up (including Adrian Lopez and some of the skate team from Zero): at the time, Blink-182 were number one on *TRL*. The show ended up shutting down Van Buren Boulevard, one of the main streets in Riverside. All without a permit or a business license. It was insane.

A FAMOUS BODEGA STORE AT A TRADE SHOW

RAY COOMER (FORMER ROOMMATE)

The first Famous store was a beat-up building. Travis turned it into a rehearsal place, and then he had his product in the front. To draw customers, they decided to have Blink play. The radio station 103.9 (X FM) got wind of that and broadcast the news. The store was right on Magnolia, with two lanes going one way, a center divider, and two lanes going the other way. Easily a thousand people showed up, covering the whole street. The cars that were parked in front of the store, they got trampled. People were sitting on them, standing on them: anything they could do to see the stage. The police came and broke it all up. I think Travis got in trouble—he never did anything like that there again.

Pretty quickly, we were doing good business and making some noise. Lots of people were shopping there—it seemed like there was always a dope Cadillac parked out in front by one customer or another. I kept working on the building, turning some space in the back into rehearsal rooms for bands. About three months after we opened, we started having a lot of problems. The police kept coming by, asking for work permits, business papers: everything I had never filed with the city. My lack of experience was obvious: I didn't even know I was supposed to have a sales

FAMOUS STARTED
OFF WITH BUCKLES —
WE SOLD ½ MILLION OF
THIS DESIGN IN THE
FIRST YEAR.

license. The police also did a walk-through of the building and searched the rehearsal rooms. They found drugs and guns—and they weren't even mine. They had been stashed by one of the bands that was practicing there.

It was obvious where this was all heading: they were going to shut down my store. So I closed it down myself before things got ugly. I was bummed, but that turned out to be the best thing that could have happened. I had basically been running a skate shop that also sold a couple of store shirts that said "Famous Stars and Straps" on them. A business like that, you spend a lot of time selling other people's stuff. You look through their catalogs, picking the right things to buy—but sometimes they don't sell. That means you have to contact the company and say, "Hey, can we do a sell-back, because these aren't moving?" I called all that work being a retail junkie. But once I closed the store, I wasn't worrying about selling other people's clothes in a retail outlet. I could put all of my energy into building my own brand.

TIM MILHOUSE (FRIEND)

We were on tour and we saw all these brands starting. The intention with Famous was to start a brand for us, something that we'd be stoked to wear. Originally it was a belt-buckle company and we made belts with stars on them. The first shirt said I LOVE ORGASMS. After I stopped being Travis's drum tech, I went on tour for the brand one time and pushed those shirts and stickers, just trying to get the word out there.

Travis started the company in one of the empty bedrooms in his Riverside house. He got a desktop computer, and we used stock fonts off of Microsoft Word. We got stickers made at a local place, S&W Plastics

FAMOUS DESIGN

line:	**FAMOUS STARS & STRAPS**	season:	**SUM 15**
design:	**MASKED FACES**	division:	**MENS**
colors:	**WHITE & BLACK**	date:	**8/29/14**
artwork by:	**RICH / MOUSE LOPEZ**	approved:	**PENDING**
special info:		sample:	**XXXXXXXX**

FAMOUS DESIGNS BY MOUSE LOPEZ

in Riverside. And then we'd go out and plaster stickers all over. I never got in trouble for doing that, but the brand has gotten phone calls. We knew we were doing a good job when cities called and complained. When that happened, we'd focus on a different area.

I rented a warehouse and started working. At first there were just two of us, me and my friend Will. We had an online business: people would place orders through the website, and we would ship shirts to people. Slowly, as the reputation of Famous grew, mom-and-pop skate shops started calling us. I didn't have any sales reps when we started: we were just reactive. The first place to call us was Electric Chair, a cool clothing store and piercing shop with locations in Riverside and Huntington Beach. They called up and said, "Look, we want to buy ten dozen T-shirts.

Can you get them to us in a week?" We printed the shirts ourselves and hand-delivered them.*

JIMMY "SHRUGGS" GULLY (FRIEND)

It was a rough beginning with Famous. Hot warehouse, no AC, peeling stickers, making shirts with heat transfers. Then we'd go out every night and sticker-bomb the freeways and the neighborhoods and the high schools. When we got big corporate orders, like when Hot Topic came around, we didn't really have the manpower. So it would be two of us doing, say, an order for twenty thousand belt buckles. Hot Topic would send us their own tags, and we'd have to hand-tag each buckle ourselves. But luckily, Red Bull and Monster would send us pallets of energy drinks, so we'd be wired all day, packing orders.

One time, we got a package of belts from wherever the belts were being made—some other country. We had thousands and thousands of belts in freight containers, and

---

* We didn't need most of the warehouse space: at the beginning, I would park my cars at the warehouse and give drum lessons there. During the height of Blink, I began giving lessons during my breaks from touring; sometimes seven or eight students in a day. It was a full-time job that I was doing when I was home. It was a way for me to keep playing drums instead of just partying with my friends, and I loved giving something back.

Some students lasted only one lesson: I would figure out that it was some thirteen-year-old kid who just wanted to stare at me for an hour, and didn't really want to learn drums. They would pick up the drumsticks, and I could tell it was their first time doing it. They just wanted to chop it up with me one-on-one for an hour. I would tell the parents, "Look, I appreciate you coming down and it was awesome meeting your child, but I feel guilty taking your money. I do meet-and-greets for free at concerts." Then there were other kids, boys and girls, who would ask me lots of questions: How do you play this song? What is this lick that you do here? And those were the best.

I haven't been able to give lessons for a while, although I'd love to take on a few students again. What I've been doing instead is posting tutorial videos on YouTube under the name "The Crash Course."

they came infested with crazy exotic roaches. So those
foreign bugs infested our warehouse for a while.

I toured with Travis, setting up the Famous booth at
all the stops and doing all the Famous promo stuff. I
figured out how to work the ladies: I'd sit onstage, on
the side of the stage, but just visible enough that the
crowd could see me. I'd sit up there for a couple of
songs and then I'd go walk around in the crowd. I had
a big bleached 'fro back then, so I was recognizable—
chicks would come up to me. It's crazy what women will
do on tour.

Famous Stars and Straps was homegrown: the business got bigger
and bigger, but it all happened organically. I always had a team of
friends working with me who were just as passionate about Famous as I
was. Originally, it was me, Tim Milhouse, Jimmy Gully (aka Shruggs),
Melissa, Will, Ryan Leonard, and sometimes my friend Jeremy.[*] We
made mistakes, but we learned as we went, with no business degrees and
no outside help. Self-made, dues paid.

---

[*] Tim, Jimmy, ans Ryan still work at Famous today.

AN ADVERTISEMENT FOR FAMOUS, ARTWORK BY LUKE WESSMAN

ABOUT TO BOARD A
PLANE TO THE
MIDDLE EAST WITH
BLINK-182

9

Pills, Broken Bones, and Wedding Rings

Whenever Blink-182 did a world tour, we flew about fifty times to get from city to city. I was doing what I loved—playing drums—and making great money. But fifty times in the space of two or three months, I also had to do something that I hated and feared more than anything. During takeoffs, I'd be white-knuckling, and sometimes Mark and Tom would laugh and make fun of me, because I'd be like, "Dude! Did you hear that noise?" It was usually the landing gear.

One time we flew to Miami, played a show, and then flew straight to the Bahamas, where we were doing something for MTV. In the Bahamas, I was smoking a cigarette when the band's manager, Rick DeVoe, told me, "You need to quit smoking, Travis. You've got to take care of yourself. Twenty years from now, you might have kids, or you might want to relax and enjoy everything you've worked for."

I said, "Man, we could die in a plane crash at any moment. It doesn't matter if I quit smoking—who knows the fucking shit that could happen?" I had been living day to day for so long since my mom died. I didn't have

a death wish, but I didn't expect to grow old—every year, I was surprised that I was still alive.

The more successful the band became, the more we flew—we even started taking private jets. I medicated myself to get through it. If we flew to London to play three days at Wembley Arena, I would put myself to sleep to get through the flight, crushing up Vicodin in my Jack and Coke. I didn't even enjoy drinking. When I started, my goal was not to do too much, so that when I landed, I still had a day to get it out of my system. But pretty soon, I was taking more and more pills.

On one flight to Australia, I had a Xanax bar. That's not a traditional pill—it's a long, skinny bar that you can break into four pieces. I ate the whole bar and went to sleep. I woke up halfway there, somewhere over the Pacific Ocean, took another one, and went right back to sleep. I slept for the whole nineteen-hour trip, and when the plane landed, they were trying to wake me up: "Mr. Barker, excuse me. Mr. Barker?" They practically had to drag me off the plane. I was so out of it that in the Sydney airport, I couldn't figure out how to put my feet on an escalator. I just stood at the top, puzzled about how I could step onto something that was moving. For about ten minutes, people kept pushing by me to get on the escalator. Finally I rode it down—and then I fell asleep again at baggage claim.

I started taking pills for fun when I wasn't flying. I wouldn't take anything before a show, but as soon as I got offstage, I liked swallowing a handful of Vicodin and chain-smoking. I loved that feeling of being so chilled out that I was almost melting.

A friend invited me to a bachelor party in Las Vegas. I was off the road, so I would have been content to stay at home in Riverside: smoking some cigarettes, smoking some weed, eating some pills, talking about cars. But he said, "Dude, just come out—it's my bachelor party, don't miss this." I said fuck it, and I decided to fly out. I brought my pal Brent—we shared a hotel room.

I took a bunch of pills on the plane. Pills do different things to different people: if I take a handful of painkillers, I'll be awake for the next twenty-four hours. I have hella energy, but all I do is talk.

TRAVIS BARKER
can i say

The party was at a strip club. I had been to ghetto strip clubs in Riverside, but I had never seen anything like this: beautiful girls everywhere, and first-class insanity. Everyone at the party was messing around with different girls. I gave a bunch of money to the girls, a couple of thousand dollars total, and told them to make sure the bachelor was taken care of—I wanted them to do the dirtiest shit to him they could. And one of them surprisingly said, "But I want you."

She was the dopest girl in the whole club—to me, anyway. So I was like, sure, why not. She gave me some intense lap dances. I was at the strip club maybe two hours, tops, and then I left with this hot stripper and her girlfriend. We went back to my hotel room and had the craziest night ever. Brent was sleeping one bed over, and he didn't have a girl, but that didn't slow the three of us down.

I had never experienced anyone so wild and free as these two. They were doing crazy things to each other, and they fucked the shit out of me. I was tripping. But halfway through, a condom broke. It went from being the best night ever to being a nightmare. The next day, I was so afraid: what if she's pregnant? I was drunk, I don't remember: did I come? It haunted me for the next year. I kept waiting for a call or a text telling me that she was pregnant.

I started to realize that I needed to watch who I was intimate with. I was safety boy from day one, but accidents can happen. I didn't want random diseases, and I was terrified of having a kid with some girl who I never actually wanted to see again.

Back in Riverside, I was still living with Gay Ray and partying at his house. There was a guy named H-Dog living in the neighborhood. We used to get H-Dog high sometimes. One time, we smoked some weed and took some pills and H-Dog left our place saying, "Dude, dude, I really don't feel right, Trav. This is fucked up, I don't feel right."

I said, "H-Dog, I'll just walk you to your place. Go lie down—you're going to be okay."

"Trav, I drank too. I don't know, man. Maybe I should call an ambulance. Man, I'm breathing crazy."

I got him back to his house and got him to lie down in his bed. The next day I went by his house to see how he was doing—I crept up to his window and said, "Wake up! It's noon!"

H-Dog hadn't gone to sleep—he was in the same position I had left him in the night before. He had been looking at the ceiling for twelve hours straight. "How do I make this go away, Travis? I don't know what to do, man." It was like a scene from *Friday*. He came down later that afternoon.

H-Dog had a complicated family situation. He had three little brothers. They didn't have a lot of money—if the kids were good, the big reward was that they could sit in the back of his truck and he would rev the engine. Then H-Dog's mom got sick and her husband left her. That broke my heart—it reminded me of what had happened to my mom. So whenever I got home from tour, I would make sure to take his mom out to dinner. Not trying to date her in a creepy way: keeping her company and making sure she was doing good.

My friend Tim and I used to go to local clubs: some of our favorites were In Cahoots, the Metro, Club Rubber, and the Baja Beach House. We'd show up and just stand there for a little while, not dancing, enjoying the scenery, hoping the DJ would play Method Man or Cypress Hill. Inevitably, girls would approach us. If we liked them, we'd tell them we were heading back to the house and invite them to come with us. They'd jump in the car.

This strategy caused some problems—sometimes a girl had actually come to the club with a guy, who didn't appreciate it when she took off with us. The next time we went to the club, some dude would be like, "Bro, that was my chick." There was too much bro stuff going on—and you always needed to get out early, because the minute those clubs closed, there were shootings in the parking lot and bullshit I wanted to steer clear of. That didn't stop me from going to the clubs, though.

A lot of those girls were pretty shallow. But I was being shallow too: I was down for a one-night stand. Everyone understood why we were there, and no one's feelings were hurt.

One night at the Baja Beach House, we met a trio we called the Platinum Girls: three girls, all hot, with platinum-blonde hair. I started talking to one of them, named Melissa, and she was smarter and more real than most of the girls I was taking home. I actually got her phone number and called her the next day. A few months later, we became a couple: I was crazy about her, and I was happy staying clear of the clubs.

MY GREEN '66 CADILLAC

I had three Cadillacs by now. I still had the one with cancer holes that had blown up on the highway—I ended up selling it for $200, because it was basically just scrap metal. Then I bought a green 1966 Cadillac and a 1970 white convertible Cadillac. I also bought a truck, and all these cars were sitting in Gay Ray's garage.* I was getting money from Blink-182, but I was hood rich, just buying one car after another. Mark, Tom, and everyone else around Blink-182 kept telling me I had

---

* Customizing cars was becoming a passion of mine. Once I could afford an old Cadillac, I preferred that to a brand-new car. There's something about finding an old car that you can design and make your own from the ground up. It's making something from nothing, like building a song or a beat. Seeing the car when you first get it—whatever condition it's in—and then watching the transformation. First bodywork and primer, then paint and suspension, and then wheels and interior. It's another form of self-expression, and I love it.

to be smarter about my money: "Dude, stop buying cars. You need to buy a house."

Eventually, the message got through to me. People in Riverside knew where I lived and were coming by the house all day long, and I got tired of it. I was hanging out with Melissa one morning and I said, "I'm going to look at houses—you want to come with me?" She knew nothing about real estate, but she was up for it.

MELISSA KENNEDY (EX-WIFE)

I met Travis at a club in the Inland Empire, when he was young and I was *extremely* young. He was just getting involved with Blink-182; I think they were about to make their first music video together. I didn't like Travis that much at first: I just thought he was weird. We got to be friends—and then, after a good night of drinking, we never left each other's side for years.

GAMBLING WITH MELISSA
AND LUKE DOG

The whole time we were together, Travis would not go onstage unless I kissed both his hands and both his drumsticks: *one, two, one, two.* And whenever we were on a plane, we had to wear the same clothes because he was so scared of flying. He had his lucky flying pants, and I had my lucky flying rock: a little worry rock. We'd pass it back and forth, depending on who was more scared that day.

One time we were in Italy—Blink-182 were appearing on MTV Italia. After they taped their interview, we went out to the van. But there weren't enough police officers, and the van got surrounded by a crowd of Italian teenagers. At the time, Blink were the biggest band in Italy, bigger than the Backstreet Boys even. These kids were beating on the windows, and it was a very scary situation—even our security guards were scared. We had to all lie down on the floor of the van so we wouldn't get hurt if the kids broke the windows. I was lying there, thinking we were going to get killed. Luckily, we got away—but one kid ran next to the van for, like, five miles. No matter how far we went, he kept up. Eventually, we pulled over and gave him tickets to that night's show.

When we got married, we had a couple of hundred guests, all our family and friends. We had just gotten back home after three and a half months on the road, so that was really nice. Travis wore Converse and a bow tie: he looked like Pee-Wee Herman.

Travis bought another Cadillac, but both his cars were old, and neither of them ran really well. Our most dependable car at the time was my 1993 Geo Metro baby-blue, three-cylinder hatchback. Travis used to call it the Roller Skate. We drove this thing around town, and Travis

WITH MELISSA

wanted to tint the windows because kids were starting to recognize him in the car. It cost more to tint the windows than the whole car was worth!

After a while, we both got really tired of driving this death trap. We pulled up to a Cadillac dealership and parked the Roller Skate out front. We walked in, bought an Escalade with cash, and drove it home. We just left the Geo on the street. I don't even know whether we left the keys in it or not.

I found a house in Corona: also in the Inland Empire, a short drive from both Riverside and Fontana, where I had grown up. It was 3,200 square feet, and compared to how I had been living my whole life, it

TRAVIS BARKER
can i say

was a palace. We agreed on a price around $325,000, I got a mortgage (having a credit history paid off), and we closed the deal. I moved in, and Melissa moved in with me. "This is the biggest, best house I've ever seen," I told her. "I'll never need to move again in my life."

Melissa had been going to college, getting a degree in psychology, but she dropped out and started going on the road with me when Blink toured. For the first time as an adult, I was learning about the benefits of a long-term relationship: when you're with a woman long enough, you feed off each other and support each other. You make each other into better people and life just gets better.

Us being on the road together all the time wasn't ideal—it's hard for any couple to be together 24/7, so I think we wore on each other faster because of that. But we were crazy about each other, and our two choices were either traveling the world together or not seeing each other for six months at a time, so we decided to be together.

MARK HOPPUS (BASSIST/SINGER, BLINK-182)

At the height of the *Enema of the State* years, we were playing in London. After the show, around three A.M., my wife and I are back in our hotel room, about to go to sleep. And then suddenly we heard *bang, bang, bang, bang* on our door. We opened the door and saw these two kids running away, rounding the corner. I called up our security guard, who was on tour with us, and said, "Hey, just to let you know, these kids just found our room and pounded on the door. You might want to let the other guys know." We all stayed in hotels under pseudonyms— the only way these kids would have found out what room we were staying in was if the hotel gave our information away. So our security guy called up the hotel security guy, who called the hotel manager at home. The manager came in, they walked the halls of every single floor of the hotel, and never found the kids.

I was downstairs in the lobby the next day, talking to Tom and Travis, and I said, "Did you guys get your room knocked on? Some kids knocked on ours at three in the morning."

Travis said, "Dude, that was me and Melissa." He was just fucking with us—they thought it would be funny to pound on the door at three A.M.

My security guy around this time was a friend named Fusi: he was a Samoan guy who lived in Carson, where he used to hang with the Crips. I used to see him loading out bands at the Palladium in LA, and he became a really great friend. It was weird that we needed security at all—it was just one more sign of how quickly we had gone from being on punk-rock tours to appearing on *TRL*. And some of the people security companies provided just sucked, and they'd be hovering over you all the time. So I started bringing Fusi with me: I knew we would have good times and stay up listening to West Coast rap together on my bus. We toured for a couple of amazing years together. There was one time when we were kicking it after the show at a five-star hotel, having a drink in the lobby bar. I went back to the room; Fusi told me he was going to chill downstairs for a while. But an hour later, I got a phone call from hotel security: "Sir, can you come down? There's an issue in the lobby." I came down and discovered he had gotten super drunk and started dancing with girls, including those who had come with dates. Nobody wanted to say no because he was a 350-pound Samoan with an underbite: to me, he was just a big teddy bear, but I understood how he was scaring people. Security told me, "He's turned the entire lobby into a dance floor and he keeps making them play Tupac."

Unfortunately, this happened not just once, but many times. Blink's manager put the brakes on and told me that I couldn't tour with him anymore: he was becoming a liability. But in my heart, he would always be my right-hand guy.

TRAVIS BARKER
can i say

WITH FUSI

About six months later, his mom passed. I went to the funeral, and it was terrible: he was the first person I knew who had lost his mom since my mother died, so it felt like I was losing her all over again. To see this huge person who had protected me in tears, it just hurt. I sat there hugging him for hours and tried to make sure he was okay.

My fear of flying wasn't getting any better. Every time before the plane took off, I would close my eyes, waiting to see a bright horizontal line that told me that everything was going to be okay—but even after I saw it, flying was gnarly. One time the band was on a flight in Europe, and as we were taking off, Melissa and I saw another plane falling from the sky. It was belching smoke out the back, and it was going straight down. We were tripping out: "Oh my God, look." The flight attendant saw what was going on and shut everybody's window shades. A few other passengers saw it, but most people didn't. The other guys in the band were saying, "Dude, you just imagined it—too many pills. You're tripping."

"No, I know exactly what I saw." And sure enough, when we landed, it was on the news: over two hundred people killed in a plane crash. That just added fuel to the fire for me. I was getting more afraid of flying every single time I got on a plane, and I was taking more pills all the time.

I didn't tell Melissa about the pills. I hid it from everyone. One of the crazy things about pills is no one can tell if you're doing it. There's no smell of smoke on your hands, there's no evidence of anything. If I was at a restaurant, I would go to the restroom, take a couple, and wash them down with some water. No one knew: I was just always in a good mood.

One time, I passed out in a club and Melissa and a few of my friends had to drag me out. Even then, I didn't tell her what was going on—I just said that I had probably drunk too much. But two or three days later, I was dizzy and my skin was turning yellow, like I was jaundiced. I went to the hospital and they gave me a spinal tap. They didn't know what was wrong, but they said I needed to tell them. Eventually I confessed, "I took a shit ton of pills a couple of days ago."

I had convinced myself that I should be taking pills all the time: I liked how I felt when I had them in my body, so it seemed like a mistake that I had never been prescribed them. I didn't even think of them as a drug anymore. It just made sense to me that I should take them every day, like a multivitamin.

MELISSA KENNEDY (EX-WIFE)

I didn't realize Travis had a pill problem. I didn't even know you could take pills and be addicted. I was naïve and I had never done anything like that. I thought it was odd that he took these pills, but they showed up in the mail, from a doctor, so it seemed okay. Sometimes he'd say, "Take one! You don't want to get up early!" I'd tell him, "Well, I'm tired, Mr. On-the-Go Guy." He passed out one time at a club, and I thought, "My God, I've got to get him out of here before the cops show up." I had a friend help me get him into the car. It wasn't to the point where he needed to go to the hospital—I just took him home and watched him all night. But still, I didn't know it was something that needed to be addressed. I apologized to him for that years later—if I had known he needed help, I would have helped him, but I was so dumb, I had no clue.

In 2000, we were doing a tour all over the world called the Mark, Tom, and Travis Show. We had a day off in Cuyahoga Falls, Ohio, not far from Cleveland. Melissa and I were bored with room service, so we took a taxi to a Taco Bell near our hotel to get some dinner. We got there and ordered our food, and then I went to the bathroom.

When I got out, there were these two large redneck dudes trying to hit on Melissa. She had been ignoring them, but when they saw that the guy she was with was a skinny, tattooed freak with dreadlocks like me, they got mad. We tried to eat, but they kept staring at us: it was a weird situation and I felt like a sitting duck. I had a bad feeling about it, so we tossed our dinners and left the Taco Bell. We went to a phone booth to call a cab to take us back to the hotel. We were standing there, waiting for it to arrive, when this red car pulls up, and one of the rednecks gets out.

This guy was freaking out—he kept calling me a "faggot" and for some reason, he took it as a personal insult that Melissa was with me. I tried to calm him down, and I said I didn't want to fight—I even showed him that my right hand was in a brace. But the guy wouldn't back off: he kept talking shit to me, and then he swung at me.

This guy was older and bigger than I was, but at that point, I had to defend myself. I hit the guy with my right hand and he went down. When he fell to the ground, I got on top of him and started whaling on him, hitting him in the face. His friend got out of the car and began kicking me—that threw me off-balance while I was punching, and my fist hit the concrete instead of this guy's face. Immediately, I knew something was wrong with my hand.

Now there were two of them, and with an injured hand, I had no way of hitting them. I tried to keep them away from me by kicking them, making a commotion until people in the parking lot came over to see what was going on. Once a crowd was forming, the two of them got back in their car and took off.

We called the police, but we hadn't gotten the guy's license plate number. When they checked with Taco Bell, they were really unhelpful— they claimed their security camera wasn't working. My right hand was hurting like crazy, so I got X-rays, and it turned out when I punched the ground, I had given myself a "boxer's fracture"—I had broken the knuckles of my pinkie and my ring finger.

The doctors put my right hand in a cast. I wanted to keep playing on the tour—I figured if Rick Allen could play for Def Leppard after he lost an arm, I could set up my drum kit the way he did, with all the electronic triggers and gadgets he had helping him. But the doctors told me I had to stop touring for a couple of months, so Mark and Tom recruited the drummer from the opening band to fill in. I stayed home in Corona, typing e-mail with my left hand, going stir-crazy from not being able to drum. During that time, I bought a pair of turntables and taught myself to scratch.

That fracture was a wake-up call: I realized I needed to use my head a little more. I couldn't get into fights; I shouldn't even go skateboarding. With a broken hand, I couldn't get dressed in the morning or take a normal shower. And I couldn't drum, which was both my passion and my livelihood.

Life is a race—leave the crashing for the dummies.

One day, Melissa told me that I had almost a million dollars in the bank. "No shit?" I said. I hadn't been keeping track of that—in a short amount of time, I had stopped having to worry about money. I played my drums, and as long as I had enough money to live on, I didn't pay attention to my bank account. I was just making decisions based on what I was passionate about. Like they say, find something you love that you would do for free, but somehow find a way to get paid for it.

I don't really have expensive taste. I've never liked to dress nice. And I wasn't interested in iced-out watches and rings.* What I really wanted to buy were nice things for my new house: stuff that I'd be seeing every day. So while I was home, I spent a shitload of money on furniture. I had always bought my furniture from Goodwill: I was living cheap with other bachelors, and it meant we could trash the place with no worries. But now I wanted the raddest furniture money could buy, from stores like B&B Italia and Minotti.

The best piece was a white Italian leather couch. It was all straight lines, and it was super modern. It cost $10,000—which I knew was a lot of money, but you can't buy a couch like that for cheaper. I couldn't even tell my friends I'd grown up with how much it cost. For that much

---

* A couple of years later, I did get an $80,000 Rolex. I wore it everywhere for a while—to video shoots, to the local gas station, even when I went running. Then, boom—I was sick of it.

money, they'd want it to drive or fly. I had a lot of respect for that couch: I didn't even sit on it. I still have it today. Good design is timeless.

Too many people knew where I lived. Not a lot of famous people lived in Corona, so I was the center of attention. And I wasn't keeping it low-key: I had friends over all the time, or I'd be rolling around town in one of my Cadillacs. Every day I used to get notes on the front door, people saying that they were my biggest fan. That was all pretty mellow.

Then one night, I heard something on our balcony. We went outside to check it out, and there were flowers and a note on the balcony, saying I HOPE YOU GET BETTER. It was creepy. The next night, there were more flowers on the balcony: somebody kept climbing up there. I had a dog—a little pug that I named Clarence—but he hadn't barked at whoever this was.

One night about a week later, Melissa and I went out. When we came home, there was a really creepy letter on the front door. It said, "I'm coming for you. Don't bother trying to escape me." It was like some scary movie shit, but I just said, "Whatever, it's stupid." We went out the next day, and when we came home, every single door in the house, exterior and interior, was open. There was another letter: "See, I told you I could get into your house."

At this point, I was pretty shook. Not only did I have a broken hand, but some asshole was going inside my house. I didn't know if this was a joke, or if this person was potentially dangerous. *Is this person a locksmith?* That was the only thing I could think of. I bought two rottweilers and an American bulldog. All three dogs lived in my backyard, which was not that big. I also got cameras and an alarm system.

Some nights, I would stay up all night with my buddy Jimmy Gully. We had baseball bats and guns, and we were just waiting for this person to show up—of course, nobody did. I had never owned a gun before: after I bought it, I started going to the shooting range every week.

Before things could get ugly again, I said, "Let's find another house." I bought a gated place on the same street as the mayor of Corona. Right next door to me lived Reggie Wright—at the time, the head of security for Suge Knight and Death Row Records. It was a dope one-story house,

TRAVIS BARKER
can i say

and I built an insane swimming pool. I had an acre of land in the back, so I got the people who did all the rock work at Disneyland to do my pool. It had skulls, and hidden caves with skulls underneath. It had twenty-four waterfalls. It cost $800,000, and it was totally worth it. We used to have massive parties. Sometimes everyone working at Famous would just come over on their lunch break to go swimming.

The day I got the cast off, I was supposed to go to physical therapy. I skipped it and played a show with Blink instead. I figured that was the best possible therapy, since pain is mostly in your head anyway. Every day after that, I would do my old marching-band drills. It was the stupidest thing I could have done, but the idea of canceling any more shows was a mind fuck for me.

I returned to the band at the end of the summer, in time for a Blink European tour: we traveled around in a double-decker bus. That fall, after Mark got married, we got together with Jerry Finn again and started working on the follow-up to *Enema of the State*. (We had released a live record between albums to keep the fans happy—it was called *The Mark, Tom and Travis Show*, and featured all of our songs at lightning speed, plus dick jokes.)

At this point, I was technically just a touring musician with Blink-182, not an official band member. Even though I had put together all the songs on *Enema of the State* with Mark and Tom, I didn't get any of the songwriting credits or the publishing money. That was fine—they had the band for years before me, and I needed to put my time in. But I had no health insurance, and I wanted to get it through AFTRA,* and to do that, I needed to be a songwriter. So I said, "Listen, if you guys don't think I'm helping out with the writing, then just write the album on your own. When you're done, I'll come and play drums on it." Of course, nobody wanted to do that, so I got promoted to unofficial partner. I was stoked to be part of the band.

We had a lot more pressure on that album than we did before, when nobody seemed to be paying attention. We had this huge success, but

---

* A union for performers: the American Federation of Television and Radio Artists.

that just made us feel like we had something to prove. Instead of saying, "Let's write some simple songs that will be huge," we thought we'd try something more technical and darker. We wanted to be taken seriously, and we wanted to challenge ourselves.

We had finished what's called preproduction, where you record demos of all the songs you have. Then we played it for people, including our manager Rick DeVoe, who basically said, "That sounds good, but it seems like there's a couple of songs missing." They wanted to hear some songs with the Blink-182 formula that everyone was used to from the last album.

So Tom wrote "First Date," and Mark came up with the basics for "The Rock Show." We hashed the songs out in a small room at the Famous Stars and Straps warehouse—and really quickly, we had the album's two hits.

We went back to Signature Sound in San Diego, the studio where we had done the preproduction on *Enema of the State*. Once again, we worked really fast and got it all done in a few weeks. We were almost at the end of the sessions—we had one day left before we had to turn the album over to the mixer—and Tom had this guitar part that went along with a drumbeat that I was messing around with. We turned that into a song, a very basic arrangement: intro, verse, chorus, re-intro, verse, chorus, bridge, double chorus, out. Tom sang the choruses and Mark sang the verses. It was simple, but it worked, and it was cool. That was "Stay Together for the Kids": like a huge percentage of America, Mark, Tom, and I all come from broken homes, so it meant a lot to us.*

When we finished the album, we called it *Take Off Your Pants and Jacket*. The cover art had three emblems, one for each of the guys in the band: a plane, a pair of pants, and a jacket. When I saw the mock-up of the artwork, all I could think was, *Please don't give me the plane—I fucking hate planes*. I wanted my symbol to be the pants or jacket, but somehow I ended up getting the plane. Fuck me.

The album came out in the spring of 2001, and it was big, if not as huge as *Enema*. We made a video for "Rock Show" that had some good success. The label gave us a budget of $500,000: we spent about $50,000

---

* "Stay Together for the Kids" hits home today, in ways that I couldn't have guessed back then. It's my kids' favorite Blink-182 song. When they told me that, it crushed me.

on the video and handed out the rest of the money to homeless people and anybody else who was walking by. We made another video for "First Date," and that did well too. Then, a few months after the album came out, it was time to make a video for "Stay Together for the Kids." The label gave us a million-dollar budget. "This video is going to be huge," they told us. "You need to get Samuel Bayer to do the video. Go kill that shit."

So we hired Samuel Bayer, who had done a million music videos, starting with Nirvana's "Smells Like Teen Spirit." He showed up for this video shoot in a fancy car, a Ferrari or a Lamborghini, and the production staff put an easy-up tent over his car for the day. It was a huge production, with cops blocking off a street in Orange County. The concept of

ALBUM ARTWORK FOR BLINK-182'S
TAKE OFF YOUR PANTS AND JACKET

the video was that we were playing inside this house while it was being destroyed. A wrecking ball was hitting the house, and everything was falling to pieces. The idea was that it would look the same way that kids feel in the middle of a divorce—like mass destruction. The only hang-up: the day we were shooting was September 11, 2001.

We were in the middle of shooting when we found out that there was a terrorist attack. Two planes had hit the World Trade Center and thousands of people were dead. We didn't know what to do, so we finished shooting the video. It was a really messed-up day. Once it was done, MTV wanted to see the footage, which looked way too much like all the painful things that happened in New York. There were pieces of houses falling and kids crying. MTV told us that it was in bad taste and they'd never play it. We had to make a special version without the wrecking ball, and without the house being destroyed.

We played "First Date" on *Late Night with Conan O'Brien*. After our song, Max Weinberg came up to me and said, "That was an amazing performance. But if you keep on playing like that, you ain't going to be playing very much longer. Your body is going to give out on you."

I thought that was crazy, but he told me about how he's had multiple injuries and back surgeries. He's an OG drummer.* It's a good thing to keep in my head, but when I get up onstage, I just play wild and hard. My body pays for it, but I wouldn't want to play the drums any other way. Being a drummer is like being an athlete: I have to train my body to play the way I do. I do what I can to be smart about it: I warm up really well and take ice baths after shows when needed.

At that time, the only exercise I got was running to the store to buy a pack of cigarettes. And I did that all the time—I went through a stage where I always had a cigarette in my mouth when I was playing. Drumstick in one hand, smoking with the other. And when it was a fast song and I couldn't hold the cigarette, I'd leave it in my mouth and play,

---

* After that, Max always stayed in touch—whenever I played in New Jersey, he'd show up. He brought his son Jay to a lot of those gigs, and now Jay's a drummer too.

drumming and chain-smoking. Later on, I replaced the cigarette with a joint. I thought I was being so cool, but really, I was just seeing how far I could turn the ignorance up.

I was diagnosed with tendinitis: they told me that I have no cartilage left in my wrists, so when I play, they just grind. Sometimes when I'm playing, I scrape my knuckles so raw, there's no skin left on them and I just bleed all over my drum kit. I learned that when I have open wounds that won't heal, I can superglue them together. But I can't do that all the time: once I got an infection in my thumb because of the superglue and they thought it was gangrene. They had to drain out all the pus. So when my hands get really bad, I use something called Dermabond: that's the surgical glue they use when they sew up a mother after a C-section. But it all comes with the territory. I could say, "Fuck, my hands are messed up and my body hurts—I should play mellow." But it'll never happen. It's just not me.

Melissa and I got married that fall, at the Mission Inn in Riverside. It's a dope spot, a historic building with crazy architecture. Before Melissa and I got married, I was constantly looking for other girls, picking them up at strip clubs and wherever else I could find them. Even on the night of my bachelor party: I wasn't married yet. Once we were husband and wife, I resolved to be good, and I stuck to that. But even walking down the aisle, it felt like I was making a mistake.

BRENT VANN (FRIEND)

Travis's bachelor party was at this little local bar called Goodfellas. We invited fifty dudes, tops—close friends of Travis. We had girls show up, and we'd let them in, but they'd bring guys, and we'd tell the guys they had to go. These girls were so scandalous, they'd go in and leave their boyfriends outside. Chicks were leaving their shifts at strip clubs and coming to the party: we just kept letting them in. By the end of the night, there were probably twice as many girls as guys.

It didn't take a lot to get Travis drunk: three or four Coronas. Next thing you know, this girl started sucking his dick on the dance floor. So they brought him up onstage and said, "Okay, let the strippers begin"—and shit started getting crazy. There were twenty strippers onstage, doing their thing, and Travis was just sitting there, smiling.

Girls that weren't even strippers came onstage and were getting naked. The strippers were getting jealous, so they started doing crazy shit. Then girls were sucking his dick again. Not one girl, not two girls, not twenty girls. Every woman wanted to suck his dick. Travis had the lips of at least thirty to forty different women on his dick, two days before his wedding.

The next thing you know, it was an orgy. Girls are getting eaten out on countertops. It was total Viking pillage and plunder. Everybody there was at the peak of horniness. It was like the Kama Sutra of the Inland Empire. It was one of the dirtiest, nastiest, most fucking awesome experiences I have ever been part of.

My relationship with Melissa had started out with lots of sexual fireworks, but it slowly turned into more of a friendship. We went months without being intimate, and Melissa started to feel more like a friend.

The other thing that messed me up was when I found out her real age. When we got married, I was twenty-six years old, and I thought she was just a year or two younger. But when she signed the marriage certificate, I found out her real birthdate: she was five years younger than me, which meant she was super young when we started dating. I felt betrayed she had kept that from me the whole time. That really fucked me up. It shouldn't have, because I was saying that I would love her for better or worse, but I couldn't stop thinking about it. The age gap also made me feel even more like a caretaker: I took her on tour, and she didn't really have anything else going on in her life. That wasn't fair to her, but it was how I felt. I tried to ignore those feelings and be a good husband.

Meanwhile, Blink-182 had some down time—we had to cancel a whole bunch of shows after 9/11. But before that happened, when we were still on the road, Tom and I had been jamming every day. I had been turning him on to some of the post-hardcore music I loved that he had never heard, like Fugazi, Quicksand, Rocket from the Crypt, and Pitchfork. It inspired Tom to explore a whole new style of music. I loved how far he had come from a few years before, when he told me that metal sucked. He was embracing this music so much that he wanted to write songs inspired by it. He played me a couple of riffs, which sounded awesome.

"Should we use these for the new Blink album?" I asked him.

He said, "I'm thinking maybe it's not the Blink album, that we could do a side thing."

I honestly thought that Tom had already had a conversation with Mark about this. They were so tight—inseparable—I couldn't imagine Mark didn't know. So Tom and I started this side project and we began writing; he brought in his friend David Kennedy to play guitar, and I brought in my friend Anthony Celestino. I told Tom that when I lived in Riverside, I had been in a band called Box Car Racer that played music like that, with my friends Billy Meyer and Alex Barreto.* Tom loved the name Box Car Racer—I figured we had never put out an album and the band was now defunct, nobody had ownership use the name. I tried to get in touch with Alex, who had been in the original Box Car Racer, because I wanted him to be in the second version of the band. But he had gone MIA—nobody could get hold of him.

* Years before, Alex played in the hardcore band Chain of Strength and in the group Inside Out with Zack de la Rocha (before Rage Against the Machine started).

I was talking with Mark one day, and I mentioned that Box Car Racer were going on tour. He was like, "What?"

"Shit. You didn't know, Mark?"

"Dude, Tom told me you guys were maybe doing an album, but you weren't *touring* it."

I felt like a dick. That was a big tour, too, with H2O and the Used. And MCA ended up putting out the *Box Car Racer* album. I hadn't thought about how it looked until it was too late: there were only three of us in the band, but two of us did a side project together, and Mark wasn't involved. And he wasn't even clued in about it. It was fucked, and it really bummed Mark out. I felt like I had let him down.

TOM DELONGE (GUITARIST/SINGER, BLINK-182)

As Blink grew, I wanted to contribute progressive elements: bring some modernism into the band and change what everyone thought we were capable of. I didn't know how to do it yet, so the best way to experiment was to get out of the normal box, where all three of us sat together to make every single decision, and see what happened when I did something by myself. That was how Box Car Racer started.

I think that record was the beginning of what Blink could do musically—but it became an issue, because it looked like two guys in the band went off to do their own thing without the third guy, and that wasn't what it was supposed to be at all. It was well received, and then we wanted to play some shows—but it was never meant to trump anything. The intentions were harmless, but it was probably at the wrong time in the band's life cycle to be doing that kind of stuff. I don't know—it's not like I *invented* side projects! Now everyone in the band's got so many side projects, it's one big weird soup.

I considered Mark one of my best friends—he had been nothing but solid, always there for me through the years. I think he thought I was a dick for doing that project, but he was ultimately more upset at Tom because they had ten years of history together *before* me. That whole episode caused a lot of tension in Blink-182. It died down when we agreed that we would just do the one tour and then leave it alone: we'd let people buy the album, but we weren't going to promote it any further.

Meanwhile, things hadn't gotten any better between me and Melissa. I was working in Los Angeles, and I met a girl at a club. Nothing happened that night, but for the next week, I couldn't stop thinking about this girl. I knew things weren't right with me and Melissa, and I had to end it. I went home to Corona to talk to her. "Look, I think we're getting divorced," I told her. "I'm over it. I'm sorry." We hadn't even been married a year, but I was already moving on.

POSTER FOR THE TOUR WITH THE
TRANSPLANTS AND RANCID

10

True Romance

T im Armstrong left a message on my voicemail: "Yo, Travis, this is Tim from Rancid. Can you give me a call? I'm starting this group with my friend S.R., you're one of my favorite drummers, and we want you to play drums. Hit me back."

I had met Tim only briefly, at a Fishbone show at the Barn, but I was a huge fan of Rancid and Operation Ivy. And I still remembered how Tim had spit on me years back when I was in the front row at Epitaph Summer Nationals. I called him back that night. He told me, "Yeah, I'm learning how to record out of my house. My friend S.R. is rapping and screaming. We need a drummer, and you're the best drummer to us. Will you come down?"

I said, "Sure, when?" And the next day, I went down to see them. It was me, Tim, and S.R.—which was short for "Skinhead Rob," the nickname of his friend, Rob Aston. Rob wasn't a racist—he just came up in the traditional skinhead scene. We all had dinner at Chevy's, a Mexican place. Sitting there, I immediately felt like I was with old friends. Everybody

loved hip-hop and punk rock, and we all understood how their dynamics are the same: they're equal parts rebellion and angst. I drove my old Cadillac there; S.R. had an old Lincoln. It was like when you meet a girl and it just clicks, because you have so much in common. Instant brothers.

TIM ARMSTRONG (SINGER/GUITARIST, THE TRANSPLANTS)

Rob was our roadie with Rancid, helping us out, and then he started singing on the side. We hung out every day and we started recording. I was doing a thing called DJ Dead Man, which was kind of experimental: "Diamonds and Guns" was originally a DJ Dead Man song. And Rob was doing harder stuff, like "Romper Stomper." One day, me and him went out to lunch. I said, "Let's merge DJ Dead Man with your stuff. I'll sing with you and we'll be a band." So we combined forces and called it the Transplants, which is what we were calling his stuff.

Then when we were making the record, I invited Travis to come down. I'd met him a few times. When he dropped in on our songs, it just exploded. We were a VW, and then he came in and we were a Ferrari. Travis is definitely a founding member of the Transplants: it was never really a band until he came in. I love that first record. I know you're not supposed to say you love your own records, but that's a wild fucking record.

Travis is the toughest motherfucker. He plays hurt. After one show, I saw his finger ripped open, with his bone sticking out. And he wasn't even fazed. I know a lot of great cats, but he's the most talented and dedicated musician I've ever worked with.

ROB ASTON (VOCALIST, THE TRANSPLANTS)

When the Transplants started, it was just me and Tim Armstrong. We didn't have any plans of releasing music or doing any shows—it was just to experiment and have fun. And then as we worked on it some more, we got a little more serious, and we decided we should get a drummer. We decided, shit, if we're gonna get someone, we might as well get the best there is.

So we got ahold of Travis. He drove up to Tim's house in Silver Lake. I used to have this mint green Lincoln Continental—it was on the cover of the first Transplants album—and we took a ride in it. In the car, we played him some of the stuff we had been working on, and asked him if he wanted to be part of it.

I told him, "Don't worry—we're not going to hold it against you if you don't want to be involved." I'm sure it wasn't the best music Travis had ever heard, but he was into it. He said, "Oh, I'm down. Let's do it."

Travis is one of those people where you can meet him and talk for five or ten minutes, and it feels like you've known him forever. I think I'm a pretty good judge of character, and Travis is a solid dude across the board. The industries that we're in are so full of shit. People in bands, people who manage bands, people in the clothing industry—there's so many people who are fake. Travis has been around the block a couple of times, so he can see through the bullshitters. I got nothing but love for that dude: I would die for him, kill for him, live for him, whatever. There's not a lot of people I can say that about.

We recorded that whole first record at Tim's house—he has a studio in his basement. The goal was to have fun: let's just make music, fuck what anyone thinks, fuck if it sells anything. The Transplants got much better when Travis joined. He's a monster. Certain drummers are good at what they do and can keep time, but there's people like Travis who take it a million steps beyond. He can play every type of music out there—it's inspiring, but it makes you want to slit your wrists, because you know you'll never be able to do that.

When we play live, Travis will change stuff that not everyone in the crowd might hear—or even everyone on-stage. But I notice it, because when we play live, I follow him. I'll be singing, and I'll expect a certain crash to happen, and he'll change it up: not because he's fucking up, just because that's what he wants to do right now. And then sometimes I'll stop singing—not because I forgot my lyrics, but because I want to watch this motherfucker get down on drums. I'm supposed to be singing, but I want to know what he's going to do next.

I came back to Tim's place three or four days later and recorded the drums for what became the first Transplants album, *Transplants*. It came together really fast, and we had lots of up-tempo songs: 187 beats per minute, to be exact. Recording Blink-182 albums with Jerry Finn, I had gotten really frustrated at how long it took to get the drum sounds. For hours and hours, Jerry would be adjusting microphones. I'd beef about it with him all the time.

"Jerry, I'm hitting the drum. Can you hear it?"

"Yeah," he'd say.

"Let's fucking record, then."

"Dude, I need to get drum sounds."

"You got 'em," I'd say. "The drum is making a sound. You're hearing it. Let's fucking go."

It drove me crazy. I'd sit around drinking coffee and smoking cigarettes, just praying that I'd be able to start playing soon. But those albums sounded great, so he was definitely doing something right. I was just impatient.

With Tim, it was a completely different process. The drums make a sound? Let's go. It was so cool and spontaneous. Tim was an incredible songwriter—and fast. Some days, we wrote two or three new songs. And then, a month and a half later, we were on tour with a couple of opening

PLAYING WITH THE TRANSPLANTS

WITH THE TRANSPLANTS. COURTESY OF ESTEVAN ORIOL

acts. When we went on the road, Lars Frederiksen from Rancid was our guitar player, and Matt Freeman, also from Rancid, was our bass player—and he's one of the best bassists in the world. Directly in front of me was the one and only Tim Armstrong. So on tour, I was basically playing drums with Rancid. My life was made. Me, Rob, and Tim were instant best friends.

We all packed into a van and drove from town to town. In Fresno, we literally played in a barn. But I've never had more fun than I did on that tour. The Transplants had this special energy because Skinhead Rob was a great front man—up until then, he had been a roadie. He worked with a bunch of rad bands like AFI and Rancid. And then with the Transplants, he finally had his shot, so he just killed it. Onstage, he'd be screaming his heart out. I couldn't be chilling on the drums—I had to give him at least as much as he and Tim were putting out. I wanted to give him more, so he could go even more nuts.

Rob was excited about every single part of the process: let's make videos, let's make T-shirts. He grew up writing on walls and tagging shit, so he had really good lettering. He would doodle on a napkin, and those doodles would end up on our T-shirts and stickers. Then Rob and I would stay up all night, driving around LA, plastering the stickers all over the streets. It was all totally homegrown, and it felt really good.

Whenever we were back in LA, Rob and I would raise hell. Everywhere we went, the velvet ropes were instantly lifted—it felt like it was harder to stay home. We were smoking a ton of weed; Rob would tell me, "Let your body relax, bro. Turn off your brain for a minute." Rob's place was a great place to get stoned: he had cool toys, he had pictures from touring with AFI and Rancid, he had glow-in-the-dark posters. We filmed the "Diamonds and Guns" video for the Transplants album with Son Doobie, from the rap group Funkdoobiest, at Rob's apartment. During the video, Rob busted out a joint that was about a foot long. That was the beginning of my smoking pot excessively and getting fucked up on the daily.

Skinhead Rob and I would go to Matsuhisa, but before we went in the restaurant, we had a tradition: we would sit outside in the car, smoking blunt after blunt in plain view of everyone. The valet guy would laugh at us and say, "Why don't you share some, señor?" So we'd share our weed with him. We tried to get away with as much as we could and pretend it was as normal as possible.

Sometimes we'd smoke joints laced with cocaine: we called them Cocoa Puffs. I never snorted coke or put anything else up my nose, but we did that just as a change of pace. I knew something was different, but most of the time, all I could taste was the weed. And we usually smoked our weed in wrappers from Backwoods cigars—that overpowered the smell of the weed and the cocaine.

One night, we were driving on Sunset Boulevard, headed to a club to meet our friend, a tattoo artist named Mister Cartoon. Rob was driving, I had the shotgun seat, and in the backseat, we had a couple of my friends from back home. Rob turned off Sunset, onto a little hill going south, and there was a truck in front of us that was going incredibly slow. It seemed like it kept purposely braking to fuck with us. So Rob started riding this truck's ass, flashing his lights, honking his horn, yelling at the dude driving the truck.

Finally, we reached a stop sign. The truck indicated a right turn, and Rob got on the truck's left so we could drive by. When we pulled alongside the truck, its driver looked into our car and pulled out a gun. I was the closest one to his vehicle, so the gun was pointing straight at me. About four feet from my face. The driver said, "You got a fucking problem?"

Rob wasn't fazed at all. He said, "Yeah, I have a fucking problem. What are you gonna do about it, motherfucker?" My friends in the backseat hit the ground—they were just hiding on the floor of the car. At this point, I figured the situation was ride or die—there wasn't much I could do, although I didn't want to make it worse. I just stared back at the guy, which meant I was looking down the barrel of a gun.

The driver looked straight at me and said, "Your friend's going to get you killed tonight. You better tell him to calm the fuck down."

At this point, luckily, traffic was backing up behind us and these other cars started to honk. The dude decided not to shoot me. He put his gun away and turned right—we drove straight. Rob turned up the stereo. Nobody said anything.

ROB ASTON (VOCALIST, THE TRANSPLANTS)

I had never eaten at a nice restaurant until I started hanging out with Travis. He turned me on to a Japanese place in LA called Matsuhisa—the best fucking restaurant in the world. They have a dessert they call a Bento Box, which is amazing. It's a round chocolate cake with chocolate lava in the middle and ice cream. We were smoking a lot of weed and eating a lot of pills, so for a while, we would go to Matsuhisa and smoke a gang of weed in the parking lot, hotboxing in either his car or mine. Then we'd go inside and order two Bento Boxes each, and just devour them.

There used to be a club next to the Troubadour, on Santa Monica Boulevard in West Hollywood. They had an enclosed smoking patio, so we used to go there and smoke. One night, Travis called me and said, "Let's roll out tonight." I got my shit together and realized I had just smoked the last weed. This was before there were weed stores everywhere, but I knew that the dude who lived two houses down from me had some, so I went over: "Hey, I need to buy a sack."

So I rolled up a couple of blunts before we left. When we got there, we went out to the back patio: I lit up the blunt and gave it to him. Travis stood there, took a hit, took another hit, and got this weird look on his face. He said, "Something's weird." I took the blunt and hit it, and there was this distinctive scent of bad fumes. I could tell it was sherm, or lovely: my neighbor laced his weed with PCP. He probably thought he was doing me a favor. People call it "lovely" because you're on the Love Boat. Another term for it is "wet," because it makes you sweat—that's why a lot of people end up taking their clothes off when they're on it.

Travis started sweating. For the rest of the night, he stood up against the wall on the patio, sweating and incredibly white. I felt like an asshole because I accidentally got Travis wet. But he was a trouper. He didn't freak out. He took it in stride and rode it out, until he had sweated it out.

At a hotel, you could always tell what room we were in because the whole floor of the hotel would reek like kush. It was always a crapshoot dealing with hotels: some are going to be cool, some ain't. One hotel, instead of complaining and sending up security, just put some air purifiers in the hallway.

We made the mistake of signing with Atlantic Records, who put out our second album, *Haunted Cities.* We went to New York and had a meeting with them, so we could play them the album before we signed the deal. We were in a conference room full of executives, A&R people, publicists, all that bullshit. We put the album on and pressed play, and then Travis gave me a look. We lit up blunts right there in the boardroom of Atlantic Records—not to be rebellious but because we couldn't really leave the room. We offered it to everyone, but they all passed, even though I knew half the people at that table smoked weed.

After Melissa and I split up, I went on a rampage. I temporarily relocated to LA and stayed at the Riot House—the rock 'n' roll Hyatt on the Sunset Strip where Led Zeppelin used to tear shit up. Pretty soon, I had a routine. I would go to Transplants practice, and then after, go out for dinner with Skinhead Rob and my pal Ultimate Ronnie.* After dinner, we'd go to a club: I'd meet a girl there and hang out with her for a while. Then we'd go to a strip club, like Seventh Veil or Girls, Girls, Girls. There'd usually be some girls who were nice enough to give me a free lap dance, and then want to give me their number, or want to hang out after work. That would lead us back to my hotel, where we'd be up all night, taking pills, smoking weed, sometimes smoking sherm. I'd watch the sun come up, and then go to sleep for a couple of hours. The next day, I'd do it all over again with another set of girls. Melissa and I were broken up, and I was taking full advantage of being single.

"ULTIMATE RONNIE" SANCHEZ (FORMER ROOMMATE)

Travis quit smoking cigarettes and started smoking weed. That was supposed to help us quit cigarettes—I don't know why we got that idea, but we did. We started smoking weed with anything we could find: we'd make a foil pipe sometimes. And we were going to all the LA clubs—he'd have me stay sober so I could drive. We used to go to the Body Shop in Hollywood: when Travis went to the bathroom, strippers would come in, stand behind him, and grab his dick while he was pissing. I was like, "Are you kidding me?"

One night, we got a hotel room and he hooked up with this chick. He told me, "Hey, in fifteen minutes, bang on the door and say we have to go because the Famous van got in a car wreck." So I sat there for fifteen minutes, and then banged on the door: "Oh my God, we have to go, the van got in an accident. Everybody's okay, but we need

---

* I knew Ultimate Ronnie from Corona—he was actually from North Corona, which is a real cow town. He ended up being the bass tech for Mark Hoppus (and also played bass for the Transplants sometimes). When Mark met him and found out he played bass, he offered him the job, which was so rad of him. Eventually Ronnie got tired of touring and settled down in Las Vegas.

to go take care of the insurance." I'm not sure she fell
for it—but she left.

When that movie *Drumline* came out, Travis kept talking
about it, because he was a part of a drum line in high
school: "This movie's going to be *amazing*." Kevin and Bean
from the radio station KROQ rented out a whole movie theater in Corona so he could watch the movie with them. But
that night, Skinhead Rob came up to Corona with really
good weed and smoked us out. We were so high, we didn't
even show up at the movie theater—Kevin and Bean drove
all the way up to Corona and had to watch the movie by
themselves in an empty theater.

One night in LA, I met Shanna at a club. She was there with her friend
Natasha. I didn't know when I spotted Shanna that she had been Miss
USA and a *Playboy* Playmate—but I immediately thought that she was
hot. Somebody told me that she was a Playmate, and I said, "Oh, dope."
We started talking, and she asked me what my name was. I said Clar-
ence, which is the name I always used when I introduced myself to girls.*

Shanna said, "Oh, it's nice to meet you, Clarence." She knew exactly
who I was, but she was playing along.

---

* When I was young I started calling myself Clarence because of the Beastie Boys' *Paul's
Boutique*. There's a line in "Shake Your Rump," after the line "Running from the law, the
press, and the parents," where somebody asks, "Is your name Michael Diamond?" and Mike D
says, "No, mine's Clarence." And then *True Romance* came out in 1993, when I was eighteen.
It was written by Quentin Tarantino and directed by Tony Scott, and it's just the dopest,
most romantic, most fucked-up, super-violent movie ever. Christian Slater's character drives
a Cadillac, which made me think of my dad, working on his Cadillac in the backyard for
years. And when he looks in the mirror, he sees Elvis Presley, which made me think of my
mom, who loved Elvis. I felt a real connection to this awesome movie, so I started using the
name of Christian Slater's character: Clarence Worley. And when I had a daughter, I named
her Alabama, after Patricia Arquette's character. Alabama hasn't seen the movie yet—I'm
not ready to explain that she was named after a hooker.

A week later, I went back to the same club, looking for Shanna. I flirted with her; she flirted with me. Then she came back to my hotel with me. We hung out that night and she went home around six in the morning.

SHANNA MOAKLER (EX-WIFE)

I was at the Standard hotel with Natasha, my best friend from kindergarten, who was interested in Rob. I was kind of her wingman—who am I stuck with? They pointed out Travis: "He's one of my friends. He's in that band, Blink-182." I didn't really know who they were—I remembered seeing them on the MTV Music Awards when they had all the little people on bungee cords. So I said, "Oh, that's the band with the little people." But he was married, and I don't mess around with married people—and he even had his wife's name tattooed on his neck.

They introduced us, and he said, "Hey, Oscar." (Somebody must have said, "That's Oscar de la Hoya's girlfriend or ex-fiancée" or something.)

I said, "No, I'm Shanna."

He had a Mohawk and tattoos, and back then, no one really had either—only punk rockers. I was like, *Whoa!*

I saw him the following week at the same spot, and at that point he was separating from his wife. I said, "Okay, I guess I'll talk to him." It was weird, because my girlfriend, who liked Rob, suddenly started to like Travis. But Natasha and I were talking to George Clooney at the bar—I was trying to hook my girlfriend up with George Clooney—and then I saw Travis at the entrance, and I went up to him. I said something stupid, like "What's your sign?"

We hit it off. When you meet the right person, there isn't anything that can keep you away from each other. He was staying across the street at a hotel, and that night we went to his hotel and laid in bed. We didn't have sex—we just fell madly in love and wanted to stare at each other for hours.

When we finally had sex, it was amazing and magical, and we never left each other's side.

We kept in contact every day after that, either seeing each other or talking on the phone. One night, not long after that, Skinhead Rob and I went to see Danzig play in Orange County. Shanna called me up and said, "I want to see you."

I told her, "Well, I'm at this Danzig show in Orange County. You can meet me here and pick me up, and Skinhead can drive home by himself. Pick me up and we'll go to my crib."

So she picked me up, and she had Natasha with her. At this point, I didn't know Shanna that well—I thought she might be crazy about me, but I wasn't sure. We drove back to Corona. (Melissa had moved out of the house by now.) The three of us were hanging out in my movie theater, talking, and Shanna said, "I'm going out to your pool. Meet me out there."

I said, "Okay, cool, tell me when you get in." Natasha and I kept talking, and Shanna didn't come back. I began to wonder: Damn, are they pulling a switch? Are they trying to set me up with Natasha instead? Because Natasha was sitting right next to me and she wouldn't stop talking.

After a while, Shanna came in, dripping wet, wrapped in a towel, really pissed. She said, "I've been naked in your pool for forty-five minutes. What the fuck are you doing?"

"Whoa, whoa, whoa," I said. "I'm sorry—I didn't want to be rude and leave your friend here."

She said, "You know what? I'm going to leave."

I said, "This is awesome. I barely know you, and we're already having our first fight." I was dying laughing: I could tell that Shanna was going to be a handful.

At the beginning, I'd just tell Shanna, "Hey, me and Skinhead are going to eat," and she and Natasha would meet us. If we ended up at a fancy restaurant, I wouldn't know half the food on the menu—I'd be asking the waiter, "You got a burrito?" Then we'd go out to a club. Skinhead Rob would hang out with Natasha; Shanna and I would be smoking, drinking, making out publicly, causing a ruckus, not giving a fuck.* Shanna and I became boyfriend and girlfriend pretty quickly, but it felt casual at first. Sometimes she'd say, "I'm going to go dance." She would, and I'd stay at the table, chopping shit up with Rob. Sometimes girls would walk by and start talking to us—maybe somebody I had met at Seventh Veil or Girls, Girls, Girls. Shanna might come back and a girl might have her arm around me, just talking to me.

Shanna would go crazy: "Who's *this* bitch?" She'd almost want to fight her.

---

* Pretty soon, Rob was saying, "Don't fucking make me hang out with Natasha anymore, Trav." I wanted him to take one for the team, but Rob's like me—if he's not having a good time, he's not going to sit and pretend that he is.

I'd have to say, "Chill, chill, chill." One time Jaime Pressly* asked me to join her after the club. Shanna found out and threw a fit: "Jaime, you're supposed to be my friend, what the fuck?"

Jaime said, "I didn't know you were with him! I had no idea—I was just talking to him!"

It was true: lots of people didn't know Shanna and I were a couple, because things were so brand-new between us. That night, Shanna got so pissed, she stormed out of the club. I followed her outside, but she wouldn't talk to me. There was a guy on the sidewalk playing acoustic guitar and serenading people, with his hat out. I gave him a hundred-dollar bill and told him to follow her singing "Wish You Were Here" by Pink Floyd—it was our song—and not to stop until she came back. This guy ran down the street after Shanna, singing the song. It was awesome. Finally, she turned around. First she cracked a smile, and then she started laughing. It was undeniable. We were falling in love.

WITH SHANNA IN MY '75 COUPE DE VILLE

I don't know if Jaime had broken some secret code of *Playboy* girls. Whenever Shanna took me to the Playboy Mansion, she ended up getting pissed off. She'd go off to dance, and some other girl would come up to me. When Shanna came back, she'd say, "Why are you talking to her?"

---

* The model-actress, who had also been in *Playboy*. She hadn't yet been cast on *My Name Is Earl*.

I'd tell her: "Babe, we're at the Playboy Mansion and you walked away from me. What am I supposed to do? Say, 'Hey, you can't talk to me because my girl's dancing?'"

SHANNA MOAKLER (EX-WIFE)

Obviously, girls always came up to him. But even if people tried to talk to him, my tongue was down his throat. We were never off each other's faces for, like, a year. We couldn't keep our hands out of each other's pants. We had sex everywhere, like we couldn't control ourselves. We pulled off the road to fuck on the side of the road. We would put our coats around each other at clubs. When we went to Disneyland, we were trying to fuck on rides.

We had some amazing times at the Playboy Mansion too, especially at the Halloween party and the Midsummer's Eve party. We got stoned in the arcade to the point where we could barely walk. We had sex in the bathroom. There's footage of us practically boning in front of everybody. It was a very sexual relationship.[*]

We went on vacation in the Bahamas, staying at a resort called the Ocean Club, and we just went crazy. We would down bottles of champagne and break into the villas where they do massages, just so we could have sex. They had a fireworks show at night, and we were in the middle of a grassy field, having sex while the fireworks went off—anyone could have seen us. We were absolutely nuts—we didn't give a fuck about anything. We were acting like rock stars.

Shanna had been in a relationship with Oscar de la Hoya, the boxer. Early on, people warned me about her: "You better be careful, bro, she took Oscar for millions of dollars." I didn't care—I was young and having a good time, and I was falling in love like I never had before. Anything

---

[*] We made one sex tape together, but somehow we lost it: neither of us could ever find it. It's a miracle it never leaked.

I COVERED MY DRUM KIT WITH SHANNA'S PLAYBOY PICS.
COURTESY OF ESTEVAN ORIOL

negative people told me about Shanna went in one ear and out the other. Shanna had a young daughter with de la Hoya, named Atiana. Shanna's mom was living with her at the time, so she took care of Atiana most of the time. Shanna would stay at my house for a couple of weeks at a time, then go home for a few days, and then come back.

The beginning of a relationship makes you feel like you have superpowers. Blink-182 started working on a new album. I didn't want to be away from Shanna, so I drove to San Diego and back to LA every day: three hours each way. I had an S600 Mercedes-Benz, and I was commuting with Daniel, my drum tech. One day, on my way to the studio, I tried to outrun a cop in that Mercedes for fun. I was speeding through a hilly section near San Diego, with lots of quick turns. This cop clocked me for speeding and turned on the sirens. Daniel thought I was going to stop—but I figured the cop was way behind me, so I gunned it instead. I was driving like a madman, going 120 miles per hour through the hills. I thought I had totally lost him, but he caught up with me. I have no idea how he did it.

The cop said, "You had to have been going really fast to go this far ahead of me."

I played dumb, telling him I had been going the speed limit and I didn't see or hear him. He knew I was lying, but he let me off the hook. Blink-182 were popular in San Diego, so he knew who I was and he was cool about it. I got really lucky.

It was a weird time in the band. Everyone was getting older: Blink-182 was no longer just three inseparable guys who were touring together. Mark had married Skye, who he had met at MTV, and Tom had married Jen, who was the girl of his dreams from high school. Both of their wives were super cool, but once we all had significant others, it added a whole different element. And once I split up with Melissa and met Shanna, that changed the dynamic again. Shanna and I couldn't go anywhere without being photographed. That was weird attention I never asked for, and it added to the awkwardness in the band.*

---

* My divorce with Melissa had turned nasty, and it stayed nasty for quite a while. If I had gotten into another relationship in the Inland Empire, nobody would have known about it. But Melissa had to see pictures of me and Shanna in *US Weekly* and *People*, which was

MELISSA KENNEDY (EX-WIFE)

When we split up, we didn't talk for a little while. The whole transition was odd, but it wasn't really rough for me. The only thing that made me mad was when he got somebody pregnant before we were officially divorced— that was annoying. After a while, we got back in touch and stayed friends. We worked better as friends than we did as a couple.

I was young and had no understanding of the world I was living in with Travis. It just seemed normal to me to be flying all around the world. After we split up, I wanted to go visit a friend in Australia. When I was with Travis, his management would have taken care of that, but now I called up the airline myself: "Yes, I'd like a business-class ticket to Australia."

"Okay, that'll be sixteen thousand dollars."

"Er, I'll have to call you back."

I still hear Travis's voice in my head sometimes. If I'm thinking about not finishing washing the dishes, or cutting a corner on some other job I'm doing, I hear him telling me, "If you're going to do it, do it right. Don't

---

toxic. Sometimes she'd come by the house to pick up her stuff, and Shanna would be there, and it was just ugly.

I felt like a dick that Melissa had to go through that—while at the same time, I was pissed that I had to break off a half million bucks for her, even though we were married only four months: we had no prenup. But as time went on, we put that behind us, and we're really good friends now. We were young and dumb when we were married—if we had met years later, it would have probably worked out.

Right before we split up, I told her that she should find a career she loved: "You're smart, you're young, you don't have job-stopper tattoos like me, you could do a lot with your life." She went to real estate school, and recently she was named one of the top thirty real estate agents under the age of thirty. She's awesome.

half-ass anything." Travis taught me that, and I still thank him for it.

When we started recording the next album, I felt inspired by what had happened with the Transplants record. I told Mark and Tom, "Let's pretend it's our first album. Forget about what people expect from us or what they heard us do in the past. Let's do what we're feeling right now. Personally, I'm feeling all these crazy beats." So Mark and Tom told me to record them, and that became "Feeling This," the first song we did for the record.

First, I got down the beat that ended up being the verse. And then I recorded the crazy cowbell part. Mark and Tom were saying, "This is funky, this is crazy—how are we going to write to this?" And then the song came together. That's still one of our favorite songs: it has these big John Bonhamesque drums and lots of cool drum parts. There's a cool intro. It's got huge verses and smaller choruses. And there's a middle part where the drums are blown out. I used five different drum kits on that song—every part of the song had a different kit. It was very innovative. There was a lot of smoking and pills going on during the recording of that song. For me, anyway.

We were trying stuff we had never done before. On "I Miss You," Mark played stand-up bass. We wanted a minimal drum sound, so I played with brushes—the only Blink song where I did that. Brushes are a totally different style of drumming that you have to learn; I knew the basics from pieces I played in jazz band in high school. The song was heavily influenced by the Cure's "Love Cats." It's one of very few Blink songs where I helped out with lyrics. We put in the Jack-and-Sally reference[*] because Shanna and I were super into *The Nightmare Before Christmas*.[†]

The band rented a house in San Diego and kept working on the album. I recorded most of my drum parts at the beginning, and then I went and

---

[*] "We can live like Jack and Sally if we want / Where you can always find me / We'll have Halloween on Christmas / And in the night we'll wish this never ends."

[†] Shanna and I would fall asleep watching movies—our two favorites were *The Nightmare Before Christmas* and *Dumb and Dumber*.

did other things. Mark and Tom have their own pace in the studio, which is more relaxed than mine, and they wanted to experiment with different sounds, so everything took a long time. I would go do other projects, and then go down to San Diego to hang out with Mark and Tom. Every time I went down, the songs would be a little more finished. I went on two full Transplants tours (one of them opening up for the Foo Fighters) and played drums for the Vandals while Mark and Tom were working on the album. I came home and the record still wasn't done. They were still tracking guitars. It was nuts.

That was a good time in my life. I was smoking *just enough* weed and taking *just enough* pills. I was playing just enough drums and working out—*just enough*. Things were cool with Shanna and me. That whole time period was really dope, even though the album took a whole year to make—we had come a long way since recording *Enema of the State* in three days. But it was worth every minute.

ON TOUR IN JAPAN

SELF MADE - DUES PAID

11

I want it all

bought some old Cadillac advertisements on pressed aluminum. When
I went to get them framed, a kid rolled up next to me in the parking
lot, filming me with a video camera. "Wassup, Trav, wassup?"

We didn't have any paparazzi in Riverside, so I wasn't sure what was
up with somebody rushing up on me with a camera rolling. I said, "Yo,
wassup, man? What's up with the camera?"

"Oh, I'm just a fan. Can I take a picture with you?"

"Yeah—let me get this framed, and when I roll back out, we can take
a flick."

I came out and took a picture with him, and this kid was selling
himself: "My name is Chris. I just moved here from Sacramento. I wash
cars: I heard you have a bunch of Cadillacs, and I'd love to wash your
cars. I'm starting a company called Flawless Auto Detailing. I do the
best job—I'll take care of you."

He gave me his card and I told him, "I'll be calling you for sure. You
can roll through sometime and do the cars."

The next day, I rolled up to the Famous warehouse, and Chris was already there, washing everybody's cars and blasting Jay-Z hella loud. At the time we had a small building, with no signs on the outside. He had just done his homework and showed up. I asked him, "How did you know where this spot was?"

He said, "I take this shit really seriously, man. I wanted to prove to you how good I can wash cars. I don't want anyone else touching your cars—I want to take good care of you."

He was a skinny white kid with a bandanna, standing five foot five, a couple of years younger than me—he looked like Eminem, but he was washing cars. We started calling him Lil Chris. At first he wouldn't let me give him money for the car washing, so I would trade him clothes or tickets to shows. But I didn't want anyone working for free, so finally I got him to take money. He would come over to my house to wash my cars, and while he was there, he'd be spraying my driveway or organizing my garage—I wasn't even asking him to do this stuff.

A couple of months later, I invited him over to my house; I hosted a pool party for the Famous crew every couple of weeks. I was at the point where I had Famous, I was in two bands, I had all these cars—I was in over my head and I knew I needed some help. I asked Chris if he wanted to be my assistant. "You need to start touring with me," I told him. "You don't have to wash cars no more."

Once Lil Chris started, he was never seen without me; I was never seen without him. He was my shadow; I was his shadow. Whatever I asked, he was there. I could call him at two in the morning and he'd say, "I'll be over in five minutes, Trav." He was much more than my assistant—he was my best friend and my brother. Chris's last name was Baker—one letter away from Barker. For some reason, I always found that kind of mind-blowing.

Shanna and I kept getting crazier. We'd go out to dinner and have such a good time. I'd drink and she'd drink—we were trying to get to that point where you're goofy and careless. We would get there very often. If I could go back in time and change how I lived, the one thing I would never, ever do is drive drunk. The last time I ever drove drunk was

LIL CHRIS, THE ORIGINAL WILD ONE

going home from Mr. Chow, a dope Chinese restaurant. I was behind the wheel of a $120,000 Mercedes, driving onto curbs, driving onto people's lawns. Sometimes when I was driving this way, Shanna was performing oral on me. We were treating life like it was a video game. I was lucky not to be pulled over—and more important, I was extremely lucky not to have killed anybody.

You can never be old and wise if you were never young and crazy.

My attention span for females had always been very, very short. Shanna and I had been together for six months and I didn't want to run away from her. I thought she might be the one I wanted to settle down with. I stopped using condoms with her: I actually thought I wasn't capable of having a baby. I had smoked so much weed, and my dick had been in so many crazy places, I figured it didn't work anymore.

Many nights, we ended up at my place in Corona, skinny-dipping, listening to Pink Floyd, and having sex all over the house. One night Shanna came over, and I had gotten us a bottle of the best wine: I was ready for a night of drunken wildness. But she said, "I'm not drinking." I thought that was weird—she loved to drink.

We went to my room, and she said she had a gift for me: I opened it up, and it was a little giraffe dressed in blue, and baby clothes in blue, including a baby-blue beanie. I was in a total state of disbelief. Finally, she said, "Say something!"

I said, "No way—you're *pregnant*?!" I was the happiest person in the world, but I was stunned: I couldn't believe it was possible for me to have kids, to create life. And we were having a boy.

DR. BRIAN WEEKS (FRIEND)

There is something so pure about Travis's heart and the way he approaches his life. He came up to me backstage at a Blink show, holding Shanna's hand. They had met just a couple of months before. He asked me, "Dr. B, if we're getting it on pretty regularly, do you think there's a good chance she could get pregnant?"

I said, "Well, Travis, are you using birth control?"

He said, "Well, no man, no."

"Well, dude, there's a really high chance she could get pregnant. I would say there's a super-high chance."

He looked at me like he was kind of puzzled. And then about three months later, she was pregnant.

To me, it was a young guy being completely and passionately in love with a beautiful woman, even though he and Shanna are polar opposites in many ways.

The day Shanna told me she was pregnant, I ran all the way to the freeway and back: a five-mile round trip. All through her pregnancy, I ran that distance two or three times a day. I wanted to be in the best shape of my life. I started going to the gym every day and learning to box with John Brays, who used to be the sparring partner for Mike Tyson. I knew I was having a son, and I was obsessed with being healthy and tough for my son.

After a year of work, Blink-182 finally finished the album in 2003. Some people think it's a self-titled album, called *Blink-182,* but Mark has always insisted it was actually untitled. Either way, by the time we wrapped it up, we really liked it a lot. It had a little bit of everything: we ventured far enough outside our genre to make ourselves happy, but not so far that we offended our fan base. It was a perfect happy medium, and it's the Blink album that Mark, Tom, and I are most proud of.

MARK HOPPUS (BASSIST/SINGER, BLINK-182)

Travis likes to come in, listen to something, do his thing, and move on to the next. On the untitled record, Tom and I were agonizing over little sounds and pieces, hemming and hawing. *What about an acoustic guitar? What about a clean electric guitar? What about this? What about that?* It was like a laboratory, while Travis is more like a surgical strike.

Tom brings ambition and spasmodic creativity to Blink-182. I bring a pop sensibility and I ground things. Travis is the X factor. Like on the untitled record, he came in one day and said, "What if we did some kind of logo, like a really identifiable pop-art smiley face?" And he spearheaded all the artwork for the record. There were smiley-face stickers and posters all over Los Angeles, and that was his idea.

Once we started exploring musically, we were also looking to push boundaries in different ways. Mister Cartoon, who did lots of my tattoos, did some of the artwork for the album.* We got Estevan Oriol, a good friend of mine, to take the photos for the album.† His style, incorporated into Blink's, didn't make us too gangster: it just gave us a bit of an edge. It was cool to feel like Blink had a dangerous side.

We made a crazy video for "Feeling This" with David LaChapelle, a controversial photographer and video director who was the It guy at the time. We played inside a chain-link cage while some teenagers had a riot in a prison. During the video, he insisted that I keep my shirt off and kept telling his assistants to pour oil on me. When I explained to them that I didn't want to be oiled because it made my drumsticks slippery, which made it hard for me to play, he got upset and greased me up himself.

Then, at last, we started touring. Every Blink-182 tour, I would do what's called a "drum gag": that's the part of the show where I not only play a solo, but something crazy is going on with the production. The first one was a moving platform that caught fire all around me. The second

---

* Mister Cartoon has also tattooed Dr. Dre, Snoop Dogg, Eminem, and lots of other great artists. I met him through Skinhead Rob, and we became good friends. Cartoon has an insane, nasty car fetish like I do, but even worse. He has full-time mechanics and painters on his payroll. We can just sit around and talk about cars all day. One Thanksgiving, when I was still married to Melissa, the Transplants, Cartoon, and Estevan Oriol all rolled their cars down and we celebrated the holiday in Corona. After dinner, Mister Cartoon tattooed the side of my head: the image of praying hands. It was the first of many tattoos I got from him.

† Estevan used to be the tour manager for Cypress Hill, but he was also known for photographing Los Angeles street gangs and rappers like Eminem, Method Man, and Dr. Dre. He and Mister Cartoon have been homies forever, and they're frequent collaborators.

one, I was in a cage that flew up in the air and turned upside down: the old-school Buddy Rich stunt. The third one, my drum kit was on cables, so I was spinning around and flipping both ways.

I would tell Daniel, my drum tech, "You decide what I'm going to do this year," and he would come up with the drum gag. We would have one preproduction day before we went on the road, so I would show up and they would harness me in for a test run. Sometimes in tech rehearsal, the rig would stop moving in the middle of the solo and I'd be stuck upside down. I'd be shouting, "Get me the fuck down from here!"

"Hold on, Travis, we got a problem."

"Obviously! Get me the fuck down, please!"

Eventually, they would get me down. The day before a tour started, I would always spend about three hours finding out how Daniel's gag worked, fixing those glitches, figuring out what I was going to play during the drum solo, and reminding people that in case of an emergency, please don't leave me upside down up there. I always said a prayer before my drum gags. It was the same routine I did before I got onto an airplane. I'd start with "Mom, this is for you," say my prayers, and then close my eyes. With my eyes shut, I could see the bright horizontal line—everything was going to be okay.

There were times when the crew told me before the show, "The weight limit was weird today—we're not going to lift you as high." Wait—what do you mean the weight limit's not okay? Why are we doing this *at all* today?

I always worried when we went to Europe, because we didn't know those venues like we knew the ones in the States, so it was harder to figure out where it was safe to do the gag. But Mark or Tom would always boost my confidence: "Dude, it's the best part of the show. Don't trip. Just go out there and kill it." It was fun once I was in the middle of it, because that was my chance during the set to spaz out.

Robert Smith of the Cure had appeared on the untitled album, singing on "All of This." And we had covered the Cure's "A Letter to Elise" on an *MTV Icon* show about the Cure. So when we played Wembley Arena in England, Robert Smith came onstage and did both songs with us. He

BLINK-182 IN A HELICOPTER ON THE WAY TO VISIT TROOPS IN KUWAIT

had the full hair and everything you would have imagined. Everyone was super stoked.

We got offstage and I was soaking wet; I don't wear a T-shirt onstage because I sweat like a monster. Then I felt somebody behind me massaging my back: I looked over my shoulder and it's Robert Smith. *Fuck, this is super awkward.* I was slimy from the sweat and he was rubbing my back—I felt really weird about the whole situation. Our road manager Gus Brant saw what was going on and somehow separated me from him, so the back massage lasted only a couple of minutes. It was all pretty funny. He's still one of my heroes.

We flew to the Middle East to play a couple of gigs for the US armed forces. It bought us even closer together to be doing something bigger than ourselves. At this point, Shanna was massively pregnant, so that was a really hard trip for me: not only was I heading off to another country, but I was going to be in a war zone. We did one show on a naval base in Bahrain, an island country right next to Saudi Arabia; the temperature hit 120 degrees, which meant that when they carried a deli tray outside for less than a minute, between an air-conditioned building and the air-conditioned tent that we were using as a backstage area, the cheese on the tray melted and bubbled.

Then we did another gig on the USS *Nimitz*, an aircraft carrier in the Gulf of Oman: to get there, we had an incredibly gnarly ride on a large military helicopter, where the back of the copter was open the whole way. My dumb ass snuck weed into Bahrain and onto the aircraft carrier. Bahrain has some really intense laws: they can execute you for possession. We weren't even supposed to bring pornography into the country, but I had gotten used to smoking weed so openly, I didn't even imagine there could be consequences. I was a total addict: I put it in a baggie inside a shampoo bottle, and I thought if they found it, they would just slap me on the wrist. Estevan had come along to take pictures,* and when he and Daniel found out I had brought weed onto the aircraft carrier, they told me I had to smoke it or throw it away. Obviously, I smoked it. There was no getting any more weed while we were out there.

There was no alcohol allowed on the *Nimitz*, but the captain of the ship had one bottle of brandy in his cabin for emergency purposes. Mark, Tom, and I convinced him that it was an emergency, and he opened it up for us. We spent twenty-four hours on the aircraft carrier, and I stayed up all night, exploring the ship and meeting sailors. I even got to work out with them. Somebody in the infirmary asked me if I wanted to get a procedure where they inject you with a chilled saline solution to bring your core temperature down. I did it just to see what it was like, but it was just like having a regular IV. But anything that brought your temperature down felt good.

I kept asking how we were going to leave the *Nimitz*, and whether it was going to dock someplace—our tour manager told me they were working it out. It turned out that when we left the *Nimitz*, they didn't

---

* Gavin Edwards came along to write about the trip for *Rolling Stone*—we got to know each other a lot better on those long plane rides, and a decade later, he's the coauthor of this book.

PERFORMING WITH BLINK-182
ON AN AIRCRAFT CARRIER, THE USS NIMITZ

put us on a helicopter: we were on a small transport plane, which was even scarier.* Because the runway on an aircraft carrier is short, they basically catapult the planes off, using a big hook underneath, so they'll have enough velocity to fly. Fluid was dripping from the plane's ceiling, and before we took off, the cabin started filling up with steam. I was out there to help our sailors, so I was going to do whatever I needed to do, but I was terrified, shaking in my seat while I waited for the plane to take off. I closed my eyes—I couldn't see anyway because of the steam—tuned into my horizontal line, and waited for it to be over. It all happened incredibly fast, and I had no control over the situation.

Soon after we landed, we got on another plane: a side trip to visit military personnel in Kuwait. There was one point during that flight when they got a missile warning and they suddenly dropped thousands of feet in elevation. It was all so sketchy—I was already scared of flying, and I was having some of the most terrifying flights of my life. On our way home from the Middle East, they kept grounding our military flight: we were too heavy with all the fuel and equipment, we had trouble getting flight paths over some countries because of no-fly zones, and then there was a blackout in England that screwed up the airports. I decided to get home by myself, because I didn't want to be sitting around waiting for the military to figure out my itinerary when Shanna was pregnant and by herself. Daniel and I left the military flight and flew back to LA commercially. We took six connecting flights and got home in forty-eight hours (it should have taken less than half that time). I ended up arriving in LA just a couple of hours before Mark and Tom did, but it was all worth it to get home to Shanna. I was so excited to see Shanna carrying my unborn son that we didn't even make it to the bedroom—we had sex on the stairs. I had met kids in the military who had never met their own children because they'd been on duty overseas when they were born—I wanted to make sure I made it home to see mine. The whole trip made me think of Pops and how brave he was to serve. I have so much respect for the U.S. military.

---

* It was called a COD aircraft: COD stands for "carrier onboard delivery."

Blink-182 went on tour with No Doubt and Cypress Hill: that was a really cool bill. Gwen Stefani and I would smoke weed together on that tour. Sometimes we'd be staying in the same hotel and I'd see her at an after-party in the lobby. I'd tell her that we were heading upstairs to smoke, and she would join us. One time, hotel security was very cool and showed us out to this little spot where we could smoke. At one point, it was her and me out there, smoking, and I was thinking *Yes!* I was really excited, thinking how it would be awesome if her security or my security didn't come to get us, or just forgot about us. She was so rad.

We would just talk. I didn't feel like the kid who grew up watching her play at Spanky's, and I didn't tell her how I fanboyed out on her back in the day, or how excited I was that time she asked me for a lighter. This was a true test of my relationship with Shanna: I wasn't looking to cheat on her, even though Gwen was my dream girl. (Not that Gwen was looking to cheat with me, either.) I was just stoked to be in Gwen's company after hanging around with dudes all day long. And then at one point, Shanna came out on tour and Gwen's old man joined her, and our smoking sessions came to a grinding halt. I was thinking, *Nooooo!* Oh, well.

Cypress Hill had to leave that tour before it was over—they had some other dates scheduled. Their last day with us, I went into their dressing room and told them what a pleasure it was having them out on tour. "It was such a breath of fresh air—you guys were awesome."

B-Real said, "It's our last day, and we have to leave during your set, so let's smoke one."

I grabbed Tom, even though he rarely smoked weed, and said, "Come on, Tom, don't be scared—come smoke with us." So me, Tom, and Lil Chris smoked with Cypress Hill: two blunts, we hit a bong a couple of times, whatever. Even at the height of my smoking weed, I had never smoked right before a gig. It was always a release after the show. About fifteen minutes later, Blink went onstage. Our shows were always high-tempo, but when this one started, it felt like everything was in slow motion. My hands were moving, but it felt like I was in a totally different place. It felt like we were floating around the stage instead of playing our instruments.

Tom turned around at one point and said to me, "I want to go home." I totally agreed. I wanted to crawl offstage, have nobody notice that I was gone, and just go home. The show felt like it lasted forever: I thought I was onstage for four hours. Tom was so stoned, he couldn't even banter with Mark in between songs.

Eventually, Mark said, "You guys are high, huh?" I think he said it on the microphone. We were not in any shape to be onstage, and we just barely got by. But what can you do when the Cypress guys leave the tour except give them a proper farewell?

Back home after the tour, Lil Chris and I were driving around in my Escalade, smoking weed, and we got pulled over by a cop. We ditched the blunts, but the Escalade stank of weed, so when the cop came over, he detained us in the back of the police car. He combed my vehicle and found my bag of weed. He let us go, but he kept the bag of weed. I wasn't sure whether he was trying to give me a break or whether he just wanted my weed. At the time, I was mostly just bummed about the weed: as soon as I got out of the back of the police car, I wanted to smoke right away.

ROB ASTON (VOCALIST, THE TRANSPLANTS)

When Travis lived in Corona, I'd drive out there to hang out with him. At the time, I was still driving my old green Lincoln Continental, which is a Ford car. And his family was exclusively Chevy and Cadillac, so his father wouldn't let me park the Continental in the driveway. I had to park down the street in front of the neighbor's house.

Whatever happens, Travis has my back. I've had to borrow money from him, which I hate having to do, but he's always there for me. I always pay him back, even if it takes a little longer than I'd like—I hate owing people money. I don't want to feel like a burden. These days, I don't have a car—I just have a motorcycle. If I need a ride, he'll say, "Take the Escalade," without me even asking. You can't carry boxes of merchandise on a motor-cycle, like you gotta do when you're in a band. Numerous times, Travis has said, "Just come to the pad and get one of the cars—take it for as long as you want." I never do, because I don't live in the best neighborhood, and I don't want anything to happen to his stuff. I'm very thankful for everything he's done for me—he's the least selfish person in the world.

He doesn't categorize himself as a rock star, or as a celebrity—he's just Travis.

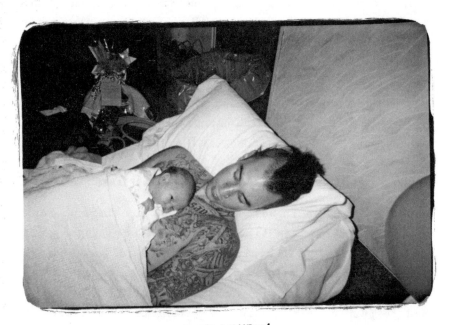

WITH LANDON

TRAVIS BARKER
can i say

People were still bothering us at the Corona house, so even though I knew I would miss the insane swimming pool, finally I said, Fuck it. Pops and Mary stayed at that house, looking after it, and I moved into Shanna's place in LA. That meant we got to spend more time with her daughter, Atiana, who had turned four. She would hide behind corners and call me "Slavis." It was really cute. I liked kids. I used to help take care of my nephew Brandt when I was growing up: I was very close to him. And I had been spending time with Atiana. So I knew that when I did have kids, it would be awesome. And I was right. When my son, Landon, was born, on October 9, 2003, I knew I could stay home every day and not work another day of my life and be content, because I loved this little dude so much. I would lie there in the hospital, just holding him and staring at him for hours.* I would listen to "Your Song" by Elton John while I rocked him to sleep in my arms. I was always desperately afraid that something would happen to Landon if I wasn't around: I used to put my face right next to his sleeping face just so I could make sure he was still breathing. Landon had eyes just like mine: when I looked at him, it felt like I was looking at a mini me.†

Mind you, at that point I was also a pill-popping moron. When Shanna was in the hospital, they gave her Percocets because she had just had surgery. She was supposed to have them for the pain, but she shared them with me—they had a little bit of a different buzz than Vicodins. I would say, "Tell the nurse you dropped the pill on the floor."

We went looking for a larger house; I sold my Corona property and had enough money to buy a house in a gated community, Bel Air Crest. I said, "This is where I want to raise my kid." So I bought a brand-new five-thousand-square-foot house: small in that neighborhood, but plenty big for us. We moved in about a month before Christmas—and then on

---

* His full name is Landon Asher Barker. He came really close to being called Elvis; we also thought about calling him Clarence (because of *True Romance* and the Beastie Boys) or Cash (after Johnny Cash).

† As he got older, I loved dressing him up head to toe in the same clothes as me.

Christmas morning, we had our first real rainstorm. We woke up and there was about an inch of water in the house.

I had to do lots of work to make sure everything was fixed and there was no mold, because somebody put a bad roof on the house. I was still taking long runs and I noticed this mansion where the lowest story was a hollowed-out garage: it looked like a fifteen-car garage. One day, I went by and some guys were doing work on it. I asked if it was for sale, and one of them said, "Yeah, but it's expensive."

"How much?"

"It's going to be about seven or eight million dollars." He told me when the work was going to be done, and my wheels started spinning. That was my dream house. Over the following months, I was working even harder, getting in the studio with anybody who asked me, and spending every other hour trying to build up Famous.

Pops was always telling me that the Corona house was too big for him and Mary, and that the electricity and upkeep was costing us a fortune. So one day I told him, "Pops, what if I sold the Corona house, sold the Bel Air house, and bought a big house in Bel Air for me and bought you a spot in Lake Elsinore?"*

"If that's what you want to do, pal."

So that's what we did. I made the guys who built my Bel Air house fix the roof and repair the damage, and then I sold that house and moved into the *big* Bel Air home.

RANDY BARKER (FATHER)

Travis came to our house one day. He said, "Dad, I got a new tattoo"—and he showed me that he had the word *pal* tattooed on his shoulder. That's what we always called each other, since he was old enough to talk. To show him that I support him, I decided that I would get the same tattoo on *my* shoulder.

---

* He had always wanted to have a place in Lake Elsinore, which is a quiet town about an hour south of Corona.

TRAVIS BARKER
can i say

I went to the Famous warehouse and picked up some stickers—we were going to do some sticker bombing. I went to see the tattoo artist, Franco, who was a friend of Travis's, and I showed him the Famous logo on the stickers. I said, "I'll let you do this one up here if you do this other one on my arm."

He said, "I'll do whatever you want." And he did the Famous F on my left arm.

I told him, "Well, Franco, those are the last tattoos you're ever going to give me. I don't care what everybody else says, it hurts."

When I showed the tattoos to Travis, I said, "Look, pal, I got a tattoo."

He said, "Dad, that's a sticker."

I said, "No, it's not a sticker. It's a tattoo." He was really excited because I finally got a tattoo.

Travis has made me very proud. I never dreamed that he would make it big like he did. I knew guys who had bands, and they had never gotten past first base. He's amazed me with everything that he's been able to accomplish.

The older Pops got, the more I worried about him. He was still riding his Harley everywhere, and I was afraid that he was going to have a serious accident. When he came to see me, it was about a hundred miles each way. I told him, "Pal, I love you but I need you to get rid of the bike."

"No way in hell am I getting rid of my bike."

"What if I replaced it with something?"

"There's nothing you could replace it with that I'm going to like. I want my bike."

I reached out to the TV show *Payback,* where you give a car to someone who's helped you for your entire life. I told them, "I want to pay back my father for taking care of me my whole life. And I want him to stop riding the fucking Harley-Davidson." So we arranged to get a Corvette for him.

The day of the show, he came down to my house, and I asked him to go outside to take care of a delivery that was coming. When he went out the front door, they were lowering a brand-new Corvette, next year's model, all customized, silver and black, just sick. He said, "You guys delivered the wrong fucking car. Travis ain't got no Corvettes."

They said, "No, sir, this is supposed to be at this address."

I came out and told him that the Corvette was for him being good to me and taking care of me my whole life. I also told him that he had to give the motorcycle to me and promise never to get back on it. He burst into tears, and he gave me the motorcycle. I sold it, and he's had the Corvette ever since.*

I wasn't home very long, or very often: Blink-182 were always on the road. For one tour, we flew down to Australia—the day after we landed, we checked out of our hotel in Melbourne and I was hustling through the lobby to get to our tour bus. Right next to me were Lil Chris and a security guard named Jake. Usually Jake helped us out with our bags, because he was a three-hundred-pound dude with muscles. But somehow, this time Chris and I had ended up with most of the luggage. I had a bunch of bags on my back, which made me lose my balance. I tripped on the sidewalk, just feet away from the bus—there was some uneven pavement—and landed hard on my right foot. I could hear an ugly snapping sound and I felt an intense flash of pain.

Gus, our tour manager, said, "Dude, just walk it off, get the blood flowing." I tried to limp around—the tour hadn't even started and I didn't want to punk out.

But Chris saw I wasn't doing well. He said, "You good, man?"

"Dude, I can't even fucking walk."

---

* He's put over 120,000 miles on it now.

We took off my shoe and my foot was black and blue. I played the gig that night: I had Daniel pick up a double bass pedal so I could play with my left foot. The next day, we hit the road, but my foot wasn't getting any better. A couple of days later, I flew home to the States to get it checked out (and to see Landon): the part of Australia we were in didn't have any MRI machines, just X-rays, plus my orthopedic surgeon, Dr. Ferkel, really wanted to make sure he took care of it himself. It turned out my foot had basically snapped in half. It was broken in seven or eight different places, and all the tendons and ligaments were torn. The injury was called a Lisfranc fracture: a lot of football players get them, and apparently it was a common jousting injury, back in the days when people were jousting a lot. I needed surgery and I was going to be in a cast for months. That was when I really began using painkillers. My foot hurt so bad, it went from taking them for pleasure and plane flights to *needing* them.

I got the surgery (three screws in my foot) and the cast, and then I got on a plane back to Australia. We canceled one week of shows, but then I toured in a cast for two and a half months. I'd get rolled out to the drum kit in a wheelchair, hop on the throne, and play with my left foot, though my right foot is my dominant foot. (Because I don't use a double bass, ordinarily my left foot just handles the high hat. It was like writing right-handed, even though I'm a lefty.) I was taking a lot of painkillers, but recalling how bummed I was lounging around at home after fracturing my knuckles, I knew it would be better for me, mentally, playing the set every day. And I had the time of my life. I even played a drum solo and got so sweaty, I had to get the cast changed once a week. It was cool to fight the fight.

Nobody cares, go harder.

I got the screws out of my foot,* healed up, and went right into another Blink tour—but I never weaned myself off the Vicodin. I had buddies who were getting it to me off the streets: for $600 to $1,000, I could buy a big bottle that would last me a couple of months, even though I was taking eight to ten pills a day.

After surgery, I was out of my mind on morphine, and I had a pocket-knife, so for no reason at all, I started cutting myself. I wasn't in a suicidal state, but my body wasn't acting the way it was supposed to, which tripped me out. I was intrigued by how I didn't feel anything: when I would cut my own flesh, it didn't hurt. If it had hurt, that would have just given me an excuse to take more pills. I was comfortably numb.

* I still have those screws today, framed on my wall.

TRAVIS BARKER
can i say

ME ON CRUTCHES, COURTESY OF ESTEVAN ORIOL

THE BARKERS AT DISNEYLAND

12

Meet the Barkers

I proposed to Shanna at Disneyland on Christmas Eve. I knew exactly what ring she wanted: she had a picture of it in her room, so I got it at Cartier. It was a four-and-a-half-carat diamond ring called the Luna that cost $150,000, so it would have been ideal to have an armored truck deliver it. But instead I kept the ring in the pocket of my big puffy down jacket; all I could think about was that I might lose it and that it would be such a fucking fail if I did. We rode all the rides we normally did, trying to make the afternoon normal. Then when it got dark, we went to the Haunted Mansion. Every year, they redecorate it for the holidays with a *Nightmare Before Christmas* theme—so it seemed like the perfect time and place to propose.

Anytime we went to Disneyland, we had a special tour guide so we wouldn't get swarmed and we could go on the rides right away. That day, I told the guide—his name was Nick—that I wanted to be able to go on the Haunted Mansion ride solo with Shanna. So we went into the

portrait gallery that turns into an elevator, and after the voice said, "Of course, there's always my way," the lights went out with a clap of thunder.

That was my time: while the lights were out, I got down on one knee. I hadn't lost the ring, and when the lights came on, I popped the question. She said yes, and then she got down on one knee and pulled

WITH LANDON AND ATIANA

out a ring of her own. We both had the same idea. We rode the rides for a couple more hours, and then we went home, got drunk, and had sex. Like pretty much *every* night.

The difference was, that very night Shanna started planning the wedding. Soon, she was filling up every day we spent together with wedding planning.

It kept getting harder to leave behind Shanna, Landon, and Atiana when I went on tour with Blink-182. While I was away, Landon took his first steps. And then when I came home, Shanna brought him to the airport and he didn't recognize me. I went to hug him and he just started crying. It killed me. When I was home, I just wanted to hang out with

Landon, sewing patches on his clothes or giving him a Mohawk with the little hair he had. And as soon as he could hold the drumsticks, I started teaching him to play the drums.

But as much as I loved the idea of never leaving the little guy ever again, I had a job to do and, soon enough, I flew down to Australia for another Blink-182 tour. Leaving my family behind was the hardest it had ever been, and on top of the flight, to get through the heartache . . . I needed to take pills. I was still taking Vicodins by the handful, but while I was down there, I got some Oxycontin, which was even crazier. Sometimes, Lil Chris and I took it together on our days off—we'd be hanging out on a couch in my hotel room, getting blurry. When I took Oxycontin, it felt like my face was melting, and that I was poured into a flat puddle all over the couch. Lil Chris was supposed to be looking after me when I did pills: I always used to say, "Dude, hit me if I don't wake up."

Now that Lil Chris was doing them with me, he'd say, "Sure. You do the same thing for me, dude." And then we'd pass out together. So I paid Jake, one of our security guys with Blink, to sit up with us and make sure we were still breathing. Jake was sober, so his job was to hang out all night and make sure we didn't die.

While we were in Australia, Blink filmed the video for "Always," the fourth single off the untitled album. The video was about all three of us dating the same girl, played by Sophie Monk: she was a singer and a model, and at the time, she was the It girl in Australia. In the treatment, I was the one who made out with Sophie, and Shanna was so pissed.

"Why did they pick *you*?" she demanded.

"I don't know, baby. That's how they wrote it. I got to kiss the girl, whatever." And of course, I wasn't mad about kissing Sophie. But I was a gentleman. I only kissed her when I was supposed to. It's weird kissing on a video: it's not the same when there's a bunch of people watching with cameras and lights, and somebody's telling you, "Okay, put a little more into it." But even with all that, it was fun. We could have hung out afterward, but I bowed out. I *was* getting married.*

---

* Years later, Sophie moved to LA and we ended up hanging out.

I got home from Australia after a nineteen-hour plane ride, out of my mind on pills—totally Xanaxed out. It was November 14, 2004, my twenty-ninth birthday. Shanna picked me up at LAX and said she was taking me out to dinner, which was cool. I was always looking for fun after a long plane ride. There were times when I would arrive on another continent and Chris and I would head out for some fun, burning the candle at both ends.

Shanna took me to this restaurant that I had never heard of. I wasn't sure why she hadn't just taken me to Matsuhisa, which was our favorite place, but she told me that it was a super-cool spot and she had wanted to surprise me with it. The first thing I noticed was that the restaurant was weirdly lit: it looked bright and awkward.

I asked Shanna if she wanted some Vicodin or some Ecstasy (I had started experimenting with E as well). She said no, but I figured it was my birthday: I took a hit of E at the table. The waiter came out and started hitting on Shanna. She was calling him honey and he was calling me the guy with the interesting haircut. (I had a Mohawk.) Apparently, he and Shanna used to date: he was flirting with her and he kept insulting my haircut.

I told Shanna that if the waiter came at me sideways one more time, I was going to say something. She went to the bathroom, and the waiter sat down at the table with me and started giving me a hard time. Finally, I said, "You wanna go outside?" I got up, ready to flip over the table. And then Ashton Kutcher came out and said, "I think we need to bring it down a notch." The whole thing was a practical joke, being filmed by hidden cameras for *Punk'd*, and Shanna's "ex-boyfriend" was Ahmed Ahmed, a stand-up comedian.

I don't think they expected me to throw down that quickly. I was feeling pretty heated, even after Ashton came out. It took me a minute to realize it was all a joke. That waiter had been riding me all night, trying to get a rise out of me. My gut was still saying "fuck this dude"—not because he had been hitting on Shanna, but because he had ruined my

buzz.* Looking back, I could see how funny the situation was. We left the "restaurant" and went to the Dime, which was my friend Andy's bar. Pops showed up and we all celebrated my birthday.

On Pops's next birthday, I was driving out for meetings at Famous and I had the idea of doing something special for him, something I had never done for him before. I told him to come down to the warehouse, and then I asked Lil Chris to hire two of the dopest strippers he could find in LA. I told Pops to wait in my office and I would be right in. The next thing you know, two smoking-hot chicks came in—Pops didn't know they were strippers at first, but when their clothes started flying everywhere, he figured it out. Chris and I left, laughing our asses off, wondering how he would react, thinking he would be timid. Instead, fifteen minutes later, one of the strippers came out in tears, saying that he had been spanking her and biting her nipple. Chris and I were shocked and impressed—we could see Pops still had some of the dog in him. I paid the stripper twice as much as we had agreed, and Pops had one of his most memorable birthdays ever.

My friend Jesse Ignjatovic came and visited us at the house. He had created the MTV show *Diary*, which showed a day in the life of various musicians. Blink-182 had appeared in one of those, so Jesse and I got to be pals. He directed the first two Transplants videos, for "Diamonds and Guns" and "D.J. D.J." The program that was super popular on MTV at the time was *Newlyweds*, with Nick Lachey and Jessica Simpson. Shanna and I had talked about doing our own reality show. Our life was already practically a television show, and I was ready to show the world how much I enjoyed being a father. Jesse was sold on the idea immediately. Within a week of that fifteen-minute conversation, he filmed a pilot, and it was dope. Back then, reality shows didn't have scripts—it was all absolutely real.

We called the show *Meet the Barkers*. I wouldn't have done it with anyone else, but I trusted and respected Jesse. The show had Chris and

---

* They edited out a lot of stuff for TV—including me popping Ecstasy at the table. Shanna told me later that she was wearing an earpiece so she could get instructions from Ashton, and she could hear him freaking out when I took the E.

me being ourselves: running Famous, playing with the Transplants and Blink-182, working all day, putting Famous stickers up all over town, creating havoc. I thought it was cool that people could see the dynamic between Chris and me, how crazy and funny we were, and how we hustled.

We were inseparable; Shanna was very envious of our relationship, and I think Chris's wife felt the same way. Sometimes I would tell Chris, "You don't need to be here until eight or nine tomorrow morning," and he'd show up at six, washing the car. I'd tell him to stop washing the car: "You don't do that no more—you call somebody else and have *them* wash the car, and you get to tell *them* that it's not clean and *they* have to do it over."

I don't know if it was because Shanna and I were doing this television show, but our wedding plans kept getting more elaborate. We had to have this high-end, high-profile Hollywood wedding planner. And it turned out to be a disaster. Something that was supposed to be festive and beautiful was turning into a huge hassle, which just sucked.

Meet the Barkers showed that dynamic pretty well.

"Trav, we got to go to this meeting for the wedding planner."

"Okay, you want me to meet you there?"

"No, I want you to pick me up."

So I'd stop recording or whatever else I was doing, go pick her up, and drive to the meeting with the wedding planner. We'd get to the restaurant for the meeting and I'd tell her, "I'll be in there in ten minutes." I'd sit in the car, smoke two blunts, and walk in high.

You can see it on our show: I am as high as a kite during any meeting with the wedding planner. I just say "Uh-huh, uh-huh, yeah, sure, yes." Just agree: that's the only way you're going to win at those fucking meetings, by making them as painless as possible. Instead of celebrating our relationship, we were fighting over what color balloons, what color rose petals, what will the tablecloths look like, what music are they going to play, whether we would build a hundred-thousand-dollar scaffold over the pool so we could get married on top of the pool. It was *hectic*.

When you're filming a reality show, people come out of the woodwork to try to hang out with you—everyone wants to be on TV. It's ridiculous.

Shanna was always shopping at this one boutique. Every time she went there, this dude would show up and try to be on TV. Finally Shanna told the owners that he needed to cool it, but she was opinionated about it: "Who the fuck is this random guy that's always here every time I'm here? It sucks, you know? It's uncomfortable."

The next time Shanna was there, he broke in on her in the dressing room and started yelling at her while she was half-dressed: "What the fuck, bitch? You better stop talking shit about me. I know where you motherfuckers live, I know where you're getting married. You and your old man better watch your back."

I got a call from Natasha, who was working as Shanna's assistant. Natasha was crying, and I could hear Shanna crying in the background. Natasha said, "I'm going to tell you something, but you gotta promise not to trip."

"Nah," I said. "You gotta tell me what it is first before I decide if I'm going to trip or not."

She broke it down, and I hung up the phone. I called the business and told them, "I don't know if you guys realize what you did, but you got yourselves in a fucking mess." I told them they needed to give me the phone number for the guy who did this. Then I called him up and said, "You and I need to meet up and talk. I need to meet with you face-to-face, because what you just did is fucked up and unacceptable."

He didn't care. He just said, "Yeah, motherfucker, you got a problem?"

"It's beyond I've got a problem. I'm ready to meet up with you. I don't care how big you are or how big your crew is. Tell me where you can meet up."

Then another dude got on his phone. He told me which gang he was part of and shouted, "What do you want, motherfucker?" Gangbangin' on me, telling me he was going to kill me, this and that.

I said, "Just tell me where you want to meet up." He had threatened me and my family—it was on.

I called Shanna and told her, "Stay home, watch the kids, lock the doors. I'm not going to be home tonight." I called my brother Skinhead Rob and told him what was up, and then we went to see our friend

Paulie, who was in one of the gnarliest biker clubs in the world. He was my boy, so we got a crew together: seven or eight of the scariest dudes I've ever seen in my life. Skinhead Rob went down the line and said, "Any of you motherfuckers aren't ready to die tonight, you need to leave right now. If anyone's going to be here that's not ready to die tonight."

DJ MUGGS, SKINHEAD ROB, ME, AND EVERLAST AT PAULIE B's STORE

We all got in a van. We had so much ammo and guns, we looked like a SWAT team. If the police had stopped us, I probably would have gone to jail for the rest of my life. Shanna and I were getting married in three days, so I wanted to get everything settled before then—the last thing I wanted was my family and friends getting shot up at my wedding.

Paulie got on the phone—he knew one of the OGs in this gang, because they had done some business together. He found out that the gang was, in fact, connected to this guy, who had them on his payroll. We tried to meet up with them at a gas station, and it was a no-show. We drove around until four A.M., but we never caught up with them. Either there was some miscommunication, or they were ducking us.*

I was carrying a gun everywhere. Lil Chris and I kept visiting the shooting range—I wanted to practice shooting because I thought shit was going down. Maybe we were smoking too much weed. But one day, Chris and I were in the range when a whole bunch of thugs came in and were staring the two of us down. We were outnumbered nine to two, and we were in a shooting range with live ammunition. It seemed like the easiest place to smoke somebody—I figured they had followed us. It turned out we were just in a bad part of town and they were staring at us because we were the only white boys in the range. I was totally paranoid.

MY FRIEND PAULIE B.
COURTESY OF ESTEVAN ORIOL

---

* Paulie (full name Paul Michael Krug) died a few years later, at the end of 2007. He had been under investigation by the ATF forever, but he had finally gone on the straight and narrow. He opened up a bunch of tire shops, and he had just had a child. But over the amount of time the feds had been watching him, his record had built up so much shit—they didn't care that he had calmed down.

They raided his place—it was going to be his third strike. Supposedly he resisted arrest, and by the time he made it to the police station, he was dead. They basically beat him to death. There was an open-casket funeral, and we could see that his face was black and blue. People at that funeral were angry—and we were all being photographed and harassed by federal agents.

WITH SHANNA: OUR *NIGHTMARE BEFORE CHRISTMAS*-THEMED WEDDING.

COURTESY OF SIMONE & MARTIN PHOTOGRAPHY

PLAYING DRUMS WITH SOLOMON BURKE.
COURTESY OF SIMONE & MARTIN PHOTOGRAPHY

So my wedding day came, and there had been no communication with these guys. Shanna and I had a *Nightmare Before Christmas* theme for the wedding—but what she didn't know was that I was walking down the aisle with a gun in my suit jacket. I was strapped at my own wedding. Bikers were there in suits and half my groomsmen were strapped. There were killers in suits there that nobody had ever seen.

"Who are those guys, Travis?" Shanna asked me.

"Just some of my friends who decided to come to the wedding."

And one of Shanna's buddies was in a different motorcycle club. So at my wedding, you've got these two rival bikers right next to each other—and normally, that would mean bloodshed. Luckily, everyone was respectful and chill.

I took way too many pills that day, so I was pretty out of it. I was trying to hold it together, because we had about three hundred people there, including Mark, Tom, and my Pops. I walked down the altar with a pistol in my jacket. My son, Landon, was running down the aisle behind me, in a little suit just like mine—and all I could think about was how awful it would be if anything happened to him. It was the hardest night ever—how had we ended up in this mess? I had two of my best friends watching over Landon the whole night. In the back of my mind, I was just waiting for gunshots.*

---

* Everyone survived the wedding—and I surprised Shanna by getting Solomon Burke to sing our song, "Don't Give Up on Me." I played the drums while he sang it to her. Then Shanna and I went on our honeymoon in Fiji. We were happily in love one minute, and bickering the next. We were going snorkeling and kayaking butt-ass naked: the majority of the trip, we didn't have our clothes on. Coming back, we were waiting in line to get on the small plane that would take us to our big plane home. She was wearing shorts and a tank top, and I could see people were staring at her: she had hickeys and bite marks all over her. Finally, one guy asked her what happened. She joked, "Oh, he beat me." I told her to tell the truth. So she said, "I'm just kidding—we had lots of good sex on our honeymoon."

COURTESY OF ESTEVAN ORIOL

13

Not Today

I n early 2005, Blink-182 broke up—for no good reason. Maybe it was because we had all become fathers and had our own families and our own priorities. I wasn't sure what Tom was thinking, but it seemed like he wanted to take a break from touring and take some time off from the band to be home with his family. Mark and I wanted to be with our families too, but we also wanted to keep going with the band—we had built up so much momentum with the untitled album. And I wanted to support my family by touring more. I was learning that you can have time or money, but you can't have both. It was the sort of thing where we should have been able to compromise and work it out, but instead the band built up bad blood.

We had stopped talking to each other, so our manager, Rick, kept polling us on what we wanted to do about different things, and we always disagreed. You had to be truly neutral if you were in the position Rick was in, but it felt to me like he kept siding with Tom, so I began to see the

band dynamic being Rick and Tom against Mark and me. Whatever the case, it was unhealthy for everyone involved. Certainly for me, anyway.

A band has to have the same goals and desires. Most important, you have to communicate. And if you don't, you're destined for big problems. I felt like the *Meet the Barkers* camera crews rubbed Tom the wrong way, but it wasn't something we ever talked about. All through 2004, the glue that kept the band together was our tour manager, Gus. He knew how the band worked, and he knew how to handle all of us. In my opinion, he should have been our manager.

The three of us were rehearsing to play a benefit for tsunami victims, and after we worked out which songs we were going to do, we started talking about what our schedule for the rest of the year was going to be. We couldn't come to any consensus, so we agreed to disagree and we headed home. But it felt like we were breaking the relationship rule that you never want to fall asleep without making up after a fight.

The next morning, Rick called me and said, "Tom just quit the band." It felt toxic—like if a girl broke up with you and doesn't even give you a reason. But given the way things had been lately between us, I wasn't totally surprised. I didn't want Blink-182 to break up, but I wasn't going to chase after him: once somebody's said they want out, it doesn't do any good to try to change their mind.

That evening, I was out with Skinhead Rob and a couple of my friends when Rick called me again. "What are you doing?" he asked.

"Eating dinner with S.R.," I told him.

"Why aren't you doing something? Your band just broke up." Eight hours later, this was his genius plan to get us back together.

"Fuck you," I told him. "You're the reason we broke up! You couldn't handle this situation." Tom never even called—he went back to San Diego and changed his phone number. We pulled out of the benefit show; Rick issued a statement saying we were going on hiatus. Days became weeks became months. I didn't think I would ever talk to Tom again. And after all those months of tension, it was almost a relief that we had gone our separate ways.

COURTESY OF WILLIE TOLEDO

I was in a state of shock that everything we had worked for had been flushed down the toilet. I felt powerless to fix it. But I didn't have time to think about why Blink had broken up: I still needed to earn money to support my family. I jumped into making the Transplants' second record, *Haunted Cities,* and then we went on tour. Rob was on a lot of drugs at that time, and so was I: we were smoking weed all day, taking Vicodin, sometimes sipping lean (aka syrup), whatever we could get our hands on. From the time we woke up to the time we went onstage to the time we got offstage to the time we went to sleep, we were smoking and drinking—and Tim had been sober for a long time.

I always wanted to spend time with both of them, so most mornings, I would smoke a blunt with Rob, then get to a gym with Tim. Then I'd come back, smoke some more weed with Rob, go play a show, get offstage, smoke about six blunts, take some pills, watch some movies on the bus, and do it all over again. Being around us made Tim question his sobriety: it wasn't healthy for him, so he ended the band and I had no choice but to respect his decision.

ROB ASTON (VOCALIST, THE TRANSPLANTS)

When Travis joined us, Blink-182 were on MTV and radio everywhere. He went from buses and first-class everything to getting in a van with us and playing small shows in small clubs. He didn't give a shit if it was ten people or ten thousand. I've never heard Travis complain about the conditions of a tour: he just wants to play music and put on a good show.

On show days, some people stretch or exercise. Some people get drunk; some people get high. Travis sits there with his practice pad for hours. He can have full-on conversations with you, or talk to his kids, and he never misses a beat. He's like a machine. He used to warm up with solid-steel drumsticks, the way baseball players will take practice swings with a doughnut on the bat.

TRAVIS BARKER
can i say

They're twenty times heavier than a regular drumstick and he'd just be going rapid-fire. And then some dipshit stole them. That's typical.

The last show of the Warped Tour 2005, we walked offstage and came down the steps. I said to Tim, "Hey, great show. Good way to end the tour on a good note."

He said, "Yeah, can we talk for a minute?"

Tim told me and Travis that he was having trouble staying sober on the road, and having trouble staying sober around us—he needed a break. We told him that his health was more important, and that he should do whatever he needed for his state of mind. And that was it: he left. Me and Trav had to tell the rest of the band and the crew that it was over. We were supposed to go to Europe and Japan a week later.

It sucked. It's burned in my memory. Everyone was in tears. When you're touring in a band, that's your family. No one is more important, whether it's the guy selling T-shirts or the members of the band. Everyone plays their part, everyone keeps it going together. So everyone was just devastated. And when you're working for a band, your whole year is mapped out ahead of you, and you spend that money accordingly. A lot of people had nothing else they could do. Me and Travis went in our pockets to help out the crew, because we knew that our breaking up fucked everyone over.

In less than a year, both my bands had broken up. That turned my world upside down, and it put a lot of stress on my relationship with Shanna. I felt like there wasn't much I could do except say that my life was changing and move forward.

Fuck being bored. You shouldn't ever be bored. You can always read and be smarter. You can always work out and be in better shape. You can always play your instrument and get better at it. Your space can always be cleaner. Blue-collar work is when you work with your hands—white-collar work is behind a desk. I'm not as grimy as my father, who made his living with a wrench, but everything I have comes from working with my hands.

TRAVIS BARKER
can i say

Famous was getting bigger every day. The MTV cameras were still following me and Shanna around. I was spending every free minute with Landon, unless I was working a late night at the studio; he was getting used to having drumsticks in his hands. I would wake up, take him to breakfast, and push him around the neighborhood in his stroller. Despite all the bad stuff that had gone down with my bands, I felt blessed to be spending time with my son. Being a dad was the best thing in the world.

WITH LANDON.
COURTESY OF SIMONE & MARTIN PHOTOGRAPHY

I was also working more and more with hip-hop artists. That started a few years earlier, when Puff Daddy asked me to appear in the video for his song "Bad Boy for Life," playing drums in a suburban garage. I hadn't actually performed on that track, but it was cool to be invited into his world. Then Pharrell Williams gave me a call and asked if I would appear in the video "Provider," for his band N.E.R.D.

"Yo, we're filming this video, riding BMX bikes around," he told me. "I want you to be in the 7-Eleven when I roll in." I was happy to do it: I stood in line in a convenience store buying beer, and Tony Hawk played the clerk. When I met Pharrell on the set, we vibed with each other and he was super cool.

I also connected with the Black Eyed Peas, back when they were playing the Warped Tour instead of the Super Bowl. Will.i.am said, "We got to get together—I have a studio and I'm always making music." Once we got off the tour and back to LA, he would call me up sometimes and say, "Yo, roll over to the studio." I would come in and do whatever they needed: he might ask for me to add to a loop with real drums, or do my own version of something he had programmed. Sometimes he might just have a cowbell in a loop, and I'd vibe with it and then make up my own drum part. I wasn't worried about getting paid: I just liked being part of the creative process, and I learned a lot by being in the same room as him. That relationship went on for years.

Amid all this chaos, my friend Nick Leo introduced me to DJ AM. His real name was Adam Goldstein, and he used to DJ with a rap-metal band called Crazy Town. They had a number-one hit in 2001 with "Butterfly," so I used to see him here and there. I had actually met AM once before—in Germany, of all places, when Crazy Town and Blink-182 were playing the same festival. I was never really into Crazy Town, but I loved what he did as a DJ, and he told me he loved what I did as a drummer. Then I went to a show in New York where I saw a DJ doing a set with an old guy playing congas. I started to think: *What if you took that a step further? What if I played on a small drum kit with a dope DJ and we did every style possible?*

One night, I went to one of AM's gigs in Hollywood. He played everything you weren't supposed to play, like Neil Diamond's "Sweet Caroline" and Fugazi's "Waiting Room," and made it sound good by mixing it with current hip-hop. The whole show, I was thinking, *AM and me, could you imagine?* I hit him up after the show and said, "We should rock sometime."

"What do you mean? Do you DJ too?"

"No, I'll play the drums and you DJ. Shit, man, pretend you're the guitar player, but you throw every genre of music at me and either I match you or play off of you. You take all the drums out and let me do the drums. And I'll be playing double-time to songs that have a slow groove, and we'll do live remixes of stuff." I had this vision of AM throwing a cappellas at me while I played live drums and 808s.

The first time we jammed, we played for seven hours. I didn't know what he was going to play because he didn't know what *I* was going to play. It was intensely satisfying. I had never gotten to show anybody all the styles I could play.

We kept jamming, and we started doing some shows together, just local club dates. My attitude was, "AM and I are going to do something that's never been done before."

Right off the bat, AM and I played a big radio show, the KROQ Inland Invasion. The next thing you knew, clubs in LA and Vegas were asking for us and we were doing Boost Mobile parties. We were having the time of our lives.

KEV-E-KEV (MANAGER)

Adam was my closest and best friend. I think he and Travis had such a connection because they're cut from the same cloth. Both of them were pretty much raised by single parents but were wild in the streets, dis- covering things. Both of them were self-made mil- lionaires who came from nothing. Both of them are adored by millions. They're both lovers of women. These two guys are,

WITH DJ AM. COURTESY OF ESTEVAN ORIOL

respectfully, two of the greatest at what they each do individually on their instruments. They would have been in high school together, separated by two grades. They grew up on the same music. All those similarities were part of their connection.

Meanwhile, the Transplants were supposed to do a track for the solo debut of Bun B: he's an old-school Houston rapper who was one half of the legendary UGK. That plan went down the hole when the Transplants broke up. Skinhead Rob told Bun, "Our band's not together no more—we're taking a fucking break. But don't worry, I'm going to have Travis make you a beat."

Then Rob called me up and said, "Yo, man, can you make a beat for Bun? You're a sick-ass drummer—you should be able to do it."

I had never made a beat in my life, but I had ideas and I'd always wanted to produce, so I said, "Fuck, yeah!" I got home and went into the studio I had set up in my basement, which was basically just drums and a Pro Tools setup. I did not know what I was doing. But like they say, problems are opportunities in work clothes. Learning how to create a mood in a finished instrumental track, not just hitting the drums, was a challenge—but an exciting one. It was my chance to give back to a genre of music that I loved. Even though I didn't rap, I found a way to contribute to hip-hop.

I had one buddy, Kevin "Sweatshop" Bivona, play keyboards with me, and another buddy, a DJ named Ryan Best, do some scratching. I did four tracks in the studio. I put aside the very first one and then I sent Bun the next three. He liked one a whole bunch, and that became the song called "Late Night Creepin'." He and Rob rapped on it and it was dope. It was such a trip when his album *Trill* came out; I was really honored to work with him. If Rob and Bun hadn't asked me, I probably never would have started making beats.

When *Meet the Barkers* hit the air in 2005, it introduced me to a lot of people. I had always been the quiet guy in Blink, but the show let people see a lot of things about me, whether it was my love for tattoos, or having the worst Cadillac and Louis Vuitton fetishes, or spending time with family and running my companies. I would buy those Cadillacs for three grand, put in another five to ten thousand dollars fixing them up, and end up with a ride I liked better than a brand-new car. I still dressed like a homeless guy (T-shirts, cutoff shorts, and old sneakers) and got turned away from restaurants, but I was discovering the finer things in life. I was smoking weed 24/7 and getting a lot more done than most people who don't smoke. The show got the attention of a lot of people in the rap community who then wanted to work with me—which I never would have guessed would happen. It also boosted the sales of Famous Stars and Straps, which was totally unintentional: I was wearing Famous clothes most of the time on the show, the way I always did, and people got to know that it was my company. At that time, we were selling about $100 million of product per year.

DR. BRIAN WEEKS (FRIEND)

Travis, even when he was popping a lot of pills, never asked me for a controlled substance. Just another thing I love about the guy. But one night, he called me around midnight on my cell phone and said, "Dr. B, I need you, I got a little situation here."

He had picked up an executive from one of his record labels—the guy had flown in from the East Coast, and apparently he was a bit of a partier. Who knows what he had premedicated on before the flight, but when he got to Travis's place, they rolled him a big fat blunt. Maybe they sprinkled a little something in it.

Travis said, "Dr. B, we smoked this record-label executive out. He took two hits, and then his eyes rolled back
in his head and he collapsed on the floor."

"Is he breathing?"

I heard Travis ask Lil Chris, "Is he breathing?"
Lil Chris said, "Shit man, no, he's not breathing."

I said, "Travis, this is a medical emergency. You need
to call 911."

"I can't call 911, Dr. B."

I tried to persuade him to make the call, but Travis was
freaking out. My own heart was going about 160 beats per
minute, because I was worried that the guy was dying on
Travis's floor. For all I knew, he had done fifty lines
of coke.

Then I heard Lil Chris say, "I got an idea!" Apparently,
he grabbed a cup of ice water and started throwing it in
the guy's face. While he was doing this, I told Travis,
"You need to call 911 and you need to start CPR. If the
guy's not breathing, he might have had cardiac arrest.
He might be dead. Are you doing coke?"

"No, no, we're not doing coke."

"Did this guy do coke?"

"I don't know, I don't know!"

Suddenly I heard screaming and Lil Chris yelling, "Oh my God!" The ice water did the job: the guy woke up, and he shot up straight, like a scene in a movie.

Travis got back on the phone. "Alright, Dr. B—I'm cool. I'll talk to you tomorrow," he said, like nothing had happened. And then he hung up.

It was hilarious—because the guy was fine. The next morning, Travis got him on a plane and got him out of LA.

Meanwhile, even with Tom out of the picture, Mark and I were still great friends who wanted to keep working together. That's how we started the band +44. I said, "We don't want to do a band that's just like Blink—it'd be weird." I suggested maybe we should do something with a girl singer, to really change it up. I had known Carol and Caryn Heller when I was living with Bill Fold in Riverside—we'd all go to punk-rock shows together. I was friends with Caryn: Carol was her older sister. A year before Blink broke up, I heard they were playing in an all-girl punk-rock band. So I called Carol up and said, "Hey, would you ever think about being in a band for real?"

She said she'd love to, so she came by my house and we did some demos in the basement. We wrote a few songs that had an electronic vibe. It ended up not working out with Carol, which sucked—I don't think the chemistry was fully there—so we needed somebody who could play the guitar really good. So we got my friend Shane, who had played in Doyt with me (the band that never got out of my family's garage).

Mark and I were both living in LA, so it made sense for us to find some space in town. We looked around for a studio and found a small place in North Hollywood, being sold by a guy who used to play guitar with Poison. Us buying that studio changed my life. Once we had that space, I no longer spent my days smoking weed, driving around in cars, hanging with the

homies, getting into trouble. I still smoked weed and got into trouble—but it was always in the studio. Mark would be in one room working on something, and I would be in the next room. It was our workshop.

I don't think +44 was exactly the band that Mark and I were supposed to be in, but even though I was content building my project with DJ AM, we both clearly wanted to keep making music together.

MARK HOPPUS (BASSIST/SINGER, BLINK-182)

As Blink-182 was falling apart, Tom was heading off to go do his own thing. Travis and I had a conversation where we said we were going to stick together and continue doing what we do. So we went in the basement of his house in Bel Air—the one that was on *Meet the Barkers*—just me and him and an engineer, putting song ideas together. That was +44.

It was good to do something with no expectations. Also, this is what I imagine it feels like for divorced people: they see friends, and everybody's always like, "How you doing? You all right?" Yeah, I'm cool, it's good. That was a painful, cathartic record—I think for both of us—but I'm really proud of it. And it was a really good experience because it allowed both Travis and me to understand what our skill sets are. That sounds really corporate.

Travis has a great singing voice. I've heard him sing maybe once or twice ever, and the last time was probably ten years ago—but he can sing. He has a sharp sense of humor too. Before, I think people just saw Travis as the quiet drummer in the background, because Tom and I were always so loud. There have always been three personalities in Blink-182, but I've gotten to see Travis branch out from being the band's drummer: he's built his company, worked with different artists, and become a personality outside the Blink framework.

The things that are important to Travis are very important to him, and the rest of it can come or go. If Travis wants something specifically, I give it extra weight, because he lets so many things go by. He's got an incredible work ethic. If it's not a musical project, it's something with Famous, or he's working out. He's really focused on whatever it is he's doing right then. He never just sits down and watches TV, vegging out.

When I went into the studio, I would do production every minute. I'd wake up, smoke a blunt on my balcony, and spend my day at the studio, locked in a room, making beats from ten A.M. to one A.M. I started a group with Skinhead Rob and Paul Wall called Expensive Taste, and we put together tracks for a mixtape.

ROB ASTON (VOCALIST, THE TRANSPLANTS)

Me and Travis continued to work on stuff after the Transplants broke up. We were talking with Paul Wall, the rapper from Houston, and told him about everything that went down. He said, "Shit, we can have a band." We started a group called Expensive Taste. Travis drummed on that album—I guess technically it was a mixtape, but 95 percent of it was original material—and he also produced almost all the songs on it. That was the beginning of him making hip-hop beats.

When we were making that album, the three of us were hanging out one night on Travis's balcony, smoking weed. We had a clear view of the street below us, and we saw a four-door Honda Accord pull up. It stopped in the middle of the street. Then the driver got out and opened the back door—and a deer jumped out of the backseat of the car. The deer took off; the driver got back in the car like nothing happened and drove away. The three of us got very quiet: we were all asking ourselves, "Did I really just see a fucking deer get out of the back of that car and run away?"

After I did the track for Bun and started working on Expensive Taste, I also started doing remixes. The very first one was for "Back in the Mud" by Bubba Sparxxx, followed by "Can I Have It Like That" for Pharrell Williams and Gwen Stefani. But it took off when Soulja Boy's label asked me to remix his song "Crank That." It had a bare, simple beat, which was great: it was like an empty canvas for me to do whatever I wanted to with the track. I took it from 0 to 100 and gave this remix really high

energy with heavy guitars and drums. Within a year's time, my remix had thirty million views on YouTube. And the next thing I knew, I was getting lots of calls like that: "Hey, we've got this song by a new artist, we'll pay you X amount of money to do a remix." "Hey, Travis, would you do a remix of 'Umbrella' for Rihanna?"

When this started, I wasn't even settled into my studio yet: for each track, I had to rent a studio to record the drums and do all the remixing. I always did a little video of me playing the drums on the remix. It didn't have to be fancy, but it had to be unedited, so people could see I was actually playing. These videos were poppin': I was getting twenty to thirty million views for each of them.

Interscope wanted me to come out with a whole album of remixes, but it seemed like a mess: too many of the artists were on different labels. Lil Chris said, "Fuck a remix album. Do your own album. We know every rapper." We had built up a lot of relationships: a lot of times when I did a remix, I'd say, "I'll do it on love—don't worry about paying me. Return the favor when it's time." So a whole bunch of people owed me a favor.

At the time, I was hanging out with a lot of rappers: Jermaine Dupri and Nelly wanted me to get on the mic myself. They would tell me, "Dude, you need to put out a rap album. We'll write for you, whatever you need—you just go do that shit." I said, "Hell no. I'm a drummer, man. I want to play the damn drums." I probably could have pulled it off, but I didn't have the passion—and making beats was more exciting to me than getting on the microphone. I didn't want to do anything that felt out of character, even for a second. And at the time, rap was still gangster. I was also getting name-checked in a lot of rap songs: Lil Wayne, T.I., Too Short, Gucci Mane, Dem Franchize Boyz, Shop Boyz. That blew my mind. I had always loved hip-hop just as much as rock, and it was amazing to be accepted as part of that community. I decided that I wanted to make an album, I wanted to produce all the tracks for it, and I wanted to drum on it—and have it feature all my favorite MCs.

Some days I would leave the studio thinking, Ugh, I'm not in love with these. Other days, I'd be thinking, These are the best fucking beats I've ever made. And every day, different artists would be rolling through. T.I. would come to town and say, "Hey, I'm playing Jay Leno, I want you to play with me." Jamie Foxx: "Hey, I'm playing the BET Awards, I want you to play with me."

If I was in the studio, Lil Chris would be partying with whatever artist just came to town, and then he'd bring 'em to the studio late at night. We had a system: every day there was somebody new in there. So in the summer of 2008, I recorded "Fuck the World" with Bun B and Beanie Sigel.* And I put together "Can a Drummer Get Some" with the Game, Swizz Beatz, Rick Ross, and Lil Wayne.

At the time, I wasn't in Blink and I wasn't in the Transplants, but my dreams were coming true. The kid who grew up listening to the Beasties, Whodini, and KRS-One was getting called by Jay-Z asking if I could play on Beyonce's album. In many ways, Blink-182 breaking up was a positive thing for me. I loved the band, but my career with them was one-dimensional: I played with Blink and toured with Blink. The band was a third leg that I was dependent on. When it went away, I had to stand up by myself. It was like when my mom died: I had been depending on her to do so much for me, but then I had to grow up.

JAMES INGRAM (RECORDING ENGINEER)

Mark and Travis had just bought their studio in North Hollywood—I showed up for an interview with Chris Holmes, the engineer, when they were still getting their gear in there. He said, "You can stay if you want." I was just doing intern stuff: painting walls, wiring, taking out garbage, picking up coffee.

The guy who owned it before had a weird psychedelic-clown motif going on. It was really, really strange.

---

* We eventually renamed that track "Just Chill."

MOM AND DAD BRINGING MY SISTER HOME FROM THE HOSPITAL

A DRAWING I MADE AT FOUR YEARS OLD
OF ME PLAYING THE DRUMS

Travis
4yrs old
1979
Tiny Tots:

DAD, TAMARA, RANDALAI, AND ME

KINDERGARTEN

NEW FRIENDS   Thomas, Kathy, Danielle, Nancy, Dana, Nathan, James, Yvette, Manuel, Windy, Wendy, Lena, Lucio, Maria, Garrett, Jennifer, Jarrat, Jason, Shane, Serenity, Sheila, Mario, Jannel, Norma, Heather, mike, Robert, Jeramy

ACTIVITIES

ACHIEVEMENTS   Read his first book "Who Am I" Counts to 50

AWARDS   Certificate in Art & Music

WHEN I GROW UP I WANT TO BE—

☐ Fireman   ☐ Astronaut   ☐ Mother   ☐ Airline Hostess

☐ Policeman   ☐ Soldier   ☐ Nurse   ☐ Model

☐ Cowboy   ☐ Baseball Player   ☐ School Teacher   ☐ Secretary

☐ Drummer   ☐ _____

SIGNATURE   Travis Barker

MY KINDERGARTEN ACTIVITY LOG

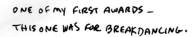

ONE OF MY FIRST AWARDS —
THIS ONE WAS FOR BREAKDANCING.

Award
of Achievement

Presented to _Travis Barker_

for _Break Dance_

an activity of the City of Fontana / Fontana Unified School District
Conducted by The Parks and Recreation Department

3-12-85
_{Date}

Department Official

GETTING READY FOR
A DRUM COMPETITION,
CIRCA 1984

ME AND POPS

CUTTING LANDON'S HAIR WITH ALABAMA'S HELP

SETTING UP FOR BLINK-182'S "AFTER MIDNIGHT" VIDEO SHOOT, WHICH TOOK PLACE IN AN AIRPLANE HANGAR

SELFIE WITH LANDON AND ALABAMA

JAMMING WITH MIXMASTER MIKE

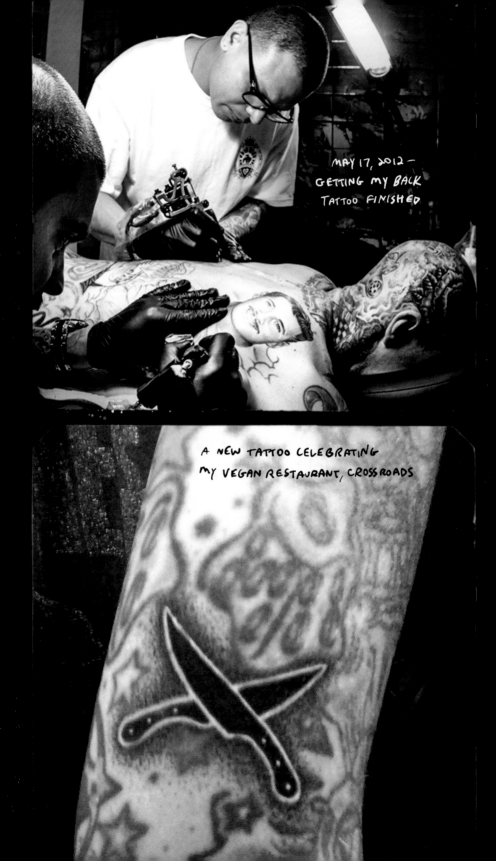

MAY 17, 2012 —
GETTING MY BACK
TATTOO FINISHED

A NEW TATTOO CELEBRATING
MY VEGAN RESTAURANT, CROSSROADS

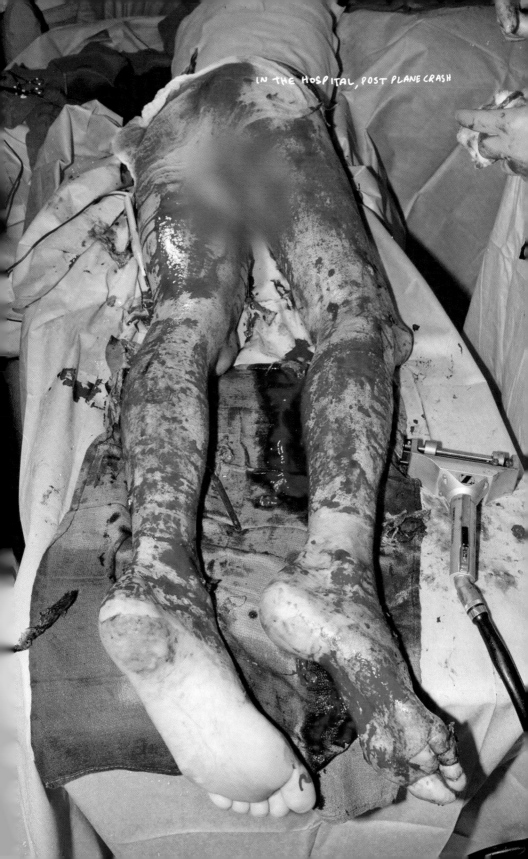
IN THE HOSPITAL, POST PLANE CRASH

COURTESY OF JAYSON FOX

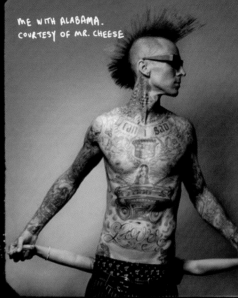

ME WITH ALABAMA.
COURTESY OF MR. CHEESE

WITH DJ KLEVER, YELAWOLF, AND BONES OWENS.
COURTESY OF CLEMENTE RUIZ

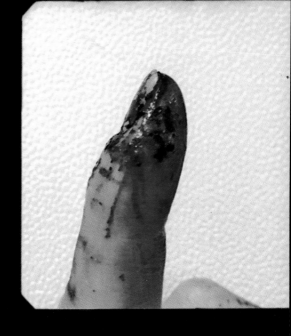

DRUMMING UNTIL
MY FINGERS BLEED

PLAYING WITH
YELAWOLF ON HALLOWEEN

OUR FAMILY'S LOVE FOR CADILLACS STARTS YOUNG.
COURTESY OF ESTEVAN ORIOL

MY FAVORITE HUMANS

MY GORGEOUS 1954 CADILLAC.
COURTESY OF ESTEVAN ORIOL

And there was this weird little closet off the side of a
bathroom. It's a drum closet now—as if the whole studio
isn't filled with drums. But when we got there, it had
a hanging light bulb in the middle of the room and a
dirty mattress on the floor. It was so gross—it was like
a weird little rape room in the studio.

About halfway through the +44 record, Skinhead Rob
came in and was doing music, and Travis was doing more
beats. We got the B room going, and they were looking for
somebody to engineer. Chris Holmes did me the biggest
solid: he said, "Oh, James can do that."

One night early on, the room was full of people—I was
trying to work, but I realized I was high because everybody was smoking so much. I turned around, and on the
table behind me, there was money and drugs and guns:
multiple piles of each. I was still pretty new in Los
Angeles—I'm a Vermont guy—and I didn't know what to do,
so I just turned back around.

One time, Too Short came in. We were working, and later
on, I found myself having a conversation with Too Short
about how to get girls to agree to have threesomes. I
thought it was great advice—if anybody knows what they're
talking about with threesomes, it's going to be Too Short.

Mark liked to come in and work on +44 stuff in the morning. Travis liked to come in a little later. And if there
was the hip-hop stuff, or the Expensive Taste stuff,
they liked to come in late. I was going in at seven or
eight in the morning to get ready for when Mark showed
up, and then if the session was going late, I'd get out
of there at four in the morning. It's not uncommon for
the music business at all, but it took some getting used

to. I've come to grips with putting in a ton of hours
and not complaining, but I've decided there's a big difference between griping and complaining.

Travis took over more and more of the studio—he pushes
boundaries. Often, he was doing projects in both rooms.
And then he started having people from Famous work out
of there so he could meet with them on the regular.

Home life with Shanna had changed as well: I would stay out all night
at the studio working, and she thought I was out fucking random girls.
We were having major trust issues for months, and then she had been
acting weird, which led to us having a huge fight. (One friend of hers
was constantly instigating fights between the two of us and making any
problems even worse.) I told Shanna, "You know what? You can move
out. This is a toxic relationship, and I'm over it."

She said, "I'm sorry," and burst into tears. "For two weeks, I've wanted
to tell you something, but I wanted it to be a surprise. I'm pregnant. I've
been weird because I've been planning to tell you." She opened the door to
our bathroom suite and there were hundreds of pink balloons everywhere,
pink flowers, pink cake. She says, "You're having a little girl, Travis."
Immediately, I melted, and I was the happiest father-to-be, once again.

I fell in love with Shanna all over again, knowing that our little girl
was inside of her. It was easy to put our problems in the past, because I
was so excited to meet my little girl. I spent a lot of time getting her room
ready. I knew how to be a father to a boy: when Landon was two, I even
potty-trained him by teaching him to pee outside.* But I knew that I'd
have to do things differently with a little girl. I had a lot to learn, but I
was looking forward to it. Both times Shanna was pregnant, I read *The
Expectant Father* so I would know what exactly was going on inside her
womb every day.

---

* He still does that today.

TRAVIS BARKER
can i say

Alabama was born on Christmas Eve, 2005.* She came out staring: no crying, just looking at me for minutes at a time with her game face, not even blinking. It almost freaked me out. I knew I was in trouble with her from day one. When I was rocking Alabama to sleep, I would listen to Stevie Wonder's "Isn't She Lovely" over and over, sometimes bravely attempting to sing along.

From the time Landon and Bama were born, I knew that I was responsible for how they turned out. Because of that, I wanted to spend every waking minute with them. I never understood what I had done to deserve the blessing of these two beautiful human beings. I was so proud and happy to be their father. From that point on, I wanted to be a great role model: I wanted to be the first thing they saw when they woke up, taking them to school, and the last thing they saw at night, putting them to bed. I was eating better, exercise had become a daily routine, and even though I hadn't stopped abusing pills—I was an addict—I was

---

* Her full name is Alabama Luella Barker. The Alabama is from Alabama Worley, of course—Patricia Arquette's character in *True Romance*. And we just liked the way "Luella" sounded. We almost called her Briar Rose—that's Sleeping Beauty's name.

struggling to be a better person and looking for a way to quit. It weighed on my mind constantly.

When we got home, I couldn't believe I had a little girl. And even when she was a baby, she had a crazy bubble butt. After all the shit that I had done to girls through my life, I knew I was cursed. With a little boy, you teach him to protect himself, teach him to protect his sisters, teach him to be tough. But with a little girl, from day one you're trying to protect her. It's the weirdest thing. To this day, when I hold Landon, he's my boy, trying to put me in a chokehold—he loves to play rough, but I still give him lots of love and kisses. But Bama will just hold on, hooking her legs around me, and say, "You're my daddy." With Landon, I had to leave on tour soon after he was born, which was really hard on both of us, but with Alabama, I was able to stay home more. So she would follow me around the house, crawling behind me, saying, "Daddy, Daddy, Daddy." And once she learned to walk, it was a wrap—she was always with me. When Bama was feeling cranky

THE BARKER FAMILY

at bedtime, I would ride around on my bike, with her strapped into an extra seat, and that would knock her right out. I would have barely left the house and she'd be asleep.

With both kids, if they were waking up at night, I would let them fall asleep on my chest. Sometimes I'd even wake them up so they could fall asleep on my chest. This worked out great for them as long as I was around—but when I wasn't there, Shanna had a lot of trouble getting them to sleep in their cribs. And with the two of us not getting along, she resented that I was always bringing them into our bed—she wanted us to have more time alone, but I cared more about being a dad.

The first year Shanna and I were together was like a movie. The times she was pregnant were magical. When our children were born, those were the happiest times of my life ever. But the rest of our relationship became a headache. I played some of the best shows of my life when I was married to Shanna, because she pissed me off so much. That energy got me high—there's no re-creating it.

I felt like having the reality show changed Shanna's character. Shanna wanted to be an actress, and I felt she started doing things just for the cameras—for attention, or maybe it was just her dramatic personality. It was turning into a variety show instead of a reality show—and in my mind, she was behaving out of character on camera, which was carrying over to her not being genuine with me. I told Jesse, the producer, "Let's just end it before it gets totally toxic." I felt like the camera crews hadn't changed me: I treated them like a fly on the wall, and I kept living my life and making my music the way I always had.

Once I saw what our marriage had become, I realized it was my time to go. Shanna was still beautiful and we still had a great sex life, but I realized we were opposites in many ways. I think I had confused love and lust. The problem was that not only did we have a show together, we were married and had kids, so this time, I couldn't just leave. I didn't really want to deal with our problems: what was there to deal with? I wasn't happy—the only thing about our relationship that was making me happy was our kids—so it was better to move on. Maybe she was growing into this new person that she wanted to be, but I didn't like who she had become.

SHANNA MOAKLER (EX-WIFE)

What was awesome about *Meet the Barkers* is that we have a video library of when we first fell in love and moments that we probably would never have captured on film. That love was genuine: it wasn't just a show.

But I think the show destroyed our relationship. I think Travis was afraid that it was now *The Shanna and Travis Show*. He had worked so hard to be taken seriously as a musician—I think he was afraid he was going to be looked on as a reality star. So when the cameras stopped rolling, he distanced himself from me in every way that he possibly could.

When Blink-182 broke up, he didn't know what he was going to do. He was going to all these new people, managers and hangers-on, trying to find a new identity. Lil Chris, who became his assistant, never left his side. I felt like I was competing with Lil Chris all the time: *Lil Chris, please go home so I can fall in love with my husband again. Please.* And no one cared. They just wanted his attention all the time.

When you're not spending enough time with someone, and then you have people purposely causing problems, and then you have drugs on top of it, you don't stand a chance.

With Shanna and me on the outs, I drowned myself in music. I was already trying to pass on my love of my favorite bands to my kids, the same way I had grown up on Buck Owens because Pops was always listening to rebel country music in the car. When Buck passed away, they did a tribute on the Academy of Country Music Awards show with Brad Paisley, Dwight Yoakam, Billy Gibbons (ZZ Top), Chris Hillman (the Byrds), Tom Brumley (Buck's band), Buddy Alan (Buck's son), and surprisingly, me. What are the chances? I have no fucking idea why they invited me. My first reaction was "Are you sure?" I never expected to be invited to something like that, but I was so stoked. And that was the one gig I made sure to take Pops to.

I showed up with a Mohawk, and I don't think everyone in the crew knew who I was. They were a little reserved when rehearsals began, but once I started playing, everyone warmed up. I had learned every lick from the original recordings—even the mistakes that the drummer had made. Tom Brumley, who also played on those records, was tripping that I was replicating those parts perfectly.

About ten minutes into practice, they gave me my freedom, saying I could play whatever I wanted and put my own flair in there. I showed up that night wearing a shirt that said FUCKING AWESOME (the skateboarder Jason Dill's brand). About three different people came up to Lil Chris saying, "He's not going to wear that later, is he? If that's all he brought, we can get him a shirt." They were so nervous I was going to walk onstage with that shirt when it was TV time. I changed my shirt; it was no problem.

Backstage, one guy in the band said, "We have enemies out here. We have people that are rooting for us to fuck up. We can't fuck up." It was gangster. That whole experience was awesome—I don't think they had any idea how excited I was.

Some people who knew me from Blink-182 said, "You're a sellout for playing country music."

I *loved* that. May my haters live long so they can see all my success.

I was never a drinker, but when I was with Shanna, we consumed large amounts of alcohol, pretty much every night. In the morning, I'd be throwing up, but I can never blame Shanna for my drug problems or my pill problems. After the kids were born, she always wanted to go out to dinner and leave the kids with a nanny. She didn't get that when I came home from tour, I wanted to be a family man, not a rock star. I wanted to spend as much time as I could with my kids because I knew all too well how quickly it could be taken away.

I was raised by my mom and my dad: no nannies. Whereas Shanna was raised by nannies. I told her that I wanted to do everything with the kids: take them to the doctor, take them to school, field trips. Anywhere I went, they went. She said, "My parents didn't do that—I'm not going to do that." But I thought what was awesome about being parents was giving your kids more than what you had for yourself.

We'd be heading out to dinner, and I would say, "Okay, I'm going to get Landon and Bama ready."

"No, baby, I just want it to be us."

And then, guess what, I no longer wanted to go to dinner. I was going to have to sit at a table with her, and she was going to complain, talking about everything she wanted to do that wasn't working out for her. She would drink wine until she was drunk, and then she'd tell me that I didn't understand her because I wasn't drinking. There were so many times when I got the check even before the food arrived. I'd sign the paper and get out of there. Sometimes on the way to dinner, she'd start going crazy and I'd just turn the car around. I'd tell her to go to dinner with a girlfriend: I'd stay home with the kids. Shanna would always be complaining about how her career was going: "I could be on this show, but I won't fuck this producer, so he won't hire me." My attitude was always "Go fuck whoever you want to get whatever gig you want—I'm cool." I hated feeling like I was holding her back.

Sometimes we would have a big fight and then she'd go out and party. She'd stumble home around five A.M., and then the next day I'd see photos online of where she had been the night before, at some party. It seemed so out of character, but when we talked about it, Shanna would say, "I moved to Hollywood to be part of Hollywood. Don't get it twisted."

I still loved drumming and I still loved to party, but having kids was changing me more than I ever dreamed. I wanted to be as good to my children as my parents were to me. Going on tour, I was doing something that I loved, but I was also busting ass to provide for our family.

Over and over, she'd remind me, "You knew what I was like when you met me. I never wanted to be a stay-at-home mom."

Shanna and I were fighting more and more, but we always had a physical attraction. We could be hating each other's guts and still have wild, crazy sex that night. Sometimes we would split up and I wouldn't see her for days—until she came to my house at five in the morning, drunk. I'd invite her in and we'd have a good time. But in the morning, when I said, "Hey, I'm taking the kids to breakfast—wake up and join us," she wouldn't get out of bed. I was spending more time with the nannies than with her. Our nannies Judy and Liz were awesome, but still. She never got out of bed once when the kids were young to walk with them or push the stroller. I was experiencing this all by myself—it was amazing and it was unfortunate she was missing out.

We would be on one week, off one week later. Looking back, I wish there had been a cleaner breakup: there would have been a lot less heartache and hostility. When we were apart, I would always make the most of that time: after numerous times at the Playboy Mansion, I had made some friends of my own. A lot of Playmates did modeling jobs for Famous.

SHANNA MOAKLER (EX-WIFE)

I think the demise of our relationship was we had a lot of third parties in our relationship, at a time when Travis was partaking in drugs and pills. These guys didn't want him with me, because it took away from their time—they wanted him to go to the clubs, because then they felt like rock stars too. There were always new people filtering in, and he and I would fight about them. I would say, "This person's not good," and he would defend him. And then a week later, he'd be gone. And there'd be a new asshole to replace him.

These guys would take him out to the club, and they were trying to get him women. We were at different tables, and I went over there: this girl was sitting next to him. They had them at different booths, but arranged so they could sit next to each other. At the end of the night, I'm going to be home with him in bed. But I was being humiliated in a nightclub—not even by him, because he should have known better, but he wasn't in a good place. These guys were doing it on purpose.

I just looked at her, and looked at him, like, Really? And I threw my drink into her face while I looked at him. I wanted to pummel her in front of all these men. Don't fuck with me and don't fuck with my family. You guys are replaceable: I'm not going anywhere. That was a big struggle in our relationship.

I threw drinks in a lot of girls' faces.

In the summer of 2006, I couldn't take it anymore: I decided I was going to split up with Shanna for good. Before I did it, I had a long conversation about my situation with AM. He said, "Man, before you do anything, I'm gonna ask you to sober up. Get sober for forty-eight hours before you make any rash decisions."

AM told me I could call him anytime, day or night—he was teaching me how to be a better person. When AM challenged me like that, I thought about how Lil Chris hadn't been looking right for a while. His coloring was off and he was falling asleep in the middle of the day. In the morning, after I hit the gym, we'd both smoke a blunt and take a pill, and then he'd drive me wherever I needed to go. Sometimes I'd look over and see he was sleeping at the wheel.

"Chris, wake up!"

"Oh, sorry, bro." But a couple of times, he drove into parked cars. I was worried about him—it seemed like he was taking even more pills than me. But it slowly dawned on me that when I looked at Lil Chris, I was looking at myself.

So I flushed every pill I had down the toilet. I wanted to get rid of all the poison in my body. During those two days, I was driving in my

'53 Cadillac, and Chris was following behind me in another car. I was about to light a cigarette, but I realized it was a mistake: I threw them out the window instead.

Lil Chris called my cell phone: "Dude, what the fuck are you doing? Your cigarettes just flew out the window!"

"They didn't fly out," I laughed. "I threw them out the window. I'm over it. I'm done." My daughter had just been born; Landon was two years old; Atiana was six. I knew it was time for a change.

I am a workaholic, and I was keeping crazy hours, which meant that Chris was keeping crazy hours too. The pills had been taking the edge off that, but I could see that what Chris was going through was more than us working too hard. Everything was taking its toll. At my lowest of lows and at the height of my drug abuse, I stared in the mirror and saw somebody worth saving: myself.

We tried to wean ourselves off the pills and help each other through the whole process. If I found pills in his pockets, I'd throw them out. He ended up going to rehab for a couple of days, whereas I basically just quit everything all at once. I had some relapses with the pills later on, and I never stopped smoking weed—but I never smoked another cigarette after the day I threw them out of my car window.

Being sober and having my head clear, it was only more obvious to me that Shanna and I needed to split up. I filed for divorce. That meant I had to leave the house and let her have the premises for two months. So I got a high-rise apartment on Ocean Boulevard in Santa Monica and lived next to the beach. During that time, I rode my skateboard everywhere. Bama wasn't even one year old, but when I had custody of her and Landon, I would put them on my shoulders and skate two miles to a breakfast place. I remember people yelling at me: "What the fuck are you doing? Get a helmet on that kid!" They were right: it was a stupid thing to do, but it felt awesome, like I was taking care of my kids and didn't have a care in the world. My marriage was over and my bands had broken up, but I had this awesome little girl on my shoulders, my mini-me Landon holding my hand, and Atiana at my side. We walked around Santa Monica, picking up acorns and hanging out at the beach.

When I came home after two months, I was alone in this huge twenty-thousand-square-foot *Meet the Barkers* house. It was just weird. I loved the house, but it had too many memories—and because it was three stories high, with an elevator, it didn't seem kid friendly. I put it on the market.* I decided that I needed to put everything behind me, live somewhere else, and start over.

---

* Avril Lavigne bought the house pretty much as soon as I moved out. Later, she sold it to Chris Paul, the basketball player. For a while, Kanye and Kim lived right next door.

HANGING OUT WITH THE KIDS

COURTESY OF WILLIE TOLEDO

14

Hey Ladies

Right after Shanna and I separated, she went on *Dancing with the Stars.* It was all over the press that she was romantically linked with her dance partner. I felt like if she was with somebody else, I was bummed, but that meant I could move on too. Meanwhile, DJ AM and I had a gig in Las Vegas, playing at the nightclub Pure. As always, Lil Chris came along with me. I was on an all-time high: *I'm single, I'm going to Vegas this weekend, I'm not going to think about Shanna, I'm going to party and have fun.*

When AM and I got done playing, Paris Hilton was hanging around. Paris said, "Come here, let me have a drink with you."

I was thinking: *Is this a setup?* I asked her, "Aren't you sort of homegirls with Shanna?"

"Yeah, I know her a little. But you guys aren't together, right?"

"No, we're not."

Paris said, "I want to take a picture with you." We did, and then she told me, "I like the way we look in pictures." While she went to get us a round of drinks, I was talking with my boys: "Lil Chris, AM, what the fuck should I do?" I couldn't believe this was happening—Shanna and I

had just broken up, and now one of the most famous women in the world was hitting on me. This wasn't my steez.

AM said, "You know what to do. Take care of that."

Stevie D, the guy who was running Pure at the time, always took great care of us. He got us a private room. We smoked a bunch of joints, and then Paris said, "Let's go to the strip club."

At the strip club, Paris and I made out with each other. We kept partying until eight in the morning. I was having such a good time that night, it didn't even register that there were twenty or thirty photographers following us everywhere.

I came home the next day to the biggest shitstorm ever. The news was everywhere that Paris and I were together in Vegas. Shanna was losing her mind and texting me constantly. Even though we had split up, seeing me out with somebody made her crazy. But she had to get used to it: Paris and I ended up hanging out for quite a while. And that so wasn't me, to be with Miss Hollywood. I never would have planned to be with her, but it just worked out that way. I was a punk-rock kid and she was my complete opposite: Why was she interested in me?

Shanna and I were so disconnected and on the outs, any kind of involvement with a female who just wanted to have fun was exciting to me. This was at the height of Paris's fame, so everything around her just seemed accentuated. For a few weeks, we did everything together. At a party in her backyard, Suge Knight (of Death Row Records) told us that he was going to marry us. You don't say no to Suge Knight.

"Paris," he said, "will you take my dude Travis? Will you suck him off? Will you ride that dick until death do you part?"

"I will."

"Travis, do you promise to beat that pussy up, in sickness and in health, and to knock out any motherfucker that messes with Paris?"

I drunkenly said, "I do."

They were the funniest, most ghetto vows I had ever heard. Suge "married" us and we went along with it.

One night, Paris and Shanna were both out at the Hyde Lounge, a Los Angeles club. Shanna spotted Paris—she walked up to her and hit her. Paris called me up from the police station, crying, saying, "I can't believe this bitch hit me." I made sure she was okay, and then I called Shanna.

I didn't want to say, "What are you doing hitting my new girl?" but more "You're the mother of my children—don't act like this." I wanted to make sure Shanna was safe, and I wanted to tell her that kind of shit was beneath her. Even though we weren't together, I felt sad and I was worried about her. But she wouldn't get on the phone with me. She did text me a message: "Fuck your girlfriend and I hope you guys both fucking die."

At that point, I just gave up. What was left of my relationship with Shanna came to a grinding halt that night.

FELIX ARGUELLES (CONSULTANT, FAMOUS STARS AND STRAPS)

One time, I was sleeping in bed with my long-term when my phone rang in the middle of the night. I pushed the button and there was Shanna going crazy, screaming.

I just let Shanna rant for a second. And I'm going, *Oh, I get it, you're drunk. And you must have thought you called Lil Chris, because Lil Chris puts up with this shit. Felix doesn't.* And I hung up on her.

And my girl said, "What's going on?" Obviously, a girl screaming in the middle of the night wakes up my girl.

I said, "Oh, Shanna was drunk, screaming to me about some message that she read on Travis's phone."

After that, Paris and I kept seeing each other, but less intensely: we were on and off for a few months. This whole time, I was also seeing Tara Conner, who had been Miss USA 2006. We had met months before when we were sitting next to each other at a club: we weren't even talking, but Shanna thought we were about to hook up, so she threw a drink on Tara, saying "Who the fuck is this bitch?" After Shanna stormed out, I apologized to Tara. We started talking and hit it off—but we never would have paid attention to each other if Shanna hadn't thrown that drink. Sex with Tara was through the roof: she was a pageant girl, like Shanna, but without all the poisonous weight and history of our relationship.

JAMES INGRAM (RECORDING ENGINEER)

Travis takes a while to warm up to people. I don't blame him—I've seen firsthand how people try to take advantage of him. So it took a while for us to connect. We have a strange relationship, because I work for him, but we spend so much time together, it's more than work.

One night early on, we went to Matsuhisa and then back to his house. There were a few tall blonde chicks, which is fine—I've dated tall blonde chicks. Travis said, "Come and check out my theater." In my head: *Cool, I get to check out the theater.* Looking back, he was getting the girls in there, but I was clueless. So we put on a movie—I think it was one of the *Matrix* sequels. I'm into the movie, because I like science fiction and shit blowing up, but I looked over, and Travis is hooking up with one of the girls. *Oh yeah, Travis is a rock star and that's Miss USA.* He was with Tara Conner, and one of her friends, another Miss USA contestant, was sitting next to me, and that's how I got to make out with her. I didn't sleep with her, and I wish I had, because, you know. But when I left, I just sat in my car. *Did that really just happen? That's so fucking insane.*

I got invited to the 2006 Halloween party at the Playboy Mansion. Even though Shanna and I had split up, I was still on the guest list. Lil

Chris and some of the Famous family dressed up like the Cobra Kai, the bad guys from the *Karate Kid* movie: skull masks and black bodysuits with skeletons on them.

Shanna and Paris were both on the guest list, but I got away with murder that night. I was in costume, so I would just walk up to girls and make out with them. I think girls might have been afraid to do that if I hadn't been in my Halloween mask, because they might get caught by Shanna.

FELIX ARGUELLES (CONSULTANT, FAMOUS STARS AND STRAPS)

In Vegas, Travis and AM always did shows at Pure. One night, we were out in Vegas and there wasn't a show—he had an appearance or a trade show—but we went over to Pure anyway; Paris was there with some of her homegirls. Because Travis had done so many shows there, our crew was well received there, and we just totally shit on the Vegas dress code: we were the only people who could storm through with hats and sneakers. Everybody would be like, "Who the fuck are these guys?" and then they'd see Trav and be like, "Oh, I understand."

At Pure, everybody loses themselves in their own zone, Travis is messing around with Paris, whatever. It's getting close to the end of the evening and I get the lean-over: "Hey, we're going to Crazy Horse." One of the good things about running with Trav is you get carte blanche to use every Batcave, every tunnel, everything. So we Batcave out of the Palm and there's three limos: one for Paris and all her homegirls, one for Travis and all of us, and then there was a tag-along one for all the people who were able to bluff their way into the crew.

Someone phoned ahead to Crazy Horse and they opened up the
back room for us. We walked in, and it was basically the
biggest night ever at a strip club, just with the people we
brought. They flooded half the talent from the front room
to the back room. This insane night kept going forever—
Vegas has never been the same for me after that.

This whole time, Mark and I kept working on +44 tracks. Making
that album was hard but therapeutic—I'm really proud of how it turned
out. After about a year, we brought in Jerry Finn to help us finish the
record, which we called *When Your Heart Stops Beating*. But after we
handed the album in to the record company, there was a lot of struggle
and shady shit going on with the label. A lot of things didn't happen the
way they should have.

We filmed our first video, for the title track "When Your Heart Stops
Beating," and during the shoot, I broke my arm while I was playing the
drums. I iced it and said, "It's going to be fine." Two days later, it wasn't
fine. Three days later, it wasn't fine. Four days later, I was in a doctor's
office, getting X-rays. He told me I had fractured my arm. I had always
hit the drums as hard as I could—but I should never have been able to
break a bone from the impact.

The doctor told me my bones were brittle: I had osteoporosis.

"Dude, how can I have that?" I asked him. "I'm not old."

"I did a bone-density test. You have the bones of an eighty-year-old."

I came clean with him: "I broke my foot and I've been on painkillers
for the last year or two. I needed them for about six months, and the last
year I've been taking them recreationally, but in abundance." Because of
AM, I would stop using pills and smoking weed when I needed to make
a big decision—but never for more than twenty-four hours. I didn't know
that Vicodin depletes your body of calcium—I had been taking so much
that my bones had become twigs.

I did have this broken arm, so the doctor took me off Vicodin and put
me on Norco, a little yellow pill.

TRAVIS BARKER
can i say

I fell in love with Norco.

I was on so many drugs that my confidence was at an all-time high. My left arm was in a cast for four to six months, but I did a whole +44 tour with a broken arm—I learned how to do everything with one hand that I usually did with both. It was the next step after doing a tour with a broken foot. I was into the head space of "I'm going to push myself. This isn't going to hold me back. I'm going to get past this and it'll be awesome."

Meanwhile, I was supposed to do an AOL Sessions gig with the Game in NYC—I was in town with +44. I should have hit him up weeks in advance and explained that I broke my arm, but the morning of the gig, I texted him, "Yo, man, I broke my arm, I don't think I'm going to be able to do the AOL Sessions with you."

He hit me back: "No man, get down here. You can do it with one hand."

My guilt trumped any good sense I may have had and I went down to the studio. I wasn't even totally familiar with the songs: I learned them on the way down. When I got there, I asked him if we should run through the songs, and he said, "No man, you got this. Come smoke with me." We smoked a couple of blunts and did it live, not even a sound check, which was insane—but I got into my zone and it came out great. This just contributed to my feeling of invincibility. That no matter how I was feeling *outside* the studio, so long as I could kick my brain into gear *inside* the studio, my playing would do the rest. I killed it.

Around this time Lil Wayne hit me and said, "Hey, I'm doing a rock album—I want to get you on my album." But he didn't know I had a broken arm. His producer came by to have me play on stuff and I had to tell him, "My arm's broke, man, I can't really play. Before I broke my arm, I was working on a couple of tracks. Why don't you take them and you can do whatever you want with them?"

When the +44 tour hit Amsterdam, Paris flew out to see the show, and she brought along Kim Kardashian. Kim used to organize people's closets, and at the time, she was working as Paris's closet girl. She would grab Paris's bags, put them in the closet, unpack them, put everything where Paris could find it. We all checked into our hotel and then rented bicycles and rode all over Amsterdam—that's what you do there. It was me, Lil Chris, my drum tech Daniel, Paris, and Kim.

We all got high as a kite at a coffee shop. Then we rode over to the Absinthe Bar, and then the red-light district. Paris and Kim kept taking photos of the working girls, and that whole area is run by the Hell's Angels, so about three or four times, a big biker came over and told them to stop taking pictures. We were having fun—running amok in Amsterdam on bicycles. Everywhere we went, a pack of paparazzi were following us, but I didn't care. I was having a blast and was happy to let the world know it. I kept on secretly checking out Kim, telling Lil Chris, "I don't care if she's the closet girl, she's fucking hot."

Four months after I broke my arm, I was back in Los Angeles; we had a short break from the tour before we went back to Europe and Japan. I visited the doctor to see the progress on my arm. He X-rayed it and said, "You're not healing."

I got scared. I went from feeling like Superman to being scared that I would *never* get better. When I got on the plane back to Europe, I was on more drugs than ever before: Oxycontin, weed, and now booze. I got to the hotel, and the guilt started to settle in. My arm wasn't healing. Landon was three and Alabama had turned one, but I was on tour instead of home with the kids. I missed them and felt guilty that I was being a terrible father. And I was masking all these feelings with the drugs and the drinking and the smoking. Even though I could get through the European tour, now I didn't want to, because I was scared. I was questioning everything. Who was I—a father or a rock star?

In Paris, I called Mark's room at one in the morning and told him, "Dude, I think I need to go home." I said that the pills were starting to catch up to me and that I was unstable. Mark, as always, totally had my back. He was really supportive of me through this whole thing. He gave me his blessing to go home; my buddy Gil came in to do the tour instead. I was in a dark place and I needed to be with my kids. Everything was catching up to me: I think I was borderline suicidal.

MARK HOPPUS (BASSIST/SINGER, BLINK-182)

Travis was taking a lot of pills, and that was not making him happy. He needed to go home, and of course I want my friend to be healthy, so you have to support the people that you care about. I've always seen Travis choose what he wants to be and make that the reality. When he wanted to stop smoking cigarettes, he stopped, and it wasn't an issue. When he wanted to stop drinking alcohol, he stopped, and that wasn't an issue. He was taking a lot of pills, but I never saw it as a problem—that's the nature of addiction, that you hide it from the people around you.

I got home and cooled out in Calabasas, which is just northwest of LA. Before Shanna and I split, she had found a one-story house there that was a lot like my old Corona house: no stairs meant it was safe for Alabama and Landon, and being a little out of LA meant I could get away from everything.* I didn't stop taking pills, but I cut way down, just enough for my body not to freak out. I was still smoking lots of weed. I even hired an extra assistant for the studio: her full-time job was rolling blunts for everybody. As a bonus, she and I hooked up most days.

Paris and I slowed way down. She was fun to party with, but our sexual chemistry was never that good; I had been having more fun with Tara. Shanna and I started talking again, and even tried to get back together. But our relationship was just as toxic as ever, and we had the same argument over and over. If I was with her, I wanted us to stay home with the kids. Then we'd fight, and Shanna would go out and party, so I'd go out too.

That was how I met Lindsay Lohan: one night, I went out to a party thrown by Sidekick phones. Lindsay was there—we had never met, so we started talking. Then she kissed me. It was way out: I didn't even

---

* I like Calabasas because it's quiet and exclusive.

know her, but I liked her. She was hot, and she was everywhere: being with her almost felt inevitable.

Luckily, the paparazzi didn't really get wind of that. Lindsay and I talked on the phone and texted each other for the next couple of weeks, and we agreed that we'd meet up again. When that time came, just as I was walking into the place, Shanna texted me: "How the fuck is Lindsay?"

Everything flashed before my eyes: How did I get caught? Even though our relationship was pretty much nonexistent, I was supposed to be trying to make it work. I just went home and told her, "I wasn't going to see Lindsay."

She said, "Yes, you were." She must have hacked my phone: she had read all my texts. After that, Shanna told me that she had been texting Lindsay: "How's my man?" "You going to meet my man?" I never pursued Lindsay again: I was too embarrassed, but we stayed friendly.

I was so bewildered about Shanna, and life, and everything. A few times, I secretly met with a therapist: Harry, the same one who was helping Chris and me sober up. He was one of the only people I could be honest with, telling him how I was confused: I have a drug problem, I just want to be at home with the kids, I don't know what the fuck to do. He told me, "You need to stop and look at yourself and ask, 'Are you the man that you would want your kids to remember you as?' And if you're not, what do you need to do to get there?" That always resonated with me.

Shanna and I kept splitting up and getting back together, announcing our status on our MySpace pages. I would do something big, like throw her a surprise birthday party, and things would be cool between us, at least for a little while.

At night, sometimes Shanna and I would sneak into the garage so we could smoke some weed away from the kids. One time, Atiana, Landon, and Bama were trying to find us: they came into the garage and it was full of smoke. I said, "Oh my God, something's on fire, you guys get out of here."

"What's on fire, Dad?"

"I don't know! Just get out of the garage and I'll make sure everything's okay." They all hustled back into the house. That was a wake-up call:

the kids were getting too old for me to be smoking blunts anywhere near them. If I was going to continue being irresponsible, I at least had to be smart about it. I knew a big change had to come soon.

When I was having some time off with Shanna, I started talking with Kim Kardashian. We had stayed in touch after Amsterdam, and she did some modeling for Famous—I hired Estevan Oriol to shoot a whole ad campaign of her in bathing suits. Kim's tape had come out and she had broken up with Ray J. She wanted to do a reality show, because she thought her family was interesting. And obviously she was right.

I respected her hustle. She was meeting with Ryan Seacrest, and she wanted to know what doing a show was like. "It's hectic," I told her. "You have no privacy—it's not just you and your family in the house. It's really personal, and it can be really fucked up."

Kim and I started hanging out. We went to dinner, we went to lunch. You might think I would be doing the worst things with this girl because of her tapes, but it was the exact opposite of any other encounter I've had with a woman: with Kim, I wanted to be nothing but a gentleman to her. It was so weird. We were around each other a lot. We used her in ad campaigns for Famous. She came to my house and went swimming. We watched the Fourth of July fireworks together. I'd go visit her and her family at their clothing store. We'd be really sweet around each other, like little kids, and then when we were apart, she'd call me and say, "I want to see you again."

"Me too," I'd say.

Shanna and I started talking to each other again, and we reunited one more time—but I really wanted to see Kim.(Shanna caught wind of what was going on—she poured a drink on Kim at a party thrown by Carmen Electra. I felt terrible.) Kim and I never touched each other. It just wasn't meant to be.

FAMILY OVER EVERYTHING. COURTESY OF CLEMENTE RUIZ

15

The Rock's Gonna Come Off

I was on my way to lunch when Mark called me with the worst news ever: Jerry Finn, who produced all those Blink-182 albums, had a massive brain aneurysm. It came out of nowhere. Mark and I went to visit Jerry in the hospital, and he was just a vegetable. He couldn't talk to us and it didn't look like he understood anything that we said. I was hoping he would get better quickly, but after a few weeks on life support, Jerry died in August 2008, just thirty-nine years old. It was really sad. The whole thing was incredibly weird and scary: it came out of nowhere, and you don't expect your friends to die young.

To deal with it, I directed my attentions to my partnership with DJ AM, which was taking off. After about a hundred hours of playing together, we started doing shows at the Roxy in June 2008, calling ourselves TRV$DJAM. We had a residency where we played two gigs on the last weekend of every month. We got really good crowds, and all that summer, I felt like I was building a new foundation to my musical

career. We even started recording music, and made a mixtape that we called *Fix Your Face*.

We played a party in Detroit for Cadillac—that was kind of a dream for me, given my intense Cadillac fetish. Before we went onstage, I told Lil Chris jokingly, "During our set, just get out in the crowd and dance your ass off." Onstage, I looked out at the audience, which had a bunch of breakdancers. Chris had started breakdancing as well: he had a circle of people around him. It was awesome.

In September of that year, AM and I were the house band for MTV's Video Music Awards, playing with everybody: LL Cool J, Katy Perry, the Ting Tings, Lupe Fiasco. It was awesome, and I loved that it was just the two of us. We could do gigs like that without having a band or all the infrastructure of a road crew. I was so excited about that gig: I brought my homie Che and all three kids to the rehearsal. The kids were especially stoked to meet the Ting Tings, and Katy Perry was super cool to them. During the rehearsal for "Goin' Back to Cali," LL Cool J told me, "If I say 'Give the drummer some,' you go bananas. If I say it again, you go *even more bananas*." During the show that night, he ended up saying it three times.

Charles "Che" Still was one of the nicest dudes I'd ever met. He was from the Inland Empire, near where I grew up. When I was busy rehearsing, he chilled out with Landon and Alabama. He was a big, muscular guy who did security for us sometimes, but despite his dead seriousness about his job, off the clock he was a huge teddy bear and, more important, a great friend.

Ten days after the VMAs, on September 18, 2008, AM and I had a gig booked in Columbia, South Carolina, playing a free show with Perry Farrell and Gavin DeGraw. It was sponsored by T-Mobile, and they were flying me and AM out there on a private plane: a Gulfstream G4.

Shanna and I were still sort of together. That weekend, she had come over with the kids, and we couldn't keep away from each other. We were so on and off and on and off, but on top of having this physical connection, we were the parents of these amazing kids. Hanging out with Shanna that weekend, I told her that I didn't even know why I was doing this South

Carolina show. I was feeling really comfortable at home: I was having a blast hanging out with the kids, throwing them around in the pool.

There was a lot of push and pull in my heart: I didn't want to be away from my family, but at the same time, I loved playing with AM. A little voice in my head was telling me that I should take a break. My exact words to Shanna were "I don't even know if I need to go." Ultimately, I kicked myself into gear and said, "This is my job, my nine-to-five. Everyone goes to work. Don't complain—just go make it happen."

I invited Shanna to come to the show. She said yes and packed her bags. Then at the last minute, she decided to stay home with the kids. "Just in case something happens," she said, "I don't want us both to be going. I don't think God would give you anything you couldn't handle. If something was to happen to you, Trav, you would overcome it." Which was kind of intense. She went on to talk about how she couldn't do the same—she couldn't handle it. I was thinking, *What the fuck are you talking about?*

When Shanna bailed on the trip, we had an extra seat. Because it was a private plane, we didn't need tickets, so I invited Che. He had been a good friend for a couple of years; now we were talking about having Che travel with me and AM full time. "It would be dope to have you out with me all the time," I told him. He came to South Carolina to check out how that might work—and because being on a Gulfstream seemed like a once-in-a-lifetime experience. So it was me, AM, Che, and, as always, Lil Chris. He had recently married his girl, Jessica, and had a two-year-old boy, Sebastian.

ARMEN AMIRKHANIAN (FRIEND)

Lil Chris was very special. Hardworking. He made sure he was there for Travis, and at the same time he tried to be there for his wife and his kid. It was really hard for him, but somehow he managed to do it. He had long days working with Trav, but at the end of the day, he would always bring something home for them—a toy for his

son, flowers for his wife—something to make them smile.
He would make me drive all the way to Trav's house to
do something small so he could leave ten minutes early,
which was always funny. Then on the way home, somehow
he managed to drive and stick his ass out of the window
at the same time. He would moon the whole freeway while
he was driving sixty or seventy miles per hour.

LANDON AND ALABAMA

Landon had his fifth birthday coming up, and Alabama was almost three years old. Bama and Landon were always bummed when I left on a trip, but they were especially frantic this time. Alabama was bawling, and just kept saying, "The roof's gonna come off, Dad, the roof's gonna come off." I asked Shanna what she was talking about, but she didn't know. Bama was frantically crying, and she wouldn't calm down. It was really bumming me out to leave her.

I still hated flying, but being on a G4 felt like we were balling. The show was dope: the promoters had closed off a block in Columbia for a street party, AM and I had a lot of fun playing, and the crowd went nuts. We were planning to stay in South Carolina that night and fly back in the morning—our flights were already booked. Chris, Che, and I were hanging out in the dressing room, just about to go party and act a fool. I was in celebration mode: it felt like TRV$DJAM was finally taking off for real.

Then AM came in and said, "Yo, man, what do you think about just getting the fuck out of here tonight?"

"Nah," I said. "Our shit's booked for tomorrow, right? It's all good."

He really wanted to leave. "Why don't we just go in halves on a private?"

Lil Chris said, "Let's just do it, Trav. We can get the fuck home. What's waiting for us in South Carolina?" He wanted to get home to his baby.

Now that I was in South Carolina, I was happy to stay the night, but it was always good to see my kids sooner rather than later. I said, "Whatever you guys want to do, I'm down for."

AM called our manager, LV. He said, "Okay, I'm going to figure something out and get you guys a plane. Everything's good." So while he worked it out, we hung out at the hotel, smoked some weed, and chilled out with some girls.

LAWRENCE "LV" VAVRA (MANAGER)

AM had been in Australia—he hadn't been home in a while. To him, getting home to get in his own bed, even for one night extra, meant so much. I was on the phone with literally ten different people, trying to find a last-minute plane. We finally found one and I remember talking to Lil Chris, saying that before I put forty grand on my credit card, I needed to confirm that AM and Travis wanted the plane. Chris had a way of getting what he wanted, not necessarily what Travis or AM wanted. Adam said yes—Travis wouldn't get on the phone for some reason, but in the background, I could hear him say yes.

LV had been AM's manager, so I hadn't been working with him very long—this was his first time booking us a plane. Gus, who had been the tour manager for Blink-182 forever, was used to me bugging the shit out of him whenever he hired a plane. I would call him and want details: "What's the history on that plane? Who's flying it? How many hours do they have?" And he would send me e-mails saying when that plane had last been serviced and who the pilot was. If the copilot didn't have experience, Gus had already gotten rid of him—he was militant about it. LV didn't know the whole get-down: he just booked the plane like anybody would.

About an hour later, we got the call from LV and headed to the Columbia airport. I felt weird about the whole situation—weirder than usual—and I smoked blunt after blunt on the way to the airport, plus I took three Vicodin and a Xanax to get right. We were all medicating ourselves, except for AM, because he was sober. We got to the airport around eleven P.M. and I did my usual drill: *What does the plane look like?* There were a couple of different planes on the runway, and I thought, "Which one is ours? It better not be that small one." Sure enough: that was the one. It was a Learjet 60, and it looked small as fuck.

I took a picture of the plane and sent it to Pops. Then I called him up in California and said, "Hey, pal, I'm just letting you know, something don't feel right. This plane is really small. If anything happens to me, make sure the kids get the house and they're taken care of. I love you, pal. I'm not sure why I'm sharing this—I'm just telling you I have a weird fucking feeling."

He said, "Don't worry, Trav. Of course, if anything happens I'll look after the kids. But everything's going to be alright, pal."

I never call up Pops just so we could say we love each other. But that night, I wanted to say, "Pal, I love you, I'm freaked out, make sure my kids are cool."

Chris took a picture of himself outside the plane and sent it to his wife and some friends. I don't know if it was a balling picture or if he was freaked out.

ROB ASTON (VOCALIST, THE TRANSPLANTS)

Lil Chris was the best. Skinny little white kid who was all heart, just gave 100 percent. Chris took care of everyone, but he didn't bite his tongue. He was quick to tell a motherfucker to fuck off, right to his face.

Che was the coolest. Probably six foot three, and in good shape. Just cool as they come, never loud or obnoxious. A team player. I can't say I ever saw Che in a bad mood.

When they were getting on the jet, Chris sent me a picture of him standing by it, just of him. I looked at it and got a weird feeling. Not "they're going to get in a plane crash," because you never think about that. That's not a normal thought. But an actual chill through my whole body, like I was looking at the past. I couldn't put my finger on it.

I got mad at myself because I didn't tell him to be careful. Not that me saying that would have changed anything or stopped anything. But it always bothered me that I didn't say, "Be careful."

The pilots introduced themselves: James Bland and Sarah Lemmon, an older male pilot and a younger female pilot. And she was really young: she looked like she was in her early twenties. We were like, Wow, that's awesome that you know how to fly planes. I asked if the weather was cool, and they told me there was nothing to worry about.

We got on the plane. I sat next to the emergency exit: I always sat next to the emergency exit. Chris and Che sat in front of me. AM was across the aisle from me. He had one of those little Flip video cameras, and he was filming us—everybody was boasting. AM said, "What do you know about a drummer, a DJ, and a PJ?"—PJ meaning private jet. Then he filmed Chris and says, "Whassup, White Noise?" We used to call him White Noise sometimes; that was his rapper alter ego. We were all showing off: "Motherfuckers, we're in a jet."

There was no stewardess—on a plane of that size, once we were up in the air, one of the pilots would come back and make sure we were all cool. We made ourselves drinks, but I was already incredibly high. I took off my shoes—and I never did that on an airplane. I'd always trip on other people for doing it: "You motherfuckers are crazy for taking off your shoes—what would you do if something happened?"

AM saw me and started talking shit: "Oh, look, someone's comfortable." My attitude was that we had a good flight going east; I was hoping to have that same good flight back home.

The plane rolled down the runway—it felt like it was taking forever. I found out later that we had been going down the wrong runway, in the wrong direction. We were taxiing for about twenty minutes, to the point where everyone else was falling asleep. I was tired, but I never let myself fall asleep before takeoff.

I said my usual prayer: "Please keep us safe during this flight. Please look after us, please get us home to our families. I love you, Mom. I love you, God. Amen." Then I shut my eyes, waiting to see that bright horizontal line that would let me know everything was okay. I didn't see it, so I kept saying my prayers over and over, closing my eyes tighter and tighter, waiting for that horizontal line, but it didn't come.

Finally, the plane stopped and I felt the engines rev up. The plane started vibrating; we were about to take off.

We moved faster and faster, hauling ass down the runway, but just before we were airborne, I heard POW! POW!

It sounded like someone was shooting at the plane, but it was the tires popping. And then the plane went out of control.

First the belly of the plane was scraping on the ground, starting a fire before we even got in the air. Then the cabin started to fill with smoke.

Then we finally took off, wildly thrusting into the air, but we kept going up and down: we would get up pretty high in the air and then we'd come down and bang on the runway again. This was happening every ten seconds or so—but it felt like minutes were going by between every impact. Every time we went down, I was watching out the window and bracing myself, because I could see the ground coming.

The smoke in the cabin turned into a fire, which kept growing. It was the most fucked-up ride you can imagine, like the craziest roller coaster in the world times ten—but in the dark, plus we were on fire.

I was yelling at the top of my lungs: "Stop the fucking plane!" The plane was shaking uncontrollably. I was tripping so hard, I started praying out loud, screaming. But nobody could hear anything. The plane hit the ground four or five times, with my life flashing before my eyes every time. In a matter of seconds, I saw decades of my life, in little bits and pieces. It was like fast-forward on a DVD: I saw my mom, I saw Pops, I saw my kids, I saw concerts with Mark and Tom, Rob and Tim. It felt like time had slowed down to show me these things.

I knew the worst was coming: I was going to die.

The plane busted through the airport fence and crossed a highway—and then our last impact was in an embankment. It felt like the strongest jolt ever, and we stopped.

I was fucked up, but my eyes were still open. I couldn't believe I was alive. I could barely breathe or see, but I unbuckled my seatbelt and through the smoke, went to AM, who had gotten knocked out—I shook him awake. Then I tried to go forward to get Chris and Che, but there was a wall of fire between us—I couldn't get through the flames and my hands caught on fire.

At that point, I panicked. I pulled the handle on the emergency exit and kicked the door open. AM was right behind me. I jumped out—right into the jet wing, which was filled with fuel. My whole body got covered with fuel and caught fire, from my legs all the way to my back.

I started running.

AM jumped over the wing, avoiding the fire. He was running behind me, seeing me completely engulfed in flames. He got his phone out and called our manager, LV. I could hear him screaming: "LV, our plane just crashed! Travis is on fire! What the fuck do I do? I'm running after him! Fucking help, fucking help!"

As I ran, I took off my shirt, I took off my hat, I took off my shorts—but I couldn't get the fire off me. I was naked, moving as fast as I could, holding my genitals—everything else was on fire—and I kept running, hoping that would put out the flames.

At that moment, I felt like I was running for my family. I didn't care about anything except being with my kids, my father, my sister, Shanna. I was in the craziest pain ever, like nothing I had ever felt before. I didn't think I was going to survive.

I ran all the way to the highway. There were cars coming—I could hear honking and screaming—and through all the chaos, somebody was yelling, "Stop, drop, and roll!"

I kept running, while more and more of my body was burning. This guy kept screaming, "Stop, drop, and roll!"—and finally, what he was saying got through to me. I

dropped to the ground, and I rolled around, butt-naked in the dirt. It felt like I was rolling for days.

I put out most of the fire, but not on my legs and feet—because this was the one time in my life when I didn't wear shoes on the plane, my socks were soaked with fuel from the jet wing.

AM caught up with me. He took off his shirt and used it to pat out the fire on my legs and feet, over and over and over again. Around the tenth try, he finally put out the flames. While he was doing that, he got burned on his arm and his neck—he had gotten out of the plane without any injuries. If he hadn't done that for me, I probably wouldn't have feet or legs today.

About sixty seconds later, the plane exploded. I was lying next to AM, screaming, *"Are we alive?!"*

THE WRECKAGE FROM THE PLANE CRASH. COURTESY OF AP PHOTO/BRETT FLASHNICK

ARTWORK BY MAXX GRAMAJO

16

Another State of Mind

"Where's Chris?!" I screamed to AM. "Where's Che?!" The cops showed up, and they were no help. They didn't even realize we had been in an accident—they just wondered what we were doing there. Then the ambulance came and they realized how fucked up we were: we were actually survivors of the plane crash.[*]

LAWRENCE "LV" VAVRA (MANAGER)

Adam called me from the ambulance, trying to explain, "I don't think Che and Chris got out. I don't know what happened." And then I heard the paramedics telling him that he needed to get off the phone so they could help him, and he said, "LV, I don't fucking get it. I was just

---

[*] Not only were these cops not very smart, they later released the dash-cam footage of me and AM, screaming in pain, still smoking—a huge asshole move.

in a plane crash, and this chick is telling me to get
off my phone." I told him to call me back when he knew
what hospital he was going to, but I don't think he did,
because they had put him in a medically induced coma.

They rushed AM and me to the hospital for emergency surgery: I had third-degree burns on 65 percent of my body. There were blood clots all through my body, so they put three filters in my legs.

The next few months went by in a blur. We moved from one ICU to another, ending up at the Joseph M. Still Burn Center in Augusta, Georgia: I had blood transfusions that lasted forty-eight hours and huge skin grafts. There were times when they were talking about amputating my foot because I didn't have enough skin on my body for the grafts.

I don't remember much from that time in Georgia. It was just me in a hospital with wires around me and staples inside me. I know my dad was there, and Mark and Skye, and Shanna and some of my closest friends. I kept asking about the other people on the plane. They told me over and over—AM's in the room next to you, Chris and Che are dead, the pilots are dead—but I was on so many medications, I couldn't fathom it.

People sent me flowers and gifts, but I couldn't see any of them because the doctors were worried about my wounds getting infected. The phone kept ringing, but I couldn't talk—I couldn't make sense of anything. A couple of kids set up drum kits in the parking lot outside the burn center and played all day for a solid week. I couldn't hear them with the windows closed, but I felt grateful that they had come out.

JAMES INGRAM (RECORDING ENGINEER)

Daniel and I put on our scrubs and went to see Travis
at the burn center in Georgia. When we were leaving, a
doctor came up to us and said, "You need to get his wife
under control. She stormed out of here a couple of hours
ago screaming and throwing her scrubs everywhere. We
had a little girl die on us already today—we don't need

this shit." Travis was saying some fucked-up shit—mind you, he was saying it to everybody. He was in a lot of pain and on a lot of drugs.

After a couple of weeks, the burn center said I could transfer to a hospital in LA. I wasn't going to fly, so I hired a bus to take me back to California. On the way, my bus driver got beaten to a bloody pulp. Apparently, when we stopped in Alabama, there were some people getting rowdy outside the bus and he told them to keep it down because there was a patient in the bus who needed his sleep. But he was an older white dude with long hair talking to six African American dudes at three A.M. in the South, and I don't know that he said it in the nicest of ways. So they beat the fuck out of him.

I woke up and noticed that we weren't moving, and from my bed, asked, "Why aren't you driving?"

He said, "Trav, I just got my ass beat, man. I'm a bloody mess."

I said, "I just got in a fucking plane crash, I don't care if you got beat up. *Drive, motherfucker.*" I was so out of my mind.

I was on about nineteen different medications when I left Georgia. A few months earlier, I wanted to smoke weed and take pills every day. Now I had a morphine clicker, two nurses, and needed to take so many meds, I never wanted to take another pill again. In Georgia, the meds and the morphine did a good job of masking the pain, but in LA, something wasn't right. I had bipolar drugs for my anxiety attacks—if I was twenty minutes late on those, I would climb the walls.

I was like the guy in Metallica's video for "One" who just wants to be put out of his misery. I would call friends and tell them, "I'll transfer however much money into anybody's account right now—I just want to die. I want someone to kill me." Finally, they took the phone out of my room and put me on suicide watch. It was like I had somebody else's brain. I didn't know why I was sticking around—I was burned and I felt like there was no reason for me to live.

I felt completely defeated.

Skinhead Rob was always at the hospital. My sisters would visit a couple of times a week. My buddy James, who engineered a lot of records I played on and was also a homie, was there a lot. Pops was always there too; he and Skinhead Rob would spend the night, sleeping upright in a hospital chair. Pops and I had a lot of late-night conversations, and he told me a lot of stuff he had always kept to himself, about my mom, about his time in the war. But because I was so doped up, the next day I would have forgotten half of it. And Shanna was there once in a while—she or the nanny would bring the kids when the hospital allowed. I really wanted to see my kids because they gave me hope—those were the best days—but I hated having them see me messed up like that.

ROB ASTON (VOCALIST, THE TRANSPLANTS)

I had my plane ticket to go see Travis in Georgia, but his managers got on the phone with me and said, "It's probably better if you just stay in LA. Travis doesn't want to see anybody right now—he's in a bad spot." Later, his drum tech Daniel told me that he was asking for me multiple times on a daily basis. That pissed me off: my best friend, my brother, was almost dead in a hospital bed, and I wanted to be there for him.

When he came out to California, I was there with him every day in the burn unit. I'd stay the night with him. It was difficult, seeing him in that state. The first day I walked in the door, I told myself, "Be strong, Rob. Keep it together." I walked in the door, and I immediately started crying. It was too much, after losing Chris and Che, seeing Travis lying there with his skin melting off, and blood and pus everywhere.

There were points where Travis thought he wasn't going to make it: he'd call me and say, "Bring a gun. I'm done. I can't do it."

TRAVIS BARKER
can i say

I'd say, "I ain't bringing you nothing." I can't blame him. I don't know what it's like to live through a plane crash. It's been a hard road for him. I'd say it was probably harder mentally than physically—and he had the fucking gnarliest burns over half his body, so that's saying a lot. For the longest time, he could only smell jet fuel.

I knew Travis was back when he started making jokes again. He said, "My dad told me the catheter turned me into John Holmes."

I went home one day, just for an hour to take a shower and change my clothes. When I came back, he said, "Homie, you will never guess who was here." It could have been anybody, because this motherfucker knows everybody and their mom. But it was Tim Armstrong. It had been three years since either of us had seen or heard from Tim.

Then Travis said, "Yeah, maybe we should do another Transplants album." He was telling me this half dead in a hospital bed. I was kind of taken aback. I said, "Man, we don't have to do anything ever again if you don't want to. If you never want to play a show again, I don't blame you. I'll be next to you no matter what."

He said, "Nah, we gotta play. We got some work to do. And I'll go crazy if I don't have music." I got humbled real quick: here's a dude who's half dead and in agonizing pain, and he's talking about making another record.

Tim and I talked. I said, "We could sit here all day and point fingers, but I want to apologize on my behalf for anything I did that contributed to you leaving the band. I know I'm not the easiest person to get along with. I got more flaws than anybody." He apologized too, and we let bygones be bygones.

It sucks that it took something like a plane crash for us to realize that life is too short. You have to value what you got—because nothing is promised except death—and do what makes you happy. And making music is what makes the three of us happy.

TIM ARMSTRONG (SINGER/GUITARIST, THE TRANSPLANTS)

I got a call from Travis's sister and she said, "Hey, Travis is at the burn place in Burbank. You should come visit him."

I said, "Yeah, how about I go down in a few days?"

She said, "No, how about now?"

I said, "Yeah. Right now." I went down there by myself. The first thing I said was, "I'm sad about Lil Chris," and we just cried.

LV, my manager, tried to visit me and I told him to get the fuck out. I blamed him for the crash, because he had booked us on that plane—I told him that I hated him and it was his fault that Che and Chris had died.

LAWRENCE "LV" VAVRA (MANAGER)

Travis wouldn't talk to me for two months. He wouldn't respond to me, and I couldn't go visit him. I think a lot of his anger was toward me because I was the manager—why did I let them get on this plane?—but we've never talked about it. It was hard, but when a guy's going through that, my feelings are the least important thing.

I wasn't eating the hospital food, especially the meat, because it was nasty. I'd give it to Skinhead Rob and say, "Dude, just fucking throw this away. It's disgusting." The medical staff saw I was losing weight, which made it hard for me to heal up. I was skinny in the first place: I was 130 pounds when they admitted me. They told me, "Look, you're not eating, so we're going to shove this tube down your throat and feed you like that." After that, I cooperated more. I had two chocolate-peanut-butter smoothies from Robeks every day and I ate meat for the first time since I was a kid. One of the nurses was this little Hispanic dude I grew to like a lot; he knew I didn't like most of the protein options. So he used to bake me beef jerky at home and bring me big bags of it, plus he gave me lots of Ensure drinks. The beef jerky was one of the only foods that tasted right to me. They wanted me to maintain a 5,800-calorie diet every day. By the time I went home, I weighed 160 pounds and I had a belly for the first time in my life.

I had twenty-six surgeries after the crash, most of them in LA. During at least twelve of those surgeries, I woke up—my body was so habituated to painkillers from my abusing them before the plane crash, they couldn't keep me asleep. I felt everything. I woke up yelling, threatening the doctors, trying to swing at them. Aside from the burns, I had actually broken my back in three places, but nobody knew it then: I told the doctors I could barely sit up, and I felt terrible. They basically said, "What do you expect? You were just in a plane crash."

They took all the skin off my back to put on my legs. So at one point I was lying in bed with no skin on my back, just raw muscles. Then I had allografts: cadaver skin, which they basically stapled to my back. If I even hiccupped, I could feel the staples stabbing into my back—and one time, I had the hiccups for twenty-four hours straight, literally burping up jet fuel every few seconds. To keep the cadaver skin wet, they had to hose me down, so I'd be lying there, soaking wet and freezing, running a fever. They'd put my blankets in a dryer, sometimes once an hour, and then at least I'd be warm for a few minutes—that was the closest I came to feeling good, besides my kids visiting me.

My pain medication just wasn't right, and after surgeries, I was in so much pain, I was using the morphine clicker every thirty seconds. My history of abusing pills had caught up with me—my body had built up so much tolerance to painkillers, nothing seemed to work now. I got so mad at the doctor in charge of my meds, one night I tripped on him and took a swing at him. And then I went off on one of the nurses who wouldn't help me. They told me they were going to release me from the hospital because of how I was acting.

I said, "Well, you're not taking care of my meds—I'm in constant pain and I'm waking up during surgeries."

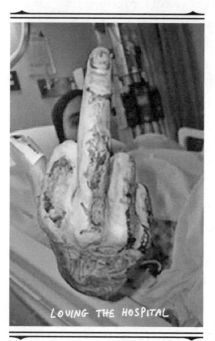

LOVING THE HOSPITAL

I ended up getting a new doctor in charge of my case, Dr. Peter Grossman. He was a stand-up guy. He said, "We're going to get your meds right, but I need you to be patient." We worked it out.

DR. PETER GROSSMAN
(DIRECTOR, GROSSMAN BURN CENTER)

When Travis arrived, I went to meet him thinking I was going to be the great calmer. I walked into the hydrotherapy room with my physician's assistant, Kurt Richards, to introduce myself. Establishing a rapport was very difficult: I think he just looked at me as some asshole doctor who was trying to tell him what to do. I tried to put my ego in check and understand where he was coming from: he had gone through not just the burn itself, but the nightmare of the plane crash and his close friends not surviving.

TRAVIS BARKER
can i say

We've seen people who have had complicating factors and have had to have their legs amputated. I don't think Travis was ever at risk of amputation—he's young and the blood supply going to his legs was pretty good. But he was very close to having some significant functional impairment. He had some really deep burns, over a large surface area. This wasn't just cosmetic—these were life-threatening injuries. When you have burn tissue, which is basically dead tissue, it serves as a nest for bacteria. Then they multiply and colonize and get into the deeper parts of our body. Organ systems can become septic and then begin to shut down.

I told Travis that we would have to go to the operating room and remove the unhealthy tissue. It's called "tangential excision": we're basically shaving away the nonviable tissue with a big razor blade on a stick. You shave away layer by layer until you get to some bleeding—your goal is to get to the bleeding, but then you have blood loss and life-threatening anemia.

I explained we would probably do this in stages and put on some temporary skin, cadaver skin, until we saw what needed to be grafted and what didn't. That was the game plan, but I was getting calls from the director of nursing on a nightly basis about how he was yelling and screaming, calling this nurse a "cunt" and this doctor a "fucking asshole." There were nurses who would not take care of him because he was being so verbally abusive.

I came into the ER right as Travis was about to go under general anesthesia, so his life was in the hands of the anesthesiologist, and he was saying, "This guy's a dick!" It was a Spicoli moment, like in *Fast Times at Ridgemont High*.

I thought, *What the fuck is wrong with this guy?* but I just said, "Dude, this guy is going to put you to sleep in two minutes. It's time to back off a little bit."

I was a completely different person while I was recovering: someone I'm not proud of. I had been through hell, and I was on so many medications. I had lived through my worst nightmare, but then I couldn't sleep for months and I kept having flashbacks of that nightmare. I was alive, but what was inside my head was scarring me. I wanted to kill myself, and it's amazing to me that person—the guy I was in the hospital—made it out alive.

During that time, I needed a massive blood transfusion—it took twenty-four hours. And I was tripping, because Dr. Grossman was out of town for a couple of weeks, and I didn't trust the other doctors: one of them was the guy I took a swing at. I told Shanna that I was really shook, and I needed her to stay with me, and she agreed to make sure that I was never alone.

During that time, my buddy James decided to do me a solid. He knew that I had lost my computer in the plane crash, so he got me a new one and set it up. He was really tech-savvy and he knew all my passwords, so he loaded the whole thing up. He brought me the computer, but I didn't get to go on it for very long. I went from surgery right into this transfusion, so I was pretty knocked out. Sometimes I would sleep for twenty hours straight.

While I was sleeping, Shanna went onto my laptop, and my e-mail accounts were all open. She saw all my e-mails from the previous three or four years, including messages from about thirteen different girls I had been messing around with in the year before the plane crash. We had been on and off in that time, but that didn't mean she wanted to know about it. We both did our own thing when we were split up, but I never would have told her, "Look, I'm banging this girl and that girl" and so on. She was my baby mama, so I tried to keep a clean slate, just in case we ever got back together.

There were plenty of girls that she had wondered about and some that she knew nothing about. And now it was all out in the open.

I was fucked.

I woke up and Shanna wasn't there. I had a bad feeling, because she had promised me she would stay, no matter what. She knew how bad the friction was between me and some of the doctors, and how important this blood transfusion was. I opened up my computer and looked at my sent e-mails—and she had written to every single girl. If they had sent me naked pictures or videos or a dirty e-mail, she went in on all of 'em. They all got a message along the lines of "Fuck you bitch, how dare you mess with my man, this is Shanna, fuck you."

JAMES INGRAM (RECORDING ENGINEER)

I got a call from Travis: "Hey, did you put a password on my computer?"

"No."

"Why not?"

I said, "Half the time you're awake, you don't even know where you are. I don't think you can remember a password."

If anyone wanted Travis and Shanna to be a thing forever, I'm the guy to blame. Well, he could have also not hooked up with other women. So there's that. But the last straw, I'll take credit for that.

SHANNA MOAKLER (EX-WIFE)

I was going through his computer and I saw a lot of bad stuff. I saw lots of women that I'd asked him to stay away from. I left the hospital that night and went home and cried. I was really fucked up over it. And I think

I was already fucked up seeing him in that condition.
It was intense.

I went out that night: I saw an ex-boyfriend. They put
it in the press that we hooked up, but we didn't that
night. So Travis thought I had cheated on him while he
was in the hospital, and I hadn't. He was in a plane
crash—I'd be there for him forever. But after I saw all
that in the computer, I didn't know if I could move forward with him romantically.

I went to the hospital the next couple of days, but there
were so many people, and his world of people don't make
me feel welcome in any capacity. I try to be nice to
everybody, but it's not fun to be around. I was afraid
to go back to the hospital, and then I did hook up with
one of my ex-boyfriends. I wasn't trying to hurt anybody;
I was just a fucking mess at that point. We didn't have
sex, but we did hook up.

Then when Travis came out of the hospital, he went to
meet us for dinner. He was holding our daughter and he
could barely walk. I said to myself, "Fuck everybody.
I'm going to take care of him and I'm going to be with
this man for the rest of my life."

I moved back into the house. They made him eat meat, so
I could actually cook for him. I would use the Crock-Pot
and bake batches of cookies. We both got fat together.
It was just the happiest time.

Then someone must have said, "She hooked up with her
boyfriend." He asked, and I lied to him. Because we
were finally in a good place, and we were a family, and
we were healing. Me saying, "Yeah, I gave this guy a

blowjob" wasn't going to help. So I lied. And he could never forgive me.

Mind you, he had cheated with probably a hundred women. Some of them my good fucking friends, who have stood next to me and smiled in my fucking face. I love him, but there's nothing I can do.

One of my worst points in the hospital—aside from the time when they were talking about *amputating my leg*—was going on my computer and seeing Shanna on a bunch of gossip sites (I tried to resist, but couldn't) with some actor. I still think she set that up as payback for the e-mails. My heartbeat was erratic; the hospital completely eighty-sixed Shanna from calling or visiting me. Justified or not, at any other time in my life, I probably would have forgiven her for anything, but after something as dramatic as the accident, I needed to systematically cut all the bullshit out of my life. Starting with her.

I slowly got better. Every morning, they put me in a big metal pan and scrubbed my burns with a metal brush. It was agony, but that feeling meant that there was progress. I had to learn to walk again, using a walker at first. After a couple of days, I could walk all the way to my first shower that didn't involve a metal pan and a metal brush. It felt orgasmic. I was standing by myself, not having five people hold me, no metal brush, feeling the water on my back. It was huge progress, because for so long, I had a catheter in my dick and I needed a nurse to help me take a shit. It had made me feel like a two-year-old.

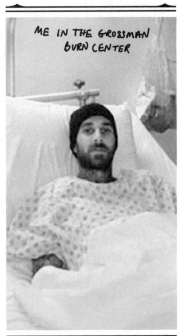

ME IN THE GROSSMAN BURN CENTER

For a long time, Alabama and Landon weren't allowed to visit me, and that was incredibly hard. I was one big open sore and I couldn't have too many visitors because I was prone to infection. When they finally did visit, Bama lifted up my hospital robe, curious what I was wearing underneath—and they saw my catheter. They got freaked out by this big tube coming out of my penis and ran out of the room.

When they finally let me leave the hospital in mid-December, eleven weeks after the crash, I knew my right foot would never be the same, but at least I got to keep it.

When I finally got home, I was on a different set of meds, and reality sank in. I had missed Chris's funeral. I had missed Che's funeral. AM had gotten out of the hospital three months before—when I got out of the hospital, I found out that he had just taken his first plane flight. I could not *believe* he was flying.

I wasn't completely healed—I still had lots of open sores on my legs. Every day, I called Kurt Richards, who was the assistant to Dr. Grossman. They had to keep checking my prescriptions—sometimes when I got my meds wrong, I took three times the amount of blood thinners I was supposed to, which meant serious internal bleeding.

My legs weren't healing, and I was sleeping only an hour a day. I was having intense nightmares and flashbacks. I didn't want to leave the house, didn't want to get in a car. Every day, my post-traumatic psychiatrist, Jonathan Simon, visited me for a session at my house. I kept calling Kurt, asking when I could get off my meds, because they made me feel crazy. He would say, "I don't know. You could be on these for the rest of your life. Many patients are."

I felt I had seen the face of death. I had dreams about dying and the plane crash. When I was awake, I was always bracing for impact, waiting for something to happen. I told Skinhead Rob that I wanted to kill myself. I knew that I needed to adapt—I came really close to checking myself into a mental hospital.

About a month later, my legs healed up, and I slowly began going on walks. Little by little, I got better, even though I was still burping up jet fuel.

When I saw Skinhead Rob, he said, "How you doing, man? You still on a bunch of meds?" I told him I was on only three or four, and he said, "Bro, I don't mean to haunt you, but you're not the same, man."

That was real: I knew Skinhead Rob wouldn't lie to me.

Then I overheard my uncle talking with Pops; my uncle was saying, "Have you noticed that Trav seems sort of slow?" I started paying more attention to everyone talking about me, and decided I needed to overcome it all. I didn't confront anyone—I just stopped taking all these meds that everybody thought I was going to be attached to forever. I needed to prove everyone wrong.

I went to see Kurt one day and he said, "Okay, what are you still taking?"

"Nothing."

"Really?"

"Yeah, man, I'm not taking anything."

"How are you feeling?"

"I'm cool," I told him. "I smoke weed from time to time, but for the most part, I'm cool."

I saw Kurt a couple more times. He told me I was healed up, and that he couldn't believe I wasn't taking the medication anymore: "I have other people that have been in really horrific, traumatizing accidents like you, and they're on these meds for the rest of their lives. So don't be too proud: if you need them, take them. It's better that you're in the right head space."

I never needed to take them again. I took pride in flushing every one of those things down the toilet. I had stopped taking pain meds as soon as I got home from the hospital, and now I was quitting the bipolar meds too. After I had been dependent on so many pills—nineteen or twenty prescriptions at a time—the idea of taking them recreationally, like I used to, seemed insane. That was the end of my pill-popping days.

KURT RICHARDS
(PHYSICIAN ASSISTANT, GROSSMAN BURN CENTER)

Our biggest concern was that Travis had severe burns to the bottoms of his feet that needed grafting. Over time, after healing, that can become a functional issue. If you get contractures—if his skin tightens—that can affect his ability to walk appropriately. And it's going to affect his livelihood, because he uses his feet to play the drums. These are concerns in the operating room: we had to take away the bad tissue to get him to heal, but not too much, because the more of his native skin we left, the lower the risk of having a severe contracture. We finally got him grafted, and his surgery went well.

By the time Travis left the hospital, he was in better psychological shape, but not great. After his discharge, I spoke with him fairly frequently: I was concerned about him psychologically. If I was horribly concerned, I certainly wouldn't have let him go, but I had the gut feeling that we hadn't reached the bottom yet.

After two weeks, Travis called me, and he wasn't doing well. There was less anger, but more fragility. He was depressed, to the point where I was concerned enough to wake up the psychologist who had been seeing him and say, "You need to call him right now, because I don't want to see him hurting himself." Travis was getting better, but emotionally, he was still lagging. I mean, he went through this horrible accident and he lost his friends.

Travis was on quite a few medications—I had a protocol to wean him off them slowly over the next few months. That was fruitless, because when he decided that he was going to quit, he just stopped. He had insomnia: it had been a problem on the unit and it got even worse when he got home. One of my biggest fears was that because of his tolerance for medication, something bad was going to happen. Celebrities are used to having the means to

get what they want, and unfortunately in this situation, there is no stamping out the pain completely. For
a couple of months after he got out of the hospital, I
was a wreck. He was always in the back of my mind.

And then it stopped. He picked himself up and started
exercising. He got on a running program, changed his
diet, and turned himself around. The Travis Barker that
I know now is a very different person from the gentleman I met when we admitted him. He's a hell of a guy.

We lost contact for a couple of years, but then he got
in touch with me because he was touring and was getting
pressured to fly by the other guys in the band. He wanted
pictures to show the guys: it's one thing to hear about
the accident, but you need to see what happened. I sent
him some pretty graphic shots, and he shared those with
his bandmates. I'm hoping they got on board after that.

If I was in his shoes? I don't know if I'd ever fly again.
If he can't get on a plane stone sober and fly, then why
do it? But I don't doubt that one day he's going to shoot
me a text with a picture of him next to a plane window.

I spent about three months in the hospital. After I got out, Shanna
and I went back and forth for a couple of weeks, but then we had our
final split as a couple. She thought of Lil Chris and AM as people that
kept me away from her, because I was with them when I went to work.
So when we were fighting, she said, "I'm happy your friends died."

I told her, "I don't care how bad I hated one of your friends, if they died,
I would never say that I was glad they were dead. That's just heartless."
She probably didn't mean it, and was just trying to hurt me because she
was angry—but that moment was still the cutoff point for me. It opened
my eyes to an anger in Shanna that I had never *really* seen before—either

because our relationship hadn't been *truly* tested, or because I was always so high.

Even during this time, Shanna was sleeping until the afternoon. I hired a driver so the kids could make it to school—I wasn't allowed to drive—and then after a couple of days, I realized they were my biggest support system. So I would ride with them to school, get driven home, and go right back to school to pick them up. I wanted to spend every waking minute with them.

There comes a point in life when you realize who really matters, who never did, and who always will.

After I got home, there were many times I would burst into tears for no reason. Shanna moved out; I was alone with the kids. I wasn't going crazy, but I definitely was suffering from post-traumatic stress and survivor's guilt. I didn't even feel right in my own body: everything on my right foot was grafted skin except for three toes, and it didn't even feel like a foot.

When I looked in the mirror, I saw a different person, even though there hadn't been any damage done to my features. I was seeing the world through different eyes. What had happened had changed me completely, and so the expressions on my face were just fundamentally different. I was really emotional and sad, and Landon and Alabama felt really helpless. They wanted to make me happy, but they had no idea what to do. They kept asking, "Dad, why are you crying?" The truth was, they were the only thing that made me happy. I could barely sleep—I was always tossing and turning—but I liked being with Landon in his room. I would lie down with him, and he would ask me if I was going to be okay. My legs were covered with scabs, and Bama would help me put my special

cream all over my legs. She used to say that she was helping the burn fairies come to help me take care of my burns.*

After the crash I felt religiously extreme, in both directions. On the one hand, I was thinking, *Who would torture someone like they just tortured me? Both my friends are dead. Sixty-five percent of my body was burned. I was in a burn center, I had twenty-six surgeries, and I almost lost my leg. My right hand is still numb. What fucking sadist would do this to someone? There cannot be a God.*

But another part of me was thinking, *I am so blessed to be here. I am still here with my kids. I am still here with my family. There must be a reason God left me here.* It was confusing. I had a lot of survivor's guilt: I was so bummed that Chris and Che and the two pilots were dead. I was having crazy suicidal thoughts, and I didn't want to be in that head space: I turned to God and asked him to protect me from myself. And then after that, I just kept praying every single day. I was literally counting the days that I had been alive since the crash—but then sometimes, I realized that every day brought me twenty-four hours closer to my eventual death. It was up to me to decide how I wanted to think about my time in this world.

I was brought up to have faith. I'd be ignorant to think that I just happen to be on this planet by accident. There has to be a larger plan—and if there isn't, I'm going to be so disappointed when I die. That just can't be it. I want to *believe.*

If Chris and I had ever had a conversation about this, we would have made a pact: if anything ever happened to one of us, the other one would figure out what it all meant. Chris would have done it, too, because Chris could make anything happen. He'd work all that shit out with God.

I still say my prayers every day. I talk to my mom; I talk to Chris; I talk to Che; anyone who's passed and is special to me, I talk to them. I have to believe that they have some ability to communicate and hear me still. I have lots of unanswered questions, but I also have a lot of faith. I pray for my dad, my kids, and my sisters.

---

* People always tell you that on their death bed, nobody wishes they had worked more—they always say they should have spent more time with their family. When I was in the hospital, that was *exactly* how I felt.

ME AND BABY BAMA. COURTESY OF ESTEVAN ORIOL.

ABOUT A MONTH AFTER I GOT HOME FROM THE HOSPITAL: MY FIRST TIME GETTING DRESSED, GOING OUTSIDE, AND PLAYING ON MY ON PRACTICE PADS. MY HANDS WERE SCABBY AND BLEEDING.

Life-changing events like my accident don't announce themselves. I couldn't understand how the world kept on going. I felt so vulnerable, but nobody around me seemed to be the same way. If they talked about going out to a bar or even picking up some McDonald's, I couldn't understand why they would take that risk. Pops would tell me that he was going to come visit me, but I wouldn't want him to do it, because that would mean driving on the freeway for ninety miles.

When I had been home for about four weeks, my hands finally healed. I had suffered third-degree burns on them, but finally, my sores closed up. That day, I called up Daniel and told him, "I want a practice pad and some sticks." He brought them over, and I set them up in the backyard—in the shade, because I still wasn't allowed to go in the sun. I watched my kids play, and I started practicing on the pad two or three hours a day.

I went into the studio, and I couldn't find my rhythm. Nothing felt right. I was still recovering from the crash—but I also wasn't used to playing unless I was high. I talked with Paul Rosenberg, who's one of my managers, a good friend, and a wise man. He also managed Eminem, and he told me that Eminem was completely sober. I was in disbelief, but he said, "It took Em a while to get right, but he's one hundred percent sober now. He's addicted to working out." I commended him—he was sober and he was still doing rad shit in this genre of music that I loved—but it felt out of reach for me.

I was scared to leave the house, and I lacked motivation to do anything. I was going into the studio just so I could feel productive, but whenever I hit a drum, I felt like it might hit me back and kill me. I saw my friend Aaron Spears: he's a gospel drummer who plays with Usher. He asked me if I had been practicing, and I said, "Nah, man, not really." He told me, "You gotta play. There are so many drummers that look up to you." He told me I should go fall in love with the drums again, and that helped inspire me.

For months after my plane crash, I dreaded getting into a car—mainly because of my fear of seeing a plane in the air. No matter how I tried, I couldn't stop imagining that any plane I saw was going to crash. I would panic and tell my friends Cheese and Armen, who were driving me around, "Please drive faster, and head away from that plane, because I feel like it's going to crash." I would imagine it flipping upside down, crashing into the ground, and bursting into flames. It took almost a year before I stopped having these visions.

After I had been out of the hospital for a few months, I was ready to see AM. We talked on the phone a whole bunch, and then we met up for breakfast. We sat there for hours, until it was lunchtime, talking about everything we remembered from that night in South Carolina. AM didn't remember anything from before I woke him up and he discovered that he was inside a plane on fire: he must have passed out, or maybe the first impact knocked him out.

I found out that Chris and Che were dead on impact from head trauma: neither one of them was wearing a seat belt. So when I tried going forward to grab them and my hands caught on fire, they were already gone—there was nothing I could do for them. When I found that out, that helped a little. It was hard to understand why things happened the way they did. I didn't even know the pilots, but I felt for them 100 percent. I spent hours researching who they were and trying to get to know them.

I went out to breakfast with LV. I told him that I was sorry: I shouldn't have blamed him for the crash. He hadn't addressed my hit list of issues when he booked the plane—but he didn't know to, so who could I blame? At the end of the day, the four of us all chose to get on that plane. I forgave and forgot—it wasn't LV's fault.

It was a long time before I looked at a photo of the plane crash. Once I did, I could see that the top of the plane was ripped off: the Learjet looked like a convertible. In other words, Alabama was absolutely right when she told me, "The roof's gonna come off."

I kept checking the Access Help website, looking for support groups for aircraft casualties, but they were oriented more for people who had lost loved ones, not crash survivors. I was both, which twisted my brain even further.

AM had been flying for months, but I couldn't imagine ever getting on a plane again. I asked him how he was doing it. Apparently, he took a Xanax whenever he got on a plane—a therapist told him that, after

TRAVIS BARKER
can i say

twelve years of sobriety, taking Xanax to fly wouldn't be that bad. But I thought it was a mistake—I knew how easy it was for that to be a gateway to more dangerous things.

I felt numb, but AM helped me a lot. He joined some support groups for people involved in plane crashes, people who had survived a crash or who had lost a loved one in a crash. He was doing some gnarly process that they called "retraining the brain." They test how your eyes react to certain things, and they try to teach your brain to loop around a piece of memory, almost erasing it. I felt like that was a waste of time for me. I would have looked down at my legs every day and said, "Fuck, I know why I have scars all over my body." I didn't buy it, but AM was a firm believer in it.

AM checked in with me every week. He was the only person I could really talk to. Whenever my friend Cheese drove me to the studio, I'd have sunglasses and a hoodie on and I would just be crying the whole way. Driving on the 101 freeway, we would pass by the burn center, and that would always set me off. Nobody around me really understood the depth of my depression. Even though AM had only an inch of his body burned, he could relate to what had happened. But he always told me, "Man, it's hard for me, Trav, because all I have is Muggsy the cat. You have those amazing kids, and you know you have to be strong for them, but I have Muggsy. I wish I had something more to live for."

He was right about my kids: every day I would be reminded that I had to bounce back for them. I had the most amazing kids, and they were my true purpose in life. I had a second chance, and I had to appreciate every minute I had left with them. They put me into survivor mode. They gave me all my strength.

MY KIDS AND MY FAMILY GIVE ME MY STRENGTH. COURTESY OF ESTEVAN ORIOL

SAYING A PRAYER BEFORE SHOWTIME.
COURTESY OF WILLIE TOLEDO

Ghost on the dance floor

When I was in the burn center in Georgia, Mark and his wife, Skye, flew out to see me right away. And much to my surprise, Tom started writing me letters. He sent me a picture of the three of us on a submarine in the Middle East, from when Blink-182 played on that naval base in Bahrain: that symbolized our past. And there was another photo, of him with his kids crawling on top of him: that was where life had taken him.

I hadn't spoken with Tom in five years. And I didn't expect to talk with him ever again. I had accepted the fact that Blink had broken up and moved on with my life a long time before. But when I got these handwritten letters, it felt obvious that he cared, even after everything that had gone down.

I called him up from the hospital; I'm not sure he was expecting to hear from me, but it was cool talking to him on the phone. He was cracking jokes about me being in a hospital bed, asking me if I was naked. After we got off the phone, I called Mark right away and told him, "Tom was cool, funny—he's the same dude we used to know. It didn't feel bad."

I hadn't seen Travis for about four or five years. When I saw him again, the biggest change was in his dedication to his family. I've been around Travis at his lowest points, and I think people would be surprised by how much of an emotional creature he is. He's got this facade that's very hard, and has bruises and scars from everything he's been through, but I've seen him when everything's stripped away, and he's very human, just like everyone else.

We had gotten the band back together and had started touring again. I was sitting in an airport, and Travis gave me a card. Inside was a message saying that he valued our friendship. It was out of left field, and it was really rad. Travis doesn't make gestures like that very often—it's not that he doesn't have those feelings, you just don't see it that much. Travis has always been quiet and reclusive. He protects himself with a lot of walls, so it can be hard to get through. But there's a little kid in there—just like with Mark and myself. Travis doesn't express anything, and I express everything.

Communication has always been hard in this band. The three of us are all like old dogs that aren't going to change. We know that this is the band that brought us everything: I describe it as a dysfunctional marriage we'll never get out of. It's not that bad—I've seen bands get in fistfights on YouTube. That would never happen to us, because we're in different hotels and on different buses. Everyone still has a lot of respect for each other, but we're constantly battling the process.

My interactions with Travis are best when I've got a guitar on. That's when I think we have an enormous amount

of respect for each other. When the three of us are playing a room together, it's the only time in my life when
I've ever been able to not think about anything other
than what the fuck is happening in that moment. When we
all walk into the room together before rehearsal, everyone's thinking about other shit and being careful with
each other. Then putting on the instruments is like the
three of us taking off all the weights of life. It's like
a translation device.

If I had never met Travis, I would not have all the greatest things in my life, except for my family. I wouldn't
have anything. That's one of those things you would never
say to each other—but it's true. That's how I feel.

In early 2009, after I had been out of the hospital for a couple of
months, Tom drove up from San Diego and all three of us sat down
together at my house. We had some heart-to-heart talks and discussed
why we had broken up. Pretty soon, we had agreed that we would get
back together. The plan was that all three of us would make Blink-182
a priority, but that we would leave lots of room for each of us to work on
our other projects. We agreed that we would get into the studio a couple
of months later and see what happened.

A week or two later, I got a call: Mark and Tom were excited to get
into the studio and didn't want to wait a couple of months. This was a
much bigger deal for me than they realized. At that point, I wasn't even
leaving the house that much. I was afraid to go outside, afraid to get in
cars. I didn't even want to walk down the street: I just wanted to lie in
bed and smoke excessive amounts of weed and hide out. But I didn't want
to tell them that. I needed to prove to myself that I could get out of my
house and that I could still play the drums.

I went very prematurely, because it felt so good to be in the studio.
I wasn't going to tell anybody the truth, that I wasn't ready to be there
yet. I still had scabs on my legs. I didn't have any feeling in my left hand,
except for my pointer finger and my thumb. I wasn't going to let Tom and

Mark know how freaked out I was, or even that my hand was numb. My hands were still healing; they bled every time I played the drums. That first day, we wrote the song that became "Up All Night."

Right after that, I worked up the courage to call my doctor and tell him that my left hand was numb. I had told him about it when I was at the burn center, but I hadn't emphasized it because I didn't want to have any more surgeries and I just wanted to go home. He told me I needed to see a nerve specialist right away: I got all these tests, and it turned out my ulnar nerve was pinched. About a week later, I went into surgery; I will probably never have complete feeling in that hand, but I can still use it to play the drums, which is what's important to me.

AM and I kept playing together. We had a special bond because we had survived that plane crash together, sharing an experience that very few people live through. We appreciated our friendship, we loved making music together, and we were grateful to be alive. We did take a Johnny Cash remix out of our set: it was "Ring of Fire," with a Black Rob beat, and AM said, "We're never playing that song again." The lyrics go, "I fell into a burning ring of fire / I went down, down, down, as the flames went higher." It was one of our most popular remixes, but it was too much.

That spring, we had our biggest show ever, at Coachella. We played for an hour, and Warren G came out to do "Regulate" with us. Anytime AM and I played, we would see if Warren G was available—if he could come to the show, we'd end our set with "Regulate" and everyone would go crazy. Warren G and his boys had never seen anything like Coachella. After our set was over, they were just watching the crowd for hours, mesmerized, checking out the girls on Ecstasy twerking on somebody's shoulders. Meanwhile, I tried to catch the Killers' set—but they had a lot of pyro, and I wasn't ready for it.

We got a lot of attention for that Coachella show. There were people who hadn't heard of us beyond "that DJ and drummer who almost died in a plane crash." Most of the DJs on the Coachella bill were people like Deadmau5 who were established DJs. And suddenly we were in the mix.

After our set I saw Bill Fold, my old roommate who'd managed the Aquabats—he had gone on to found both the Coachella festival and the promotion company Goldenvoice. He told me, "I heard you guys had a little buzz going, but I didn't know what it was going to be like. The last I knew, AM was playing top-forty stuff in clubs. I booked you guys out of love. And my jaw just dropped. You guys were fucking amazing."

Before the reunited Blink-182 played any shows, we did our first photo shoot, with Michael Muller. I showed up, and his idea was for us to stand there holding fireworks in our hands. I'd been out of the burn unit for about two months, so it was hitting way too close to home, but I didn't want to make waves or make Mark and Tom feel weird. I lit my flare and I tried to be a team player, but I had to stop and say, "I can't do it. I'll do a normal photo shoot, but I don't want to be holding something on fire." Being engulfed in smoke and fire, it felt like I was joking about the fact that 65 percent of my body had been burned. Once I said something, everyone was cool about it.

In July, Blink-182 kicked off a reunion tour in Las Vegas. We didn't have a huge production: no big light show, no mystery keyboard player on the side, no guy playing guitar behind a curtain. That's what most rock bands do these days. It was just the three of us, doing what we were supposed to do. That night, I played with the band at the Hard Rock, and then AM and I did an after-party show at the nightclub Rain, playing our Coachella set front to back, with full production. We had a blast.

AM and I got offstage, and my hands were a bloody mess from playing over four hours in one night. We were bullshitting, having all of our postshow fun, and then AM said, "Trav, I'm fucked up, man. I feel like doing mad drugs and just saying fuck it." I thought he was just talking about our normal state of mind after the plane crash, which meant not doing so good. We were both mentally fucked up, but at this point, AM was doing worse than me. When he said that, I remembered how he used to come to my practice room when I had pounds of weed there. He'd grab the weed and stuff his face in it, smelling it, and say, "One day, one day . . . I'll be able to smoke a blunt on the beach." He knew that he had an addictive personality—back when he was using lots of drugs, he had weighed three hundred pounds. He knew what his life was like when he lost control, so I didn't think he meant it when he said, "I feel like doing mad drugs and just saying fuck it"—but those were the last words he ever said to me. They echo over and over in my head.

The next couple of weeks, I was on tour with Blink. I tweeted that it felt great to be back with my brothers and playing shows. He tweeted me back saying, "I hope that doesn't mean we're not gonna jam no more, bro. I know you like playing with them better than me, but I hope we still get to do our thing."

I told him, "Are you kidding me, bro? I love playing with you. I wouldn't change it for the world. I'm just saying it feels good to be back with the band."

Then the tour got to New York, and I sent AM a message: "Yo, I'm in New York, let's meet up." I didn't hear back from him.

I was having morbid thoughts of my own a lot of the time, so I tried to fill up every minute of the day. On August 29, Blink had a concert scheduled in Hartford, Connecticut, so during the day, I went in the studio with the rap group Slaughterhouse, working on a track for my solo album. I had sent them a beat a couple of weeks before and they loved it, so we were getting together to work on the track.

They were on a short break from laying down their verses, and I saw a bunch of people clustered around a computer, talking. I walked over to see what was up. Daniel just handed the computer to me and said, "I'm sorry, Trav."

There was a news story saying that AM was dead from a possible drug overdose. I was in shock: I felt like there was a rock in my throat that I couldn't swallow. The Slaughterhouse dudes tried to comfort me—they knew AM too—but I couldn't even speak. I felt like a piece of me had just died. I burst into tears and left the studio.*

AM had gone to New York, but he didn't invite anybody to come with him. Usually one of our managers would travel with him, and he had a

---

* Joe Budden of Slaughterhouse rapped about that moment on a track called "Pray for Them": "Reminded my past is darker / Cause when AM died, I was starin' at Travis Barker / Wishin' there was something I could say to make him cheer up / And so I prayed, and he teared up."

TRAVIS BARKER
can i say

girlfriend at the time, but he purposely went by himself—from what we could figure, he wanted to get fucked up without anybody stopping him.

They found ten Oxycontin in his throat. One Oxycontin will have you melting, so I wondered: Did he just not know the new drugs? Did he misjudge because back in the day when he was using, he was three hundred pounds and needed to do a lot more drugs to get fucked up? Did he do it on purpose? To this day, I still don't know. I think about it all the time.

LAWRENCE "LV" VAVRA (MANAGER)

Adam was one of the best human beings you'll ever meet. He was a sweet guy, although he cared a little bit too much about the wrong things. He loved making money, he loved spending money, he loved socializing. He was a ladies' man. We would check in to a hotel and he would be on his different devices, texting and instant-messaging with sometimes three or four girls at a time. On long flights, he never wanted to talk about his career: it was always, "Yo, what do you think about this chick?"

The thing that was such a shock when he passed away was that he was the last guy that you'd expect—the way he helped so many other people, you thought that if he was going through something, he'd be able to reach out for help. He helped my brother get sober. He tried to get Travis sober twenty times.

I've never had this with any other artist: he would remember something I was going through and call me to say, "How are you doing today, man? Did everything work out?" You don't get that from musicians—they're inherently selfish people. I'll hear from Travis once in a while, which I think is the trickle-down effect from AM doing it to him.

Looking back, and seeing what's happened in the world of electronic music and DJs—if the plane crash hadn't happened, and if Adam hadn't passed away, they would probably be a top headlining electronic dance act making four or five hundred grand a show. Travis and Adam had become good friends, and the sky was the limit for them.

After AM died, I was the only one left alive from that Learjet: it felt like I was starring in a real-life *Final Destination,* where I cheated death and fate was going to catch up with me. I was afraid to get on the bus with Blink-182 and go to the next venue: it felt like I could die at any time. When AM was alive, it felt like because he had survived, I could survive too. Now my support system had died; I could talk to any therapist in the world for hours, but it wasn't the same because they hadn't lived

ME AND DJ AM. COURTESY OF ESTEVAN ORIOL

through that plane crash. My connection with AM went way beyond having a special bond: when he died, it was like I had lost part of myself.

We played the show, but I was a mess. I just stayed in my bus up until the time we played, crying all the time. I came out, went through the motions, and went right back to the bus. After that show, we stopped the tour so I could go to AM's funeral in California. I had missed Che's funeral and I had missed Chris's funeral, because I had been unconscious in a hospital bed in the burn center, but I wasn't going to miss AM's funeral. I didn't care if they threw me out of the band: I needed to go do this.

I rode in the bus back to California, going for four days straight, only stopping for gas, crying all the way.

The funeral was even harder than I expected: it felt like I was burying AM, Chris, and Che all together. Most of the funerals I went to when I was growing up were open casket, and although I didn't want to see AM dead, I wanted to see him one last time—but because he was Jewish, his casket was closed.

Then I turned around and drove east for four days straight to get back to the Blink tour. Those were some of the toughest shows of my life. We did a tribute to AM during the show, with some pictures of him up on the huge LED screens. There would be a moment of silence and then we'd play "Ghost on the Dance Floor."

I just wanted to hide. I was scared to go outside; I was scared to be riding the bus. I just wanted to curl up in a ball and escape from everything. Somehow I made it through the next three weeks, until the tour was over. I didn't come out of the bus; I didn't do sound check. I just played my show every day, usually with my head down, crying through the whole set. The last day of the tour was the one-year anniversary of the plane crash. I was alive, but I wasn't really living.

COURTESY OF WILLIE TOLEDO

Can a Drummer get some

When I got home from the Blink-182 reunion tour, I finally did the X-rays and MRIs I should have done the year before, and they revealed that my back had been broken in three places. The doctors asked, "Why didn't you say anything? You must have been in severe pain."

"Well, yeah, but I figured I was in a plane crash, so I didn't think I'd feel one hundred percent *ever*." In the hospital, they told me it might be two or three years before I was functioning properly, and that I might never feel exactly the same—I should just feel happy that I was still here. That resonated with me—I tried not to complain, or whine, or take anything for granted.

A powerful mind-set is the most powerful weapon you can have.

I ate a lot of meat in the hospital to help my body heal, and even after I got out, I was trying out steakhouses with Shanna and the kids: I didn't like any of them. But once I could go back to being a vegetarian, I wanted to go even further, and I became a vegan.* There are lots of ways to get protein into your body that don't involve eating meat, and I just feel like my body runs better when I'm vegan: I never feel heavy. But eating vegan isn't enough: you also need to eat *healthy* food. You can be a junk-food vegan. I used to live off Red Bull and bean-cheese-and-rice burritos, and I never drank water. I was a vegetarian, but it was gross. Now I try to juice every day; good food in your body means good energy.†

After the crash, my left hand was numb for a long time: I had multiple surgeries on it, and I wasn't sure if it was ever going to work again. But even if I wasn't able to play the drums ever again in my life, I wanted to finish my album. That was one of the goals that kept me going: I wanted to finish it because Lil Chris had been so passionate about it. He really encouraged me: "Trav, man, all these artists want to work with you." He probably motivated me more than any of the managers I ever had. Making a solo album meant that I could do whatever I wanted musically—and what I wanted was to collaborate with all my favorite MCs and musicians, giving back to the genre of hip-hop that I love so much.

---

* It's not just a personal choice; being a vegan is important for taking care of the planet. 2,500 gallons of water are needed to produce one pound of beef, and growing feed for livestock consumes over half of the United States' water supply. An acre and a half of farmland can produce 37,000 pounds of plant-based food or 375 pounds of meat, while a farm with 2,500 dairy cows produces the same amount of waste as a city of 400,000 people. Animal agriculture is responsible for more greenhouse gas emissions than all transportation.

† I also am now an investor in an amazing vegan restaurant, Crossroads. My friend Toby Morse from the band H2O introduced me to its chef, Tal Ronnen: he's cooked for Bill Clinton, Oprah Winfrey, and Steve Wynn, and he did Ellen and Portia's wedding. The vegan world's pretty small—when there are chefs like Tal, you hear about them. So I knew about him and I knew that he was all about punk rock. He approached me at a Bad Brains concert, saying he wanted me to be involved in the restaurant. (Not only is he a great chef, he has great taste in music.) He spilled his vision of the restaurant and I taste-tested the food, and it was so delicious. I felt confident that if he had his own restaurant in LA, it would be successful, and it's a huge hit. So I'm an investor in three restaurants: Crossroads, plus two Wahoo's Fish Tacos franchises.

I was spending all my time at the studio Mark and I bought—the official name for it was OPRA, but we just called it the lab. It had two rooms, Studio A and Studio B, and I had drum kits set up everywhere, so I could go back and forth between recording a new album with Blink and working on my solo album. Plus, we got the Transplants back together, and we started working on new material—every Tuesday. (Most of that material became our third album, but one track, "Saturday Night," ended up on my solo record.) The Transplants are probably the most productive band I've ever been in: Tim can write a hook in minutes, and it's awesome pretty much 100 percent of the time.

TIM ARMSTRONG (SINGER/GUITARIST, THE TRANSPLANTS)

Transplants Tuesdays has become a new stage in this creative thing we've created: we all have our crazy schedules and lives, but every Tuesday, no matter what, we show up at ten A.M. I think that was my idea, to have one day where we can get back to what we did in the first days in my basement: just celebrate music and have fun, not even have a record in mind. It had that great vibe of friends making music for the hell of it, with no real agenda. I don't even know the real name of Travis's studio. We call it the lab—he's the mad scientist. Basically, he's got four drum sets—I'm pretty sure they're mic'd up at all times. Not a lot of preproduction goes into him putting down a drum track. I keep a guitar there, because I'm left-handed. I'll go down there at a moment's notice to write a hook or whatever.

I would be at the lab all day, only going home when I was starting to fall asleep. In the morning, I would wake up and rush back.* With

---

* A typical day for me is to wake up in the morning, eat, train, drum, eat again, drum, train, and go to sleep—I wouldn't change it for the world.

all the action going on in one place, exciting things could happen. The Blink-182 song "After Midnight" is based on a beat I had recorded for the rapper Yelawolf. It's this crazy beat: it has really fast double strokes on a high hat. I had recorded some beats for Yela to listen to and some other beats for Blink to listen to. When the engineer who works with Blink was playing back the beats, he played back the wrong session—but when Mark and Tom heard it, they freaked out. I told them it wasn't even meant to be for Blink, but they said, "No, we love this." So we started writing to it, and that ended up being one of my favorite songs on that album, *Neighborhoods*.*

I asked Slash to play on my solo record, and he said, "Fuck, yeah." I grew up on Guns N' Roses, and I had played a couple of events with Slash for his charity, which helps at-risk teens. Whenever I went onstage with him, I'd play drums the whole night, and he'd rotate in other musicians: major players like Flea and Ozzy Osbourne. So I sent Slash three songs to choose from, and he liked the Transplants song. He is such a humble, grounded dude: he came into the studio with no handlers. He just carried in a guitar and an amp and murdered it. Slash knows he can call me anytime and I'll do whatever for him.†

Tom Morello was the same way on a track called "Carry It," which also had Raekwon and RZA from Wu-Tang Clan: he came in, plugged in, and started making dolphin noises out of his guitar that you couldn't even believe. The Cool Kids came in and we worked on "Jump Down"; one of their MCs, Chuck Inglish, played drums a little bit. So we set up two kits. I played on the cocktail kit—cowbells and toms and stuff like

---

* That was a hard album to make—it was very strange to be in the studio without Jerry. He had such a good ear, and he was the fourth member of the band. He could always be honest with us. Sometimes, if one of us says something about how to improve a song, it might not get through to the other guys—but when Jerry said it, we always said, "Okay, sure, Jerry knows what's up."

† Sometimes his wife, Perla, will call me and say, "Hey, this guy is throwing a party at his house—he'll pay you and Slash thirty grand if you guys go play for forty-five minutes." Sure, no problem.

that—while he played on the main drum kit. We came up with a rhythm together and banged out the track in a day.

Some people came into the studio; others would just record verses or hook ideas and send them to me. I had thirty-five guests on the album, including most of my favorite musicians and MCs: Lil Wayne, Snoop Dogg, the Game, Swizz Beatz, Rick Ross, Pharrell Williams, Busta Rhymes, Lupe Fiasco, Dev, Ludacris, E-40, Slaughterhouse, Yelawolf, Twista, Lil Jon, Kid Cudi, Tech N9ne, Bun B, Beanie Sigel, and Cypress Hill. I called it *Give the Drummer Some*—which is something James Brown used to tell his band. I was worried that it might be too obvious, but people really liked the title.

KEVIN BIVONA (KEYBOARD PLAYER)

When I was eighteen, I joined the Transplants as their touring keyboard player. That tour ended, and the Transplants were done for a while. I had nothing booked,

ME WITH SLASH. COURTESY OF ESTEVAN ORIOL

so I got a job as a telemarketer, which sucked. But one day, I got a call from Travis—he was working on a Bun B session and he wanted me to come down to the studio and play keyboards. I had done some hip-hop stuff before, so I was familiar with the vibe. Then Travis started working on his solo album, *Give the Drummer Some*—I played on tracks and then eventually we were making beats together.

One time, we were driving from LA to Austin to do South by Southwest. I had a studio set up in the front lounge of the bus, and we were making hip-hop beats together. At one point, Travis lit up a joint and we started smoking. Then the bus stopped. The driver looked back and said, "We're at a checkpoint at the New Mexico–Arizona border." We were like, *Fuck*, because they're both zero-tolerance states. We opened the window, and clouds of weed smoke were going out. Travis was like, "Dude, light up a cigarette. Light up two cigarettes!" I was smoking two cigarettes at the same time, trying to get the smell of weed out of there. I put them down like they were incense sticks and lit up two more, just power-smoking the cigarettes. Luckily, no one came on the bus, but it could have gone really badly.

The drum track that I had given to Lil Wayne when my arm was broken had become part of the track "Drop the World," which Wayne did with Eminem. It was cool to hear the finished track: I had no idea how they would end up using my parts. And when the Grammys came around that year, Em and Wayne performed with Drake (doing his song "Forever"), and they asked me to play drums with them. My jaw dropped: I knew Em had his own drummer, Wayne had his own drummer, Drake had his own drummer. That was one of my biggest musical accomplishments ever.

I started off playing in clubs for a hundred people. Or sometimes ten people. The Grammys seemed like they were on another planet. We had

one practice: three of the best rappers in the business, a dope band, and me. It was competitive—Em was making his comeback, Wayne was at the height of his career, Drake was hungry because he didn't even have his album out yet, although he was really starting to buzz—but everyone was super professional.

On Grammy day, we showed up to this big, empty building. The seats all have pieces of paper with people's faces on them: I realized that the place was going to be packed with a who's-who of the music business. Every one of my idols past, present, and future was going to be there. You can't think too much about it, because you'll mind-fuck yourself.

I had also played the BET Awards with T.I., right after he got out of jail. I had done the show once before, with Jamie Foxx, but with T.I. it felt crazy, like going into a fistfight. It was just emotional, knowing this dude had been locked up for a year and I was going to be part of his first performance back. He's really quiet and really serious—very determined.

FIRST GRAMMY AWARDS PERFORMANCE.
COURTESY OF ERIC VOAKE

He's probably the only person I didn't get on my album that I wish I would have. I think it was just a communication breakdown.

The crazy thing about those BET Awards was that they were the same weekend as the Electric Daisy Carnival festival, and I was playing both. I had been doing some sets with A-Trak, the DJ, as a tribute to AM. We got invited to play EDC, which is a full-on rave: people dressed like lollipops and SpongeBob. So when I left rehearsal with T.I. to do a sound check with A-Trak, I was walking down the street in downtown LA, and I went from seeing rappers with gold chains arriving in Escalades to seeing girls dressed as fairies and guys in bunny suits. Downtown LA looked nuts, and I loved that I participated in both worlds.

Around that time, I got a call from Ron Fair, a famous producer and record executive: "Mary J. Blige is going to do this cover—she really wants you to be a part of it."

When I got down to the studio, I found out we were covering Led Zeppelin's "Stairway to Heaven." I was like . . . Oh, man. This is kind of no-no territory. But then Mary sang it—not on tape, just singing it in the room—and her interpretation of it was so good. I was thinking, *This sounds really, really good.* We figured out the arrangement at Capitol Studios and recorded it all in one day. There were great musicians—Steve Vai, Orianthi, Randy Jackson—and Mary was such a pleasure to work with. So humble and such a great singer.

I didn't want to just play John Bonham's parts—what would be exciting about me doing that? So I went in and just did me. We recorded it live: we were all good enough players that we could play it straight through. We weren't trying to be Led Zeppelin, but I was in the best possible company to even take a *stab* at it. A week and a half later, we performed it on *American Idol*, where, because the show is live, we had even more room for interpretation and improv. We couldn't be edited.

The day we recorded it, we all discussed what the lyrics were about. Nobody knew.

Before my album dropped, I put together a mixtape to get everyone warmed up for it. DJ Whoo Kid was the guy who orchestrated that whole thing, saying, "I'm going to send you seventeen tracks," and I told him we

had to get it done within two weeks so that it would come out a bit earlier than the *actual* album, so that one wouldn't interfere with the other. He would say, "I'm getting you verses and choruses from Wiz tomorrow," or "I'm going to be sending you something from Tech N9ne," and every day he would send me something new. I'd be in my studio waiting for the e-mail: when it came through, we'd pull it up on the board, plug it into Pro Tools, and I'd start drumming.

Fifteen days after I handed in the record, I got a call from my rep at Interscope: they thought the album was too hip-hop, which made no sense to me. Everybody was pumped on the album, and we were getting ready to film our first video.

Two days later, they called me back. Now they were saying that the album wasn't hip-hop *enough*.

What the fuck is wrong with these guys? I thought. While I knew it would require managing a bigger operation, I paid for the video myself, which would guarantee I would have creative control. The most important thing, in my mind.

But that whole experience helped me cross a threshold as it made me more confident in putting out any of my future music independently. When you get with a label, you have so many people putting their two cents in—and these days, in the Wild West of online music distribution, the thing you need most from a label, the team's ability to sell albums, has proven to be a big problem. Earlier in my career, while disagreements did occur, of course, I felt like as a creative person, I was trusted by the

ARTWORK BY FRANCO VESCOVI.
COURTESY OF LASALLE RECORDS

labels to know what I did well and to go out and kill it. If it didn't work, at least it was on me. Maybe they were nervous, but I never felt that. At least not as much as I do today, where I feel like the folks whose primary responsibility is marketing, distribution, and *sales* are just interfering, trying to dictate your career and the sound of your music.

When I recorded *Psycho White* with Yelawolf two years later, I released it myself, taking care of everything down to the Internet marketing and the street snipes. I've already paid myself back, and I own the masters for the rest of my life. Interscope *still* owes me money for *Give the Drummer Some.*

YELAWOLF (RAPPER)

I knew about Blink, but I really became interested in Travis when he started popping up in hip-hop videos. It was like, "Damn, this dude is doing that? That's fucking sick." I was a fan from afar—I remember seeing Travis popping up at trade shows with Famous. I networked my way up to meeting him. Travis is from the West Coast and I'm from the South, but we're really cut from the same cloth: car cultures, rebelliousness, a love for hip-hop, a love for rock 'n' roll, a love for street culture.

If you play with Travis, he takes that record to another level. The first time I performed with Travis, I had a record called "Pop the Trunk" that was buzzing. I had played it with Questlove, who I don't want to disrespect: he's a genius. But when I did "Pop the Trunk" in LA with Travis, it was like bombs going off. Strictly my opinion: I think Travis is the best drummer when it comes to playing behind hip-hop acts. And Questlove would be second. They're both amazing.

Travis understands a metronome and a click track far beyond anyone else. He has power, loudness, and consistency in sound—the sound of his snare is always the same. He can't be touched when it comes to keeping a kick-snare pattern on top of triple-time high hats. And he does something that no one else is doing: he'll tap

the kick drum with his toe, and he'll hit an 808 synthesizer with his heel.

"Push Em" on *Psycho White* was a record where he laid down these synth drums that had a punk-rock pattern—or, in my brain, bluegrass. So we started building on it and it became this toxic mix of rhyme patterns and playing: this is you, this is me, this is what we sound like when we're going apeshit. There was no one around to say how they felt—it was just me and him rocking. Then Tim Armstrong and Skinhead Rob came in and did the ad-lib hook. That record is special. You've got to have the right setting to play it—some shows, kids lose their minds.

LAWRENCE "LV" VAVRA (MANAGER)

We didn't know what to expect with a white guy from
Fontana doing a hip-hop album, but he sold over a hundred
thousand copies in six months—in the nineties, that
would have been two million copies. We kept wanting to
orchestrate more radio-friendly singles, and he wouldn't
let us. He kept saying, "The first one's for me and the
next one's for everybody else." We could have had Dr.
Luke producing him with Katy Perry on the hook, but he
didn't want to do that.

The first single was "Can a Drummer Get Some," with verses by Lil
Wayne, Rick Ross, Swizz Beatz, and the Game. The day of the video,
they all showed up—but then Wayne stayed in his trailer. His assistant
told us, "Wayne's not doing his verse. Something's up."

I asked him, "Can you grab Wayne so I can chop it up with him?"

Wayne came out and told me, "That verse was the old Wayne—I need
to do a new verse. That's not the verse I want people to hear." He had
recorded it before my plane crash, and before he went to jail. "I would
never say that stuff now," he said. He didn't really get into why, but he
said, "Don't trip—I'll record this verse and I'll send it to you. I'll also
pay for my part of the video since I'm not going to do it today." And he
did. He was a man of his word.

About a week after that, Wayne asked if I wanted to go on tour with
him. This was his I Am Music II tour in the spring of 2011, with him,
Rick Ross, and Nicki Minaj. I played a set with Mixmaster Mike and
Yelawolf, I played drums with Rick Ross, and in every city, different
artists from my album would come onstage with me, like Paul Wall, Bun
B, Jay Rock, and the Cool Kids. Landon and Bama were out of school for
spring break; I brought them with me and we had the time of our lives.

Nicki Minaj taught Bama how to dance. Bama would also pray with
Nicki and her dancers every night, joining their huddle before they went
onstage. Landon taught Wayne about snapback hats. Every day on that tour,

we'd watch Wayne play. Sometimes before his set, he'd come grab Landon from our dressing room. Wayne would take him to his dressing room under the stage and Landon would pick out the clothes that Wayne was going to wear onstage. And then Landon would kick it with him until he hit the stage, and security would bring Landon back. Wayne is such a good dude.

Lil Chris and I had met Rick Ross early on, when he was breaking his "Hustlin'" single. He acted like the kids' long-lost uncle: after he got offstage, he would get the kids and roll around the arena. He'd be dripping sweat, and he'd put his iced-out Maybach Music chain on one of the kids.

I loved having Landon and Bama with me, and I think it's important for them to meet all kinds of people. My kids are growing up hanging out with the Boo-Yaa T.R.I.B.E.—American Samoans who are three times the size of ordinary human beings—and meeting people with tattoos on their faces. I don't want them to be sheltered; I don't want them to judge. They've met everybody and they've seen it all.

I am who I am by choice. Society rejects me because I'm different: I reject society because they're the same.

The night of the last show, Nicki's assistant came into my dressing room and said, "Nicki's been wanting to do this for a long time."

"What's that?"

"She wants to give you a lap dance onstage tonight."

"Shit, you don't have to twist my arm." She gave a lap dance onstage every night: to Wayne, to Drake, to a person from the audience. She's rightly known for her beautiful ass: it was the best lap dance of my life.

When I go on tour, I won't pack until the morning I leave. I take as little as possible. I wear the same shorts every day of a tour: camouflage shorts with patches and blood all over them. I bought those shorts used,

CHILLING WITH ALABAMA ON THE TOUR BUS.
COURTESY OF WILLIE TOLEDO

at an army surplus store: I don't like to wear anything that's new. I won't put on a T-shirt until I've washed it a couple of times. Or I'll wear the same one for months, until it's old and faded.

My tour shorts are perfect: I've had them for years, and I don't wash them until the tour is over. After thirteen or fourteen shows, I've been known to walk into a room and say, "Oh my God, what stinks?" And it's my own shorts.

Going on tour is almost like a vacation for me, just because I don't have as many interruptions. I still work like I'm broke. I don't have to go to the studio every day, I don't have to work every day—I could probably just chill. But I'm still hungry. I want to stay busy, stay productive, stay creative—take advantage of every minute I have.

I think I got my work ethic from Pops, because I saw him work his ass off. He was trying to give our family the best life he could—and even today, he still works hard. I bought him a nice house and basically retired him, but he won't stop. He's still doing stuff for me, like going to the bank or the warehouse, even when I tell him he doesn't have to. He's happiest when he's working. And I'm the same way.

Work hard, play hard.

THE KIDS WITH NICKI MINAJ. COURTESY OF CHRIS ROQUE

• THE FAMOUS FAMILY

19

C.R.E.A.M.

The height of Famous Stars and Straps was around 2007, after two seasons of *Meet the Barkers*. When the TV show aired, that blew our business through the roof, and for a while we couldn't keep up with orders. Famous has always been an independent machine: we never, ever, ever went to anyone for help, subcontracting out our business. I hired more people, we rolled with the punches, and the brand just kept growing. At that point, we were doing about a hundred million in sales a year.

Then I had my plane crash, and the company got into a bit of trouble. I wasn't able to answer questions or do anything for Famous for about six to eight months, while I was in the burn centers and hospitals. The way the clothing business works, planning seasons well in advance, my absence had consequences for years. I was so out of it at that time; I couldn't think clearly.

I've had to get rid of some faulty people in the company over the years. That plane crash exposed who really knew what they were doing. They were trying to keep everything running without me, trying to make good

decisions, but some people couldn't function day-to-day unless I was calling the shots. Now that I'm better, I'm involved in the design aspect again, and everything from A to Z is approved by me. When I'm on tour I do everything through e-mail, but when I'm home, I spend one day a week at Famous. We've gotten annual sales back up to over $40 million.

We've gotten big enough that we've had some substantial buyout offers. I've considered them all seriously—when somebody offers you $100 million, you have to at least think about it—but ultimately, I've always decided that I want to keep Famous. I've always been afraid of what somebody else might do to it.

Here's the classic scenario when somebody buys you out: they're trying to make as much money as they can to justify the price they paid for it. So they start selling your merchandise to lots of big-box stores that you'd never dream of selling to in a million years. That works for a while, but when it doesn't keep making the money they want to make, they widen distribution to low-end discount stores. So instead of your main business being with your retailers that you really like, your A retailers, you start doing the majority of your business with the discount retailers, just trying to get that number every year. Whoever bought you out doesn't care about the integrity of your brand, or what it meant to you when you built it. That's not their job: they want to squeeze as many dollars as they can out of the brand, then move on to the next one. Whereas my goal with Famous has always been longevity. I'm proud that after sixteen years, we're still around doin' the damn thing.

In 2006, at the height of everything, Puff Daddy called me about buying Famous. We talked twice and I told him, "I'm flattered you love the brand, but I'm not looking to sell or looking to partner . . . I have a vision for what I'm going to do with it." I've got nothing but love and respect for Puffy: he's one of hip-hop's smartest businessmen—and he was the first person ever to stick me in a rap video, "Bad Boy for Life."

Then I got a call from Tommy Hilfiger's brother: "Hey, Tommy wants a meeting with you. We want to bring you into the Hilfiger family, and put you in our distribution network." I had a meeting with Tommy while I was out in New York, playing a show with AM. His offices were totally elaborate—five floors with crazy kiosks and displays—but at the end of the day, it wasn't my thing.

The buyout that came the closest to happening was with DC Shoes. I had a signature shoe with DC, and a good working relationship with Ken Block, one of the company's founders; they had made tons of money off my signature products. We wanted to get into the shoe market, and I wanted access to their factories in China and their technical department. We went through months of them looking at our financials: they knew everything about my company, the insides and the outsides, to the point where it was a little invasive.

Right before my television show hit, they were supposed to be putting an offer on the table for thirty million dollars; we were ready to counter at forty or fifty. Then on the day when they were supposed to send their offer over, DC Shoes got bought by Quiksilver, and that was the end of it. It was probably a blessing the deal didn't happen: I was always concerned they might have made Famous into an action sports brand, whereas I was shooting for a lifestyle brand more rooted in music.

One of our best-selling items ever is a simple T-shirt: it has Benjamin Franklin from the hundred-dollar bill, with a bandanna over his face like he was a stickup artist, and it says GET MONEY. There's been tons of robberies all over the world where the perpetrators were wearing that design on a T-shirt or a hoodie. We had many news channels calling us for comment, claiming that we were instigating people to steal money. But it was just a motivational slogan: Go get yours. Get some. *Not other people's.*

At this point, Famous is my idea of a well-oiled machine: we have about fifty employees, including a sales team, customer-service reps, the print shop, shipping and receiving, and warehouse employees.

A BEST-SELLING FAMOUS T-SHIRT: "GET MONEY"

People know that we have the infrastructure, and we're showing over and over that we can deliver.

In 2005, Johan Espensen and Rob Dyrdek came to me: they had this idea for shirts printed with a pattern of guns—machine guns and pistols. They had built all this hype around this would-be brand, and they already had seventy or eighty thousand dollars in orders, but they had no way to fulfill them. They said, "Let's become partners," and I agreed. We called the company Rogue Status. We turned the key, and bam—by the end of the first year, it was bringing in somewhere between $4 million and $10 million. We went on to merge Rogue Status into another brand called DTA, which Johan and I still own today. DTA stands for Don't Trust Anyone: don't trust the government, don't trust the cops, don't trust your scandalous ex-girlfriend.

GREG wEISMAN (GENERAL COUNSEL, FAMOUS STARS AND STRAPS)

There was a period in the late '90s, early 2000s, when every single music artist, especially in hip-hop, decided they wanted an apparel company, the way every celebrity in the '80s had a restaurant. It's no coincidence that it happened during a period when the music industry was undergoing tectonic changes. Dollars were no longer coming in as easily as they used to from the traditional sources. All the agents and managers who derive their income from trying to put money in the pockets of their artists said, "We'd better move into consumer goods because you can't make money selling a CD anymore."

So you saw a gold rush of artists, particularly musicians. Well, Travis had organically started this brand in '98-'99, before that big gold rush, and he did it out of a passion for the lifestyle that he grew up living, and that his disciples were all wearing. The passion for Famous is as deep as anything I've ever seen. There's hundreds, maybe thousands, of individuals who have the Famous Stars and Straps badge of honor logo tattooed on their bodies. Rick Ross, among others, has the Famous logo tattooed on him.

FELIX ARGUELLES (CONSULTANT, FAMOUS STARS AND STRAPS)

Anything that Travis is about, he tries to implement into his brand, which is cool. He once told me something, and I made it the eleventh commandment: "Band dies, brand dies." He's not going to be the face of the brand, waving the flag. He could give it a boost, but he doesn't want to, because when "band dies, brand dies." Spiritually, if you want to leave something behind, your days are numbered. But once you disconnect from it, you start to notice that you have an opportunity to do something greater than you.

JEREMY "TWITCH" STENBERG
(FREESTYLE MOTOCROSS RIDER AND OFF-ROAD TRUCK RACER)

I first met Trav on the Warped Tour in 1999. We were riding on the tour, and we tried to watch Blink play every day. Sometimes we would run into them leaving lunch. It was cool, because they were pumped on moto, just like we were pumped on them. After that, I ran into Trav a couple of times—we'd randomly hang out at a release party for twenty minutes. Then one of my deals ended, and I thought,

"Man, it'd be dope to ride for Famous." So I hit up Trav, and now I'm going on my fourth year with Famous.

People look at us and think we're assholes because of the tattoos. But if they take the time to talk to us and figure out our personalities, we're normal people. Travis is the humblest, nicest dude. I see people come up to him and try to be hard, and he's still the same dude: "Hey, what's up, man? Thanks for coming to the show." He has never put on a front and I admire that.

With a clothing brand, it comes down to creating a movement. How do people perceive your brand? When they buy one of your products from a retailer, do they feel a connection with you? A lot plays into that: how you market yourself, who you affiliate with, how good your brand is, how good you are to the people who buy your products.

We're very careful about the people that Famous sponsors: we don't want just the dopest athlete or the hottest musician. We want the guy who not only kills it at what he does, but clicks with us. Our entire Famous family hangs out together. Yelawolf and Hopsin go skateboarding all the time with our skate team. Twitch—Jeremy Stenberg—is a motocross rider, but he also has a gang of tattoos and a car collection. I work with Datsik and Hopsin: we all have similar interests, and when Twitch is riding in the X Games, we're all there watching him and supporting him. When A Day to Remember plays in LA, the entire Famous family shows up.

TIM MILHOUSE (FRIEND)

Blink got to a point where it was so big and such a machine, there were three drum techs. Travis needed to get somebody who knew what the fuck he was doing, so I stopped being his drum tech. I started a punk-rock band called the Kinison, and Travis's record label LaSalle ended up signing the band. I quit right before the band got signed. I was making a pretty good living with a real job at a university, and I was going to have to quit to get fifty dollars a week on tour. It just didn't make sense.

Travis was more in the party scene at that time, hanging out in LA and going to clubs. We kept in touch, but our lives were going in two different directions. But then somebody who was around at the beginning of Famous tried to sue Travis, saying *they* had started the brand. Out of nowhere, I got a phone call from Travis's lawyer about testifying on behalf of Travis and Famous about how the brand was started, because I was the only person in that room besides Travis and this other individual when the contracts were signed. I was on standby to come to court, but I never needed to: the case got thrown out or settled.

I heard about the plane crash, of course, and tried to call Travis. His voicemail was full and his e-mail was full. And then I started seeing interviews about Travis on MTV News by people like Jermaine Dupri. I thought, "Man, he's unreachable now."

But five months after that, I just e-mailed him: "Yo, what's up?"

Travis replied back right away: "What's going on?" And we started hanging out again. We reestablished our friendship and eventually I started working for Famous again; now I'm the marketing manager.

Personality-wise, Travis has stayed the same. His sense of humor has stayed the same. Money changes you—you can't help that. But I don't think he's forgotten where he comes from. He's stayed as grounded as you can at the level of success he has. He's always had a passion for girls, tattoos, music, cars. Now he just has bigger houses and more cars—it's just exaggerated.

AT A TATTOO SHOP: EARLY YEARS

Take Warning

Recently, I was driving to pick up my daughter from school. I was obeying the speed limit, and I wasn't even in a flashy car, like my Rolls-Royce or one of my lowriders. A cop was headed in the opposite direction, and I think the way I looked fucked him up. He pulled me over with his speakers on: "Put your hands out of the car!"

The cop came to my truck and started asking me what neighborhood I was from, what gang I was in, where I had done prison time, if I was still on probation, whether I had any weapons in the car. About four questions into this, I said, "What is wrong with you? What am I being pulled over for? You've got to be kidding me."

That was it: he made me get out of my truck, threw me up against his car, patted me down, detained me, put me in the back of his car with handcuffs on, and combed my car looking for weapons, drugs, anything. For the next forty-five minutes, he was pulling the seats out of my truck, he was looking under the carpet, everything—but there wasn't anything to find. I just sat in the back of his car, getting more pissed.

The cop looked through my wallet: "Okay, where did you get all the money from? I can't find anything in your truck—where did you hide it?"

"Hide what? What the fuck is your problem?"

"Where did you get all the money?"

"I *worked* for the money."

"What do you do?"

"I'm a musician—I play the drums."

"Yeah, right. For who?"

"Different bands."

"What bands, then?"

"Sometimes I play in a band called Blink-182. Other times I've played with Too Short, I've played with Eminem, I've played with T.I., I've played with the Transplants."

He began to realize he made a mistake. "Why didn't you say that when I pulled you over?" he asked.

"Officer, you didn't ask me if I was a musician when you pulled me over, or even give me a chance to speak. You asked me if I was a drug dealer, what neighborhood I was from, and where I had done prison time. You didn't once give me an opportunity to tell you I was a musician—not that it should matter who I am."

"That's bullshit!" He was acting like I had been trying to trap him.

"It's not bullshit—you were being unreasonable."

"Do you have any idea what I go through on a daily basis?"

"I don't care what you go through on a daily basis. You're a cop and that's what you signed up for. You were in the wrong, man. You looked at my tattoos and assumed something that wasn't true. My friend back home is a cop and he doesn't act like this."

He uncuffed me and claimed that he had pulled me over because I didn't have a front license plate. He kind of finger-wagged me like he was trying to make me feel guilty for the infraction—as if he wanted me to apologize for *something*. But I wouldn't.

"You have issues," I told him.

"If you have anything else to say," he said, "I'm going to have to detain you and take you in."

I just walked away.

Anytime I'm having a bad day, I know things could be much worse—I experienced that firsthand. It takes more energy to be negative than to be positive: I try to turn all my negative energy into something positive, even when it feels like everything sucks. Everybody has highs and lows, but I've decided that how we overcome bad situations defines who we are as human beings, and I'm trying every day to be a better human being.

My kids go to a nice school, and sometimes, when I pick them up or drop them off, the other parents look at me sideways. On Landon's first day of school there—he just had orientation for a couple of hours, so rather than drive all the way home and back, I hung out in the parking lot, sitting by a bush, playing on my phone—a security guard came over and said, "Someone said they saw you smoking and peeing in a bush."

I laughed and said, "Look, man, I imagine I look different from every other parent that has a kid at this school, but I wasn't peeing in the bush and I wasn't smoking a cigarette, so please don't accuse me of that."

"Well, other parents said they saw you."

I was annoyed, but I just said, "No, I'm sorry, that's not what happened. I'm just standing outside, killing time until my son gets out."

They were mostly cool after that; years later, I donated one and a half million dollars to the school so they could have a music program.

I do my best to learn from my mistakes and teach my kids accordingly, but while I do my best to maintain my cool—for *their* sake, at the very least—Lord knows I have been tested.

I had a big confrontation with a gang of paparazzi in Calabasas. When I moved in, it was a pretty anonymous neighborhood, but a couple of years later, other celebrities started moving in. Britney Spears bought a house near me, Justin Bieber lived next door to me for a while, and now his old house is occupied by the Kardashians. It's a gated community, but the paparazzi cluster outside the gates so they can follow stars' cars when they drive out. So sometimes I would leave home with the kids, just to get breakfast at a local place, and a whole convoy would follow us.

THE KIDS GOOFING OFF

One day, I walked up to one of these photographers: I knew he was the leader of this whole crew of paparazzi. I said, "Look, I know you got a job to do, but I got three kids. And sometimes you guys run up with eight guys, and you really scare my kids. If you really need to take my picture, could you tone it down? Like, come with *two*. I won't even be a dick. I'll let you take a picture; I'll let you film me."

He said, "Travis, I'm sorry, absolutely."

The very next day, it's 7:30 in the morning, and I'm walking into the breakfast place with Bama, Landon, and Atiana. Some photographer got in my face with a camera. "What's up, Trav, what are you going to do now?"

I said, "Dude, what's your problem? Get out of here—get your fucking camera out of my face."

"Why? What are you going to do?" This guy thought he was intimidating me, and he was pushing me to the limit. So I pushed him out of the way and I spat on him.

He said, "What the fuck, man?"

I said, "Meet me out here in forty-five minutes, after I finish my breakfast, and I'll show you what I'm going to do." I went in to get breakfast—while I was eating, I looked out the window, and I could see a gang of seven paparazzi out there. So I called Skinhead Rob and Cheese and told them to roll down. I explained what had happened and said that I was going to put a stop to this once and for all. I also called the kids' nanny, Judy, and told her to meet me at this restaurant.

When Rob and Cheese arrived, we walked out together. Of course, the hotheaded guy who was sticking the camera in my face was nowhere to be seen. But there was a whole bunch of other dudes, including two sitting in a car who I recognized from when they had been hassling my family before.

Cheese, Rob, and I pulled the two of them out of the car, and it turned into a pushing and shoving match. I was trying to get them to hit me so we could settle it once and for all, but they wouldn't even push back.

It's all on tape—they were filming the whole time. As soon as they saw us walking up, they pressed "record" on their cameras. It's bad footage, because the cameras ended up on the ground. People were leaving the parking lots and screaming. Judy was taking my kids to the Escalade—unfortunately,

before they left, they had a plain view of everything that was going on and they were scared to death. I felt awful that they were witnessing the confrontation, but I had been pushed to my limit.

Eventually, the police showed up. They took a statement from the paparazzi and then came over to me. "They said you stole a camera," the policeman said.

"Yeah, we took a camera," I told him. I had no problem giving the camera back, but I explained, "These guys got in my face and basically challenged me to a fight. If I'm out acting a fool with some girl or doing something stupid, they have every right to document me—I have a good rapport with paparazzi in other parts of Los Angeles who are cool and respectful. But I'm sick and tired of these guys running up on me, following me home, coming up eight deep and antagonizing me when I'm taking my kids to lunch. I've had it, man."

The cops basically told everyone to go home, and nobody pressed charges against anybody—and the paparazzi never bothered me in Calabasas again.

After that was when I started training in mixed martial arts. I've learned both boxing and jujitsu. They became my new addiction and gave me discipline I never had before.

A week or two later, I was in the car with the kids when another driver cut me off. I was heated.

Bama freaked out, saying, "Oh my God, don't do it, Dad!" She thought the whole thing was going to play out again. I knew I had caused that, and it felt awful. *You know what?* I thought. *If somebody cuts me off, big deal. I'm with the kids in the car.*

I told her I wasn't getting out of the car, and I wasn't getting into a fight. Then I started learning: even when I didn't have the kids in the car, it was no big deal. I can't control everybody else on the road, or anything around me—except for myself. I'm a big believer now in PMA—positive mental attitude. Even when I'm not consciously thinking about it, I have to set a good example for my kids. That goes for everything from my work ethic to how I handle hostile situations—who I am today determines who they will be in the future.

COURTESY OF CHRIS ROQUE

Lets start today

In January 2013, I got an e-mail from my homie Z-Trip, a DJ who had also been really good friends with AM. It said, "Hey, Trav, LL Cool J and I are playing the Grammys and he wants to know if you'll be down to rock with us. Tom Morello from Rage Against the Machine is going to be part of it as well, and Chuck D from Public Enemy." It was only January, but I was already fucking *loving* 2013.

A week before the Grammys, we all got together in my studio to rehearse LL's song "Whaddup." Z and I were there first: we were reminiscing about old times with AM. Then LL showed up: that was cool, not only because he's LL and I grew up on him, but because I was playing with somebody else who had history with AM and me, from the time we did the MTV Video Music Awards together.

We started figuring out the song. LL told me, "Fuck, Trav, if I have you, I want you to go crazy on the drums to this shit. I want it to be wild in the end—but it has to have a crazy intro too. Within the first twenty seconds, I want you to do a drum solo. And then I want the song to keep

building and building and building." I was sitting there, trying to figure out what the definition of *wild* was. What it ended up meaning for me and Tom Morello was double-timing at the end while the sound got bigger, almost like how a Rage song would end up. We played through twice—it wasn't even the final arrangement, but we could tell it was rocking. And we didn't even have Chuck D yet—LL said, "Chuck's going to come through, but he's at Home Depot right now."

LL called up Ken Ehrlich, the executive producer for the Grammys, and told him how hyped he was. So the fourth time we ever played the song together, the Grammys' main guy was standing there witnessing it in my studio. The next day, I showed up for rehearsal and LL was wearing a Famous "Family" shirt. I was thinking, *Damn, this is awesome.* Rehearsal went great and LL invited me to the official Grammy dinner, but I was on dad duty that night with the kids. We ran through the song five or six more times: Chuck D was there, and every time he said, "Let the drummer get wicked," it was like my childhood came through the wall, smashing me in the face. When we weren't practicing, I was listening to the song everywhere I went, for hours and hours, and figuring out what I wanted to do in my drum solo. Landon and Bama learned the song and would bounce off the walls and do karaoke, pretending they were LL and Chuck D. I loved that I was exposing them to great music—and in this case, legends.

The day of the Grammys, we agreed to meet backstage before we played and make sure we were all on the same page. LL was busy hosting the show, but the rest of us got together. Tom and I played that section maybe twenty times together to get in sync. And the next thing I knew, somebody with a walkie-talkie said, "We're ready to walk you out." Once you're out on that stage, there's no room for thinking, and there's no room for error. You just go out there and kick some ass.

Nothing against the other people who played, but we had the craziest performance of the night. I had LL and Chuck D crowding around my drum kit, and Chuck D hyping me up, pointing at me to do my solo. Z-Trip was rocking, and Tom Morello was making the craziest sounds on the guitar. There were no spaceships or people floating from the rafters. It was white lights and us rocking the fuck out. When we got offstage, I said to myself, "If I never played another gig, I could be happy." I guess I had that feeling every time I played the Grammys.

Blink-182 were doing an annual tour, heading all around the world and even headlining festivals in Europe for over a hundred thousand people. But Tom wasn't going out of his way to make anyone feel like he wanted to be there. He'd show up just before the tour started and act introverted. Then, as we started playing shows and money started coming in, he'd get excited about Blink again.

Around this time, he abruptly quit the band; he e-mailed me and Mark saying that he was through with the band, and with us. Then the next day, he e-mailed us again, saying that we should forget everything he just said, and he wanted Tony Robbins to do group therapy with the three of us. He even had his manager forward Tony Robbins all the e-mails we had been sending back and forth. Apparently, he and Tony had a conversation about it, but we had no interest in meeting with Tony.

A few months later, the Transplants finally finished our third album, *In a Warzone*. Rob and I had been smoking more blunts than ever before: maybe ten or twelve a day, for a couple of months straight, all Backwoods. I loved everything about them, down to the paper they were wrapped in. Smoking weed had never seemed like heavy drug use to me, especially since I had stopped using everything else: I was just lighting up a plant, something that was produced by the earth.* But about a week after we

finished the album, I had a weird feeling in my throat, like there was a piece of food stuck there that I couldn't get out. I went so far as to stick my fingers down my throat and vomit, but it didn't go away, and I couldn't figure

WITH TOM MORELLO, Z-TRIP, AND CHUCK D
AT THE GRAMMY AWARDS.
COURTESY OF ERIC VOAKE

* Pink Floyd's *Wish You Were Here* was the soundtrack to my life for a decade.

out what it was. I kept stressing about this bump in my throat: it was beginning to haunt me. I didn't feel like I was sick: it just felt like there was a lump in my throat, or like somebody was trying to choke me.

Then I started having anxiety attacks. One day at the studio, I felt so weak, I could barely stand up. In the middle of the night I would wake up, having full-blown panic attacks. So I went to an ear, nose, and throat doctor. I visited him three times. He kept doing procedure after procedure, sticking shit down my throat, and at the end he didn't really know what it was: he said maybe it was an infection or maybe my sinuses, but it felt like he was just guessing. He even thought it might be because of the tattoos on my head: when he said that, I just laughed and found another doctor.

After visiting several other ENTs, I finally went to see a gastroen-terologist, and the first thing he said was, "We need to get you on an IV—you look terrible." So I got admitted to this little hospital for three hours while he put me on an IV and did blood work. Then he said, "I think we need to do an endoscopy on you—I hate to think that it's a GI problem, but if your ENT isn't finding anything, we need to check it out." So I agreed to the procedure. I went into surgery the next morning: they knocked me out and stuck a tube down my throat so they could look at my stomach and esophagus.

The next day, he called me and said, "You have eight ulcers and a syndrome called Barrett's esophagus. There are precancerous cells lin-ing your entire esophagus." He immediately put me on medicine for the ulcers, told me to stop smoking right away, and ordered an endoscopy every three months.

I called up my friend Dr. Brian Weeks: "He says I have Barrett's esophagus—what does that mean?"

He said, "Trav, that is a huge warning shot. I suggest you listen to it. Barrett's esophagus is irreversible, so there's no chance of it ever get-ting better: your esophagus doesn't repair itself like that. But there is a chance of it getting worse. And once you develop esophageal cancer, your chances aren't good."

So that was it: I needed to sober up. After my plane crash, I wasn't taking any other drugs—but I figured if the one thing I did was smoke

weed, it wasn't that big a deal. I had always pictured myself being like Willie Nelson, smoking into my eighties. But apparently the combination of excessive smoking and crazy stress was a problem. I stopped smoking right away and I've never smoked since: I heard that warning loud and clear, and I respected it.

Life is like a credit card. Whatever you put on that card, you're going to pay for it. Tomorrow's not promised, but whatever you do to your body, however you spend your time—if it's not good for you, you'll end up paying the price someday.

I had to relearn how to do everything sober. I hadn't been sober for almost twenty years. I had to drive sober, I had to go to sleep sober, I had to face my problems sober. Finding my rhythm in the studio was especially painful. I had to go on tour sober, go on live television sober: I didn't have anything to mask any of my nervous jitters. It was all gone.

If I like something, I get addicted to it. A buddy of mine told me that he liked to have a cigarette now and then, every couple of weeks. The thing is, if I smoked one cigarette, I'd be out the door before I finished it, heading to the store to buy a carton. Everything in my life that I've ever had, I wanted in abundance: pills, sex, weed. So when I finally got sober, I replaced it all with working out and drumming—even more than I used to. They became my new addictions.

I was already running every day, but I started taking boxing classes, learning jujitsu, doing an hour and a half of cardio a day. Those give me a major buzz. I started off not knowing anything about jujitsu, but I love learning. I love training hard, and I like seeing people work hard at something they love. I don't watch reality TV where someone's going shopping or starting arguments: I like to watch shows like countdowns to UFC fights and *All Access,* where boxers and mixed martial artists train for seven or eight weeks, get ready for a fight, and then win. Most of my life, I call the shots, whether it's with my clothing company or a solo album. I like taking a martial arts class where somebody is pushing me around and kicking my ass. I don't always want to be in control.

Even though I was forced out of smoking and drinking, I'm proud of myself for staying clean. Recently, I went to a party in Vegas, and it was chaos. A bunch of girls at my table were asking me to do shots, and it felt weird not to be part of it. For a moment, I thought it might be okay: *I've been sober a year and a half, I could have a shot.* There was nobody telling me not to, but I just didn't let myself go down that road. I filled up my shot glass with water and began taking shots with the girls. They had no idea.

After nights like that, I have user dreams that I've started smoking weed again: they're actually nightmares, because I don't know how I'm going to quit and I'm crushed by the guilt from being a terrible father. I'm addicted, I know the kids are going to find out, and I'm so disappointed in myself. It's terrible to think that I might grow old and die without being the person that I want to be—even when it's only in my dreams.

I was recently chopping it up with my buddy Kurt Sutter.* It's been inspirational getting to know him: I don't really have friends who are sober, other than Tim Armstrong and Toby Morse, but Kurt has been clean for twenty-five years now. The day that would have been AM's forty-second birthday, I told Kurt how on days like that, days that are particularly profound for me like the anniversary of the plane crash, I

---

* The creator of the excellent show *Sons of Anarchy.* He's a cool motherfucker.

SELFIE WITH ALABAMA AND LANDON

just want to smoke a joint or take enough pills to fall asleep. But I've come to understand how my drug use was just a vicious cycle: it masked my problems, but it didn't solve them. I always had excuses for why I needed to be taking drugs. Kurt said to me, "Substance abuse keeps us away from the love and it distances us from the truth. You're a fucking seeker, Travis, and you've got a lot more to discover."

I love being clearheaded and attentive. When I used to be high all the time, I couldn't work out or go running any time of the day, because I was so high and numb, and sometimes I couldn't answer questions or figure things out. It feels so good to actually be living life without drugs controlling the experience—and to be able to remember what happened the next day. AM used to tell me, "Sober up and really feel your feelings"—I've been much happier since I followed that advice. I need to stay clean, and I need to stay healthy. Landon is eleven years old and Alabama is nine. I was only thirteen years old when my mom died—I want to make sure that I'm around for them much longer than that. The best feeling in the world is being with my family and kids. We listen to the same music—everything from punk rock to hip-hop. We dance, we sing, we skateboard, we ride dirt bikes, we drum, we laugh. There's nothing I enjoy more than being with them.

The kids see me get tattoos all the time: sometimes I'll have two or three artists come over and work on me at the same time. They understand how they're a permanent part of who I am. I'm not into removing tattoos. They're all memories. Some people say "Fuck, man, it would be so dope to get rid of everything and get tattooed all over again." But they're all experiences that I went through. I got them all for a reason. Getting rid of them would be like tearing a page out of a book. It's not going to happen, so I keep them all.

The kids are welcome to get tattooed themselves when they reach the legal age of consent—I just want them to come to me first, since I know so many of the world's best tattoo artists. Landon and Alabama have already tattooed me themselves: one time when Chuey Quintanar and Franco Vefovi were working on me, they asked if they could use the equipment and then they took over a section of my left thigh.

When Alabama was just three, she made up a song that she sang around the house: "Daddy's in my way-way / Mommy's in my way-way / Ati's in my way-way / Landon's in my way-way / Woof-Woof's in my way-way / Diamond's in my way-way / cat's in my way-way / apple's in my way-way . . ." From a young age, she knew she was the boss! And when Landon was six, he got upset and wrote a song of his own: "Water in my eyes / Nothing can disguise / Just me, myself, and I / Just me, myself, and I." From an early age, they were both songwriters full of self-expression.

Shanna and I will never be a couple again, but I'm connected to her for the rest of my life: she's the mother of my children. I'm really happy that she's moved on and got a new boyfriend. Even though things didn't work out with me and Shanna, we ended up with these amazing kids. I wouldn't take back having them for anything. For them, I would do anything, and I would go through the worst parts of my life all over again. For my kids, I would be in a plane crash again. For their sake, I want everything to go well for her.

GETTING BLASTED BY BIG SLEEPS AND CHUEY QUINTANAR AT THE FAMOUS BODEGA.
COURTESY OF CLEMENTE RUIZ

SHANNA MOAKLER (EX-WIFE)

I wish Travis would allow himself to enjoy everything that he's worked so hard for. But I've seen him grow into a really awesome, strong man. I think he's a phenomenal father. He's really romantic and really thoughtful when he wants to be. One time he put a thousand purple balloons in the foyer of the house and then had a purple limo take us to the Prince concert. Now he puts all that love and attention on Alabama.

Even though Shanna and I haven't been together for years, Atiana is still part of my family. Many weekends, when I have custody of the kids, I take her too. She's come on tour with me, she goes to Disneyland with us, she goes to the Grammys with me. She's sixteen now, and I've always tried my hardest not to alienate her, even after the divorce. She's my daughter and I love her.

Since the plane crash, I haven't gone on a tour without my kids: it's good for them, and it's good for me. I haven't flown since my crash, but I built a bus called the Stormtrooper that became our traveling home.* That only works for the United States, so whenever I'm playing gigs in Europe, I take the *Queen Mary 2* there and back: it takes seven days each way. You can have time or money, but you can't have both: that's doubly true when it comes to your family.

GUS BRANDT (FORMER TOUR MANAGER FOR BLINK-182)

When the band got back together after the crash, Travis took the *Queen Mary 2* from Brooklyn to Southampton. It was funny because cruises, especially this one, are filled with people who have saved up, and it's very nice and ornate. Travis had his own enclave at the front of the ship, with his own butler, who was in charge of getting him vegan food. When we checked in, John Cleese was one line over—I didn't tell Travis until later, because he was in his own world with the kids. It was him, two kids, the nanny, a security guard, and Jack, his assistant—and everyone was wearing Famous clothes. Travis had all his Louis Vuitton luggage, and then trash bags full of toys and food. It was the funniest juxtaposition with these prim and proper people on the cruise—all very Beverly Hillbillies. They were looking at him like he was a scum-bag, when he could buy and sell them a hundred times over.

People who have any preconceived notion about Travis are almost always taken aback, because he's so soft-spoken and quiet. He has a temper, but I've seen it very rarely.

---

* This is probably a bad idea: I have a Google Alert for plane crashes. My psycho ass always wants to know about them, but I always trip when I read about them, because I've been through it.

TRAVIS BARKER
can i say

On my first transatlantic crossing, though, the *Queen Mary 2* wasn't available for the trip home, so we took a slightly smaller cruise ship back to the States. The weather on that trip was awful: thirty-five-foot waves and winds going 170 miles per hour. It went on for day after day; at least when a plane hits turbulence, it's over ten minutes later, maybe an hour tops. But this went on for six days. That's when I started to think, *Maybe I should have flown.**

Then I imagine the worst-case scenario: if the plane crashed over the ocean, I'd be exactly where I am right now. And at least *this* motherfucker floats. Traveling is difficult for me in general: I'm always expecting the worst or bracing myself for impact. On the ship, I put all our life vests right by the bed—just in case. If anything happened, I wanted us be the first ones on the lifeboats. When you take the *Queen Mary 2* west, from Europe to America, they have a party when you reach the location where the *Titanic* sank, playing the soundtrack from the movie—which is spooky and uncomfortable.

Even on the boat, I'm always training and playing drums to stay on my A game, but I never know what for. My kids used to ask me, "Dad, what are you practicing for?"

"Just to practice."

"You don't have a show this week."

"That's right. I don't need to have a show. I have to be good at what I do and continue to get better." They understand that you don't just wake up one day and you're a great musician and you're famous. Recently, when I got off the boat in New York, I got an e-mail from Daniel, my drum tech, asking if I wanted to play on *America's Got Talent*. I got the music less than twenty-four hours before the performance, and performed on live TV with a crazy acrobatic group called Acro Army. These last-minute appearances are usually the most fun things in my career: playing with Steve Aoki on *Jimmy Kimmel*, doing a YG show at the House of Blues,

---

* It bums me out, but there's no good way for me to go to Australia, Japan, and South America without flying. There are some cruise ships that go to those locations, but only as part of an around-the-world tour. So if I went to Australia for a tour, I'd have to spend five months traveling west to get back home. Maybe someday.

playing on Chris Brown's big comeback performance on BET after he got out of jail—I practiced that one a hundred times, but when it was live, I just freestyled it. Those are usually my favorite performances.

Just a week later, Demi Lovato sent me a text, inviting me to come to her show with the kids. The night before, she asked me if I would play with her. I got the music, and when I got there, I found out she and I were doing a drum solo together. It ended up being awesome, and it wouldn't have been as much fun if there had been a week to practice.

After growing up watching wrestling with my father, it was a dream come true to play halftime at WrestleMania 31. Kid Ink asked if I would play with him, and then a week later, Skylar Grey asked if I would play with her. We decided to combine the two performances to make a more spectacular show. I went to San Jose: there were 80,000 people in that stadium alone, and another seventy million watching on TV. And it wasn't just kids—in the front row, I could see Jimmy Iovine and Rick Rubin. It had more intense production than any rock show I had ever played: we would finish a song and pyrotechnics would go off all over the stadium.

Right before the last Blink-182 tour, Tom sent me a message, saying he was going to be in LA the next day. I told him to hit me up: we ended up going to my restaurant Crossroads, and we had a really cool time. We chilled and talked about our families. Halfway through the dinner, Tom said, "Do you know I've never gotten to eat a dinner with you?" All those years we've known each other, we had never just kicked it like that. It was great to finally hang out together, not on a tour, and really connect as people again.

It didn't last. Blink-182 were supposed to go into the studio to record a new album in early 2015—we hadn't released a full album since *Neighborhoods* in 2011 (although we did put out a holiday EP called *Dogs Eating Dogs*), and we kept promising fans that new music was on the way. I thought it seemed weird to keep touring with no new material, like every day was Throwback Thursday.

Tom didn't want to go into the studio unless Blink had a new record deal, so we got one lined up. We agreed that we would start recording on January 5th: we were booking space and setting everything up. The idea was that we would take over an entire house, just like we did with the *Blink-182* album. At eight PM on New Year's Eve, I got an e-mail from Tom's manager, saying that he was out. We sent a bunch of messages back and forth, and the bottom line was clear: Tom didn't want to record. He wouldn't be doing anything Blink-related in 2015. The manager said he didn't know if he ever would be doing anything with Blink again.

In some ways, it was a relief: after years of back-and-forth with Tom, we knew where we stood. You can't make people do something they don't want to do: I genuinely wanted Tom to go do whatever was going to make him happy. And since this was the third time he had abruptly left the band, it was pretty clear what he wanted. But we had one gig lined up: the band had committed to play at the Musink Festival, a tattoo/cars/music festival that I was curating. We met Matt Skiba of Alkaline Trio for lunch at Crossroads and asked him if he would play the show with us. His response was "Fuck yeah!" We issued a statement saying that Tom had left the band indefinitely and Matt would be playing the show with us; Tom then denied he had quit the band.

Even practicing for that show was a blast—I was having more fun playing those songs than I had in years. Matt was excited to be there, and that made a huge difference. We did some warm-up shows, and the fans were chanting "Skiba! Skiba!" every night. We had great chemistry, and at Musink, we killed it.[*]

We want to get in the studio with Matt as soon as possible. There's legal issues to work out with Tom, but I'm excited to make new music. Last year, I was dreading these sessions, but now I'm stoked. Blink-182 isn't the only thing I do musically, but I still love and respect the band, and when I play with Blink, I don't try to make it sound like one of my side projects.

---

[*] Curating Musink has become one of my favorite things. Bill Hardy invited me to do it in 2014, and I had such a great time, I ended up becoming part-owner. It's a festival/convention that encompasses everything I love: tattoos, classic cars, and music. We have five hundred of the world's best tattoo artists setting up shop. We showcase over forty drop-dead gorgeous cars. And the bands in 2015 included Yelawolf, Prayers, Bad Religion, Off!, Ignite, Rancid, The Interrupters, Sick of It All, and Blink-182's first show with Matt. It's a different feeling when you're surrounded by friends and family, not just some random bands that you booked.

I owe Tom a lot, starting with the day that he thought I would be a good emergency fill-in drummer. He'll always be an important person in my life, and I hope that he finds the happiness he's looking for.

Every morning in LA , when I'm driving home from dropping the kids off at school, I talk to my Pops. When I was a kid, I was just such a fucking donkey sometimes: I was a pain in the ass, and I think he was worried I was going to amount to nothing, so he was constantly having to yell at me or discipline me. It makes me really proud that I not only met his standards in my life, but hopefully have gone beyond. I love my father and we're closer than we've ever been.

I want Pops to be able to chill, but he has no interest in retiring. He works for Famous, and he helps me take care of my car collection because we share the same passion for cars. Just recently, the steering column in my '63 Impala was loose, so he took it upon himself to send it to some guy back east who specializes in rebuilding Impala steering columns. Right now, I'm helping Pops with his 1957 Cadillac Coupe de Ville. We're putting an LS3 motor in it, courtesy of my friend Delmo, and painting it black cherry. We're enjoying our classic car addiction—together.

Not long ago, Pops had a health scare: he collapsed on the floor of my house. I rushed him to the emergency room, and he stayed for about two weeks while they did tests and tried to figure out what was going on. He was in the same hospital in Fontana where my mom died: I tried to move him to Cedars-Sinai, but he didn't want to go. Whenever I pulled into the parking lot, it was the weirdest downer. But that whole experience underlined how important our time together is, because it could be taken away at any point.

I have a ritual before I go onstage: I say a prayer, name all the people I've known and loved who have passed, and think about them. It used to be very short, and my mom was the only person on the list. But I've lost a lot of people along the way, including Chris, Che, and AM. Now I have to stop for several minutes and run through the whole list—but it reminds me how lucky I am to be alive, and how much those people have meant in my life.

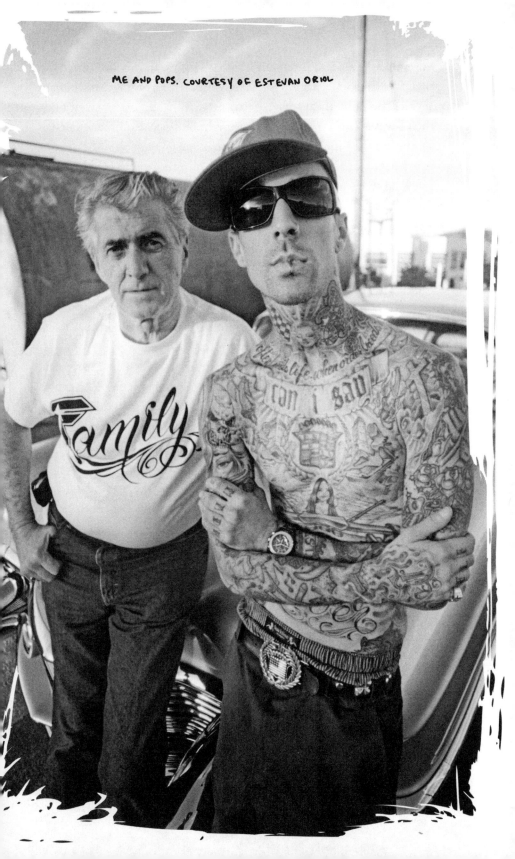
ME AND POPS. COURTESY OF ESTEVAN ORIOL

I've always wanted to remain humble and grounded. I've never for-gotten where I came from. No matter what success brings, my biggest priorities are (and always have been) my family, fans, and loved ones. When I was a kid, I dreamed that I might be a pro drummer someday, even if it was just for a night. I hoped that maybe, just once, I might be onstage in front of a thousand people. What my life has turned into is so far beyond that—once I achieved my dreams, I worked so hard to keep them alive, and to go even further, outdoing my own expectations. One of the greatest things about my success is that I can give back to my family: I help out my sisters, and I make sure Pops has a nice house to live in.

I want to spend as much time as I can with my children. I don't know how long I'll be around; tomorrow isn't promised to anyone. But as long as I'm alive, I want to be with them and to guide them. I get to introduce the kids to everything I love: teaching them drums, taking them to car shows, drawing fake tattoos on them.

I have trunks filled with every piece of art they've ever made. I love stay-ing home with the kids. I'll shave Landon's head and give him a Mohawk, and I'll braid Alabama's hair. My sisters taught me how to braid hair when I was a kid, so there are times when I feel like I'm Mom and Pops at the

SATURDAY MORNING MUSIC LESSONS AT THE BARKER HOUSE

LANDON DRUMMING ONSTAGE WITH ME.
COURTESY OF CHRIS ROQUE

same time. But I wouldn't trade it for the world—I even take Bama to get her nails done sometimes.

Every day starts with waking up, getting the kids' breakfasts ready, and taking them to school. Then I head to the studio or the gym, depending on what day it is. We do all the after-school activities as a family. Mondays, I pick them up from school and we play tennis together. Tuesdays, I pick them up and we go to boxing. They do the kids' class and I do an adult class. Wednesdays, it's jujitsu. Thursdays, Alabama has cheerleading and Landon has basketball. Fridays, Alabama has gymnastics and Landon has boxing. On Saturdays, Alabama has cheerleading in the morning: adults aren't allowed to watch, so I'll sit in my truck, drumming on a practice pad. On Sundays, the kids have singing lessons and drum lessons.

I give the drum lessons: both of them want to do what Dad does. They see how hard I work.

There is no glory in practice, but without practice, there is no glory.

At Landon's tenth birthday party, he played a set on drums with a young DJ, E-Fresh, who's ridiculously good. They played three songs: Eminem's "Berserk," House of Pain's "Jump Around," and the Beastie Boys' "(You Gotta) Fight for Your Right (to Party!)." I got them a stage, and they were really serious about it. A bunch of their friends all wanted to be roadies and drum techs. I thought I was going to be coaching Landon during the set, but he was killing it—I didn't need to say anything to him the whole performance.

I could see Pops over to one side during Landon's set: he was crying. At the end, he came up to me and said, "Pal, this really brings back memories for me. It makes me think of when you were young." Everything came full circle: my father used to watch me pound on the drums when I was a little kid, and now we were both watching Landon. I call Landon "pal" and I call Alabama "cookie"—the nicknames of my parents. Everything comes around. Pops made a man out of me. I love him for that, and I can't thank him enough for how he raised me. I hope I can do the same for my kids.

When I go to Alabama's cheerleading competitions, I can't even scream her name, because I'm so choked up—but I can't get too emotional, because I'm supposed to be her dad, supporting her. I'm unbelievably proud of her: everywhere her team goes, they seem to win first or second place. Landon and I are always there: we root for each other as a family. I can't even believe that my kids are doing the things that they're doing, and performing in front of other people—I know what that's like.

It kills me how fast they're growing up. I want to keep them young as long as possible. Landon is already having play dates and sleepovers at other people's houses. He likes the same music as me now: I can't put on Radio Disney to make him happy anymore, because he thinks it's babyish. Bama walks around the house in high heels and I overhear her talking about crushes she has at school. But both of them still think that Santa Claus is real. They argue about it sometimes, but when they do, I tell them they're crazy. They fight me on the Tooth Fairy, and I say, "No, that bitch is real. She comes to the crib late at night."

Alabama made up a family kiss. First you do a butterfly kiss (with your eyelashes), then an Eskimo kiss (rubbing noses), and then a regular kiss (with your lips). That's how we kiss each other: they don't like to do it in front of their friends now, but if either of them ever leaves the house without doing the three-part kiss with me, they'll say that it feels weird and come back to do it.

I am always proud to take the kids on tour: sometimes we've been in arenas with Blink or Lil Wayne and sometimes we've been in dirty punk-rock venues with the Transplants, but either way it's fun as hell. On a day off, we'll break away and spend the day at a water park, or get on our bikes and go exploring. Every day I wake up, I'm living the dream. The other night, I played drums with the Misfits and Run the Jewels, all within a single hour. I love what I do. Every single day, my goal is to be the best father, musician, friend, and person that I can be.

When I was growing up, I never thought I'd make it to my twenty-first birthday. When I turned twenty-one, I thought I'd die before I turned twenty-three, and so on down the line. I never once worried about the consequences of anything. I just did what I wanted. Once I said that I wanted to die before I got old—boy, was that stupid. Now I've made it to thirty-nine years old, and I'm the happiest I've ever been.

I've got a lot of life to live—I'm only halfway done. This book isn't the end of my story.

ME AND THE KIDS

OUR FAMILY'S BELOVED FRENCHIES

Acknowledgements

'd like to thank God, my amazing mother Gloria (RIP Cookie); my amazing dad (Pal) and Mary; my awesome sisters Randalai and Tamara; my humans Landon, Alabama, and Atiana; Brandt and Kelsie, Britney and Brandon. And thank you to Mark Hoppus, Lawrence "LV" Vavra, Paul Rosenberg, Kev-e-Kev, Sophie McNeil, everybody at Deckstar, Killer Distribution, Famous Family, Tim Milhouse, Felix, Luca, Angel Rubio, Jason Redwood and the entire art team, my brothers Skinhead Rob and Tim Armstrong, DTA Posse, Dr. B, Matt Skiba, Noel Paris, Randy Stewart, Frank Velasquez, Mike Ensch, Dana White and the UFC, Steve Aoki, my brother Yelawolf, Twitch, Dominick Cruz, Travis Browne, Mix Master Mike and Dianne, Neal H. Pogue, James Ingram, Daniel and Kristen Jensen, everybody at Zildjian and OCDP, Remo, Brian (Big Bass) Gardner, Christian Jacobs and all the Aquabats, Jack "Cheese" Altounian, Armen Amirkhanian, Pascal, Paul Wall, my awesome attorney Lisa Socransky Austin, Greg Weisman, Chuey Quintanar, Franco Vescovi, Mr. Cartoon, Willie Toledo, Estevan Oriol, Mark Vaillancourt, Big Boy, Chris Roque, Kevin (Shock) Bivona, Jimmy (Shruggs) Gully, Deora, Afrojack, John Sanchez, Chris Siglin, Ruben Marietta, Jaycen Joshua, Ryan Leonard, Chris Light, Ryron Gracie and the entire Gracie family, Lil Wayne, Tony Jeffries and everyone at Box n Burn, John Caleb, James Rasmussen, Killer Mike and El-P from Run the Jewels, Cedric and Omar from Antemasque, Tim Wade, Liz Catana, Judy Nduati, Joanie Morris, Y.G., Meg Dieter, Brian McClellan, Peter Grossman, Kurt

Richards, everyone at Grossman Burn Center, Bun B, the Game, Big Egypt, Big C. Dreads, Ezec (Danny Diablo), Gus Brandt, Chad Noyes, Clemente Ruiz, Darryl Eaton, Terry Doty, Edgar Sanchez, D Face, Jeff Gelinas and the whole Gelinas family, Shepard Fairey, Flea, Bill Fold, Paul Tollett, Skylar Grey, DJ Ill Will, Kid Ink, Rick Ross, Ice-T, Jesse Ignjatovic, Rodney Jerkins, Josh Brenner, Sabina Kelly, Dr. Khalsa, Kojak, Demi Lovato, Puff Daddy, Bad Lucc, Problem, Modsun, Toby Morse, Rip Hayes, Rafael and Dave from Prayers, everybody at LaSalle Records, Jody (Riffraff Highroller), Laura Walter, Samantha, Jonathan Simon, Aaron Spears, Keith Sutter, Timo, Tyga, Ty Dolla $ign, Iamsu!, Wiz Khalifa, Usugrow, Cy Wallace, everybody at Active Ride Shop, Z-Trip, Huero, Wacks, Power 106, DJ E-Man, Eric Dlux, Jeff G., Krystal Vee, Myles Kovacs and everybody at Dub, George Keshishyan and everybody at Platinum Motorsports, Will Power (Supa Hot Beats), Tilly's, Luke Burnett and Charis, Dalton at Hillview Customs, Dell Uschenko at Delmo Speed Shop, KROQ, Ray Coomer, Brent Vann, A-Trak, Shanna Moakler, Big Sleeps, Slaughterhouse, Mouse Lopez, Rudy Ruiz, Woody Dutton, Melissa Kennedy, and Ultimate Ronnie.

A *big* thank you to Gavin Edwards. I couldn't have written this with anybody else. You made life into a book, you are fucking awesome!

R.I.P.: Thank you Che Still, Lil Chris Baker, Adam "DJ AM" Goldstein, Trigz, Paulie B, Stuart Teggart, Gary Haber, and Proof for all the good memories. Forever miss you, my brothers.

SELECTED DISCOGRAPHY
AND GUEST APPEARANCES

COURTESY OF WILLIE TOLEDO

THE AQUABATS, *THE FURY OF THE AQUABATS!* (1997)

This was the first real album I recorded—the closest thing before that was the Feeble demo. It was in a real studio with professional microphones and a drum room—when you record drums, the room has to be big enough to get good sounds. We got into a rehearsal space in Orange County, and we wrote for a week. Bill Fold and Paul Tollett would just come down and listen to our progress—it was special for them, because it was their first release too.

BLINK-182, *ENEMA OF THE STATE* (1999)

This album was fueled by black coffee and Marlboro Lights. I treated it like a race: I wanted to get my drums recorded as fast as I could. We felt like we were making something great. We were well rehearsed and our songs were all figured out; not like today, when most bands write their material in the studio.

BLINK-182, *THE MARK, TOM AND TRAVIS SHOW*
(THE ENEMA STRIKES BACK) (2000)

This live album was compiled from a few different shows on our *Enema of the State* world tour: we didn't know during those shows that it might turn into an album. We played the songs at lightning speed, and the dick jokes were at an all-time high. It was a perfect representation of what we sounded like and who we were at that time.

BLINK-182, *TAKE OFF YOUR PANTS AND JACKET* (2001)

The pressure was on. We had just come off a couple of very successful albums, and because of all our commercial success, we felt like we had something to prove. Some of our songs became darker, and we showed off more technical playing—there were some people who didn't realize we were making fun of boy bands in the "All the Small Things" video, so we needed to show that we weren't a boy band ourselves. We had huge success on MTV, and we loved that, but we were still a small punk-rock band from Southern California.

BOX CAR RACER, *BOX CAR RACER* (2002)

On tour with Blink for *Take Off Your Pants and Jacket,* I always had a practice kit in my dressing room, and Tom started bringing in an amp to jam. We started doing these slower, heavier rhythms—he had been listening to a lot of Fugazi, and I got him into Quicksand. Everything was so fast with Blink, and it was cool to play something slow and heavy with Tom. Then we worked on the rest of the ideas in my warehouse in Corona. We worked out 80 percent of the album before we went into the studio. "Cat Like Thief," the song that featured Tim Armstrong, had this really weird beat where it almost felt like the measures were turned around. The Transplants were starting around the same time, and it was a really cool time—I was messing around with so many styles, and I felt free and creative.

TRANSPLANTS (2002)

The Transplants' first album was like a huge box of fireworks. We melted so many genres that didn't fit together, but they all complemented each other on this album. When I first heard it, it was on really rough demos, but it was really powerful. The call-and-response between Tim's and Rob's voices was genius. "Diamonds and Guns," "Romper Stomper," "117," "We Trusted You"—it's not even fair to mention some of the tracks but not others. I would think the album was a classic even if I didn't play on it: it's a must-have for anyone who grew up on punk rock and hip-hop. The artwork was done by Mister Cartoon, the photographs were by Estevan Oriol, and there were guest appearances by Son Doobie (Funkdoobiest), Davey Havok (AFI), and Danny Diablo. The whole album was done in Tim's basement—it was dark as fuck, there wasn't even a light in there. Some of the songs had crazy loops, some had my live drums on top of it—the whole thing made you want to drive too fast, or punch somebody, or find some other way to break the law.

BLINK-182 (2003)

This was my favorite time in Blink-182. Side projects such as Box Car Racer and the Transplants had started happening; boundaries and walls were being torn down. We were really open-minded and happy to try new things, but we still knew who we were as a band. Everything we did on this album was different, down to the studio, which was just a house we rented in San Diego. I smoked a lot of weed in that house, hotboxing multiple rooms—which felt weird, because I knew it was an actual family's house, but that's life. I started boxing around that time, so when I was stoned, I'd hit a speed bag for hours while Mark and Tom worked on their parts. I also took guitar lessons in that house, from a local teacher. It took over a year to record, but it's our best work to date, in my opinion.

PINK, "UNWIND" (ON TRY THIS, 2003)

Tim Armstrong hit me and said, "Look, I'm working with Alecia* and we want you to play drums on these songs." He wrote some songs just for her, but a lot of them were songs or ideas that didn't make it onto the first Transplants album. We had recorded maybe thirty songs for that record. He switched some of them up—it was pretty crazy, because I was used to hearing Tim and Rob sing them, and now Pink was singing them. But she killed it.

She was a trouper. We were finishing up in the studio with her, and then the Transplants were booked on the Warped Tour. So she came with us, and she and Tim worked on stuff on the bus. Warped Tour

---

* Pink's real name is Alecia Moore.

is more of a pop tour now, but back then it was a punk-rock tour in dirt parking lots with punkers and skinheads, and she was super cool. Alecia would vibe with us, and we recorded some stuff on the bus. I recorded some drum tracks in the hallway. There was just enough room for a bass drum, but I couldn't fit a snare stand, so Skinhead Rob would hold my snare and somebody else would hold the high hat. Some sessions, you have to make up your drum parts without knowing what the vocals are going to do: just be mindful, don't overplay, and leave room for everybody else.

BUN B, "LATE NIGHT CREEPIN'" (ON *TRILL*, 2005)

Who wouldn't want their first beat to go to Bun? I grew up loving hip-hop, and it bugged me that I couldn't be more involved with it than turning on albums and rocking to them. What's cool about this beat is that all of the percussion is live: real shakers and real tambourines. I didn't own a drum machine then, and I couldn't program anything. I had an eighteen-inch bass drum that basically sounded like an 808 drum machine: it was much easier for me to play everything live than it was to learn how to program.

THE TRANSPLANTS, *HAUNTED CITIES* (2005)

This was the Transplants' second release: this album was much more rooted in hip-hop and had guests like B-Real and Sen Dog from Cypress Hill and the Boo-Yaa T.R.I.B.E., who were like family to us. We did some work at Tim's house, and some of it on our tour bus, but most of it was in a studio. We continued to mesh genres: the Transplants always had the grimiest, most dangerous parts of gangsta rap mixed with the unpolished feel of punk rock. We got people from all walks of life at our shows, from punks to criminals. We broke up after doing one tour behind this album, but I'm confident that if we had kept touring, it would have been a huge success.

T.I., "YOU KNOW WHO" (ON *KING*, 2006)

T.I. was such a big influence on me. For a while, every morning when I woke up, I'd work out while I was watching BET—before I smoked a blunt. T.I. had a song called "Motivation" that was such an anthem for me. I related to a lot of lyrics and his hustle. When Blink toured, if I had two days off in Atlanta, I'd be hanging out with T.I., his manager Clay, and his whole crew. If they were filming a video, they'd say, "Trav, roll down, be in the video." I'd come down, smoke some weed with them, and be in their video. They'd send me tracks that they wanted me to play drums on—I think on that record, he sent me two. I played on both, and they picked one.

Sometimes rappers will send me a track with futuristic synth sounds, and it doesn't really need live drums and would sound weird if I played on top of it. But this had horns, guitar, some piano, and a laid-back Motown feel—it was the perfect fit.

+44, *WHEN YOUR HEART STOPS BEATING* (2006)

Mark and I were picking up the pieces after Blink and the Transplants broke up. We made the decision to keep making music together. Even though there was a lot of melody and a lot of sing-along choruses, this album was really dark. Mark and I were finding ourselves, finding the rhythm with just us two. "When Your Heart Stops Beating," "Chapter 13," and "Make You Smile" were my favorites. The album was recorded at our studio, OPRA. Most of it was live, but I programmed some of it on the SP-1200 drum machine. It was cool to be back in a band with Shane Gallagher, who had been in Doyt with me years before. We did our fair share of touring—until I had to stop because I was doing too many drugs. The shirt I was wearing in most of the press photos said it all, and predicted some of the bad times to come: HOW TO MURDER YOUR LIFE.

DJ SKEE PRESENTS: EXPENSIVE TASTE (MIXTAPE, 2007)

The Expensive Taste mixtape was basically me, Paul Wall, and Skinhead Rob. I produced everything. I was spending twelve to fifteen hours a day at the studio making beats, and then Paul and S.R. would jump on most of them. We didn't know if we were going to put it out on a label, and we didn't want to wait around on a deal. We ended up showing the tracks to Skee, who was a friend of mine—he offered to put it out. It was my first shot at making beats, learning how to program and using different keyboards—my introduction to doing something I loved.

AVRIL LAVIGNE, "I DON'T HAVE TO TRY," "RUNAWAY," "I CAN DO BETTER," "ALONE" (ON *THE BEST DAMN THING*, 2007)

I got e-mails simultaneously from Dr. Luke and Avril—they said that I was one of Avril's favorite drummers and they wanted me to come play on some tracks. I said that I'd love to, no problem. I went in and they played me the songs: Josh Freese had played on them, and obviously he's great, but they weren't happy with the drums. I said, "Okay, I'm not going to play what he played, because you're having it done over. You guys steer me in what direction you want, but I'm going to do my own thing." We did six or seven songs, and killed those tracks in a day. I made the verse of "Runaway" a little funkier by adding a couple of offbeats, but they were all guitar-driven pop-punk songs in four-four time; it was easy for me to go in and play along. She had already recorded her parts, so I knew the vocal cadence and I could complement her.

Dr. Luke was there. It's always nice when you go into those situations and someone is clearly wearing the production hat and saying, "This is what I want." He was very clear. Avril was there too. It was an easy session.

DANNY DIABLO, "LIVIN' BY THE GUN" (ON *THUGCORE 4 LIFE*, 2007)

He's a New York legend in punk rock and hardcore, also known as Lord Ezec. He's a good dude, no matter how scary he seems when you google him. He had been in really rad bands like Crown of Thorns, and he was a homie, so we put out one of his albums on LaSalle, my label. I'm credited as the drummer on this, but it's actually Tim Armstrong, who was the producer, looping something I played for him. The other day, Tim told me, "Trav, I have about nine minutes of you playing at 120 BPM." I don't care what he uses it for—it's Tim and I trust him.

THE FEDERATION, "BLACK ROSES" (ON *IT'S WHATEVA*, 2007)

They're a hyphy band: hyphy is a movement out of the Bay Area that's upbeat hip-hop. They have their own dances, and the genre will always be around in the Bay. E40 is the king of it. These guys were the young guns—they were really hyped at the time, and they're still good friends. I still talk to Goldie all the time.

TRV$DJAM, *FIX YOUR FACE* (MIXTAPE, 2008)

AM and I spent countless hours practicing, but most of the time when we played, we did a forty-five-to-sixty-minute show. This documented the set we were playing during our first year of playing shows, an assortment of every genre we ever loved, but especially New York hip-hop. We put out the mixtape so when people came to our shows, it would be like hearing an album in its entirety: we played it from front to back.

THE GAME, "DOPE BOYS" (ON *LAX*, 2008)

I found out about the Game through DJ Skee, who is always on top of everything before it pops. He put out the Game's mixtape, where the Game just murdered the streets. Everybody was talking about him, and the next thing you know, everyone has a bidding war over him. Interscope signed him and made him part of G-Unit. I think 50 Cent saw that this kid was going to outshine even him. They ended up beefing to the point where they were shooting at each other: it was someone's-going-to-die shit.

I met him right around that time, when I was having everyone in my studio. He came through—we were homies forever before we ever recorded anything together. He was one of the people that was by my bedside after my accident, and he gave a big speech at Lil Chris's funeral.

This track has big rock drums, open high hats, a big two-four backbeat, and fast snare-tom fills. A lot of producers like to add programmed drums to my drums to fill out the sound, but sometimes on this track it's just me. And at the end, he had me go crazy with some fills. This was a big single—it was awesome.

THE CENTERFOLDS, "GOODBYE" (ON *THE CENTERFOLDS* EP, 2008)

The Centerfolds were a cool little three-piece punk-rock band from Riverside. When I first joined Blink, I tried to help them out as much as I could. I put 'em on shows, and I even acted as their manager for a couple of months, just trying to help. I still talk to Tim Floyd: he's a high school principal now. His wife, Holly, was Melissa's best friend when I was married to Melissa. They were recording a demo and they asked if I would do a song with them. No problem: I went into this really small studio in Riverside, called Love Juice, heard the song a couple of times, rocked it, and we were done in an hour.

Tracks like this can almost be a mind fuck because they call for a certain type of drum pattern, but you don't want to sound like everybody else. It's real easy to play along: what's hard is being creative without doing a disservice to the song.

WALE, "OG'Z" (SINGLE, 2008)

Interscope hit me up, saying, "We have this new artist named Wale—he's a really dope rapper." I was already a fan of his. I had seen him play; he was from DC and he had a go-go band backing him, and I was sold. They asked me if I would play on this record and sent me the music. It wasn't a totally rocked-out record: it was something funky where I could almost do a go-go part on top of it.

TRV$DJAM, *FIX YOUR FACE VOL. 2* (COACHELLA 2009) (MIXTAPE, 2009)

As time went on, AM and I were getting ready for Coachella and decided to update our set. It became more EDM-based; AM was heavily getting into electronic music like Daft Punk, Glitch Mob, and Justice, but we included some of our favorites by Johnny Cash, Queen, and the Zombies. This tape was a huge eye-opener for a lot of people: I still meet people who tell me that it's their workout mix. Around the time of Coachella, we played this set at the KROQ Weenie Roast—we closed the night, and I think they expected us to be walk-out music, but we ended up turning the whole thing into a massive party.

SELECTED DISCOGRAPHY AND GUEST APPEARANCES

SKILLZ, "CELEBRATE LIFE"
(ON *THE WORLD NEEDS MORE SKILLZ*, 2010)

He's Jazzy Jeff's hype man when Jazzy Jeff DJs: he has an old-school style. He's always been a dope MC, but he's famous for his year-end "rap-ups": he'll rap about every topic that mattered in the previous twelve months. He was Adam's really good friend, so after Adam passed away, he did a song called "Celebrate Life." It was really touching, and it hit me hard. He asked me to play on it—obviously, I was going to do whatever he needed me to do. This didn't call for a bunch of big drums: I just spiced it up a little.

LIL WAYNE FEATURING EMINEM, "DROP THE WORLD"
(ON *REBIRTH*, 2010)

Wayne and I first met through Famous: we saw photographs of him wearing Famous hats. He was always interested in skateboarding and Famous, and we've had a skate team since the day we started.

Eminem had reached out to me after AM died. We hung out for a little bit, took some pictures, chopped it up. And then he asked me to play some shows with him. I was still smoking weed at the time, but everyone said that I shouldn't smoke around him because he was sober. So I didn't bring any and got a peek at what I could be. Not a white rapper from Detroit, obviously, but sober. In this industry, so many people are on drugs, and so many of our idols, from Jimi Hendrix to John Bonham, die of an overdose. Eminem is one of the best rappers of all time, and he's sober now. He was a good role model and a positive influence for me.

RIHANNA, "ROCKSTAR 101" (VIDEO, 2010)

I had done a remix of "Umbrella" back in the day, but I had never met Rihanna. My friend Lisa would always say, "I got to hook you and Rihanna up."

I said, "Shoot, anytime—she's awesome." Then I was out in New York with Chris and a couple of the homies, playing a show with AM. It was party after party that night—it might have been Fashion Week. There was a huge Kanye West birthday party at Louis Vuitton: I was coming up the stairs and she was coming down.

She saw me and said, "I love the remix you did. You fuckin' killed it—I like it more than the original."

"Oh, thank you."

Then she asked me to be in the video for this song called "Rockstar 101." I did that, and then about two weeks later, she said, "I want to learn how to play drums so I can do the Sheila E. thing on my next tour." So we got together and she showed me this stand-up drum kit that she put together, and seriously—she caught on so quick. She picked up everything so fast: she's very musical. I could tell that she wasn't meeting with me for the novelty or to hang with me: she wanted to learn how to play drums. Someone was videotaping the whole time so she could remember everything—but of course, our lesson ended up making its way onto YouTube.

A couple of weeks later, we went to see her in concert, and she murdered it. She came out in the middle of the crowd, and would drum, using all the little licks that I taught her. It was really cool.

She was totally down-to-earth. We hung out a couple of times—when I went to Vegas, we'd party together. We liked smoking a gang of weed and talking music. We partied together after one of my friends, Dominick Cruz, won the UFC bantamweight belt. Rihanna came out with us all night and danced and partied. She's awesome.

MICKEY AVALON, "THE FAST LIFE" (SINGLE, 2010)

I made Mickey a song called "The Fast Life." I took this sample from Black Rob, looped it, and came up with this idea for a song. (Later on, I substituted Skinhead Rob singing the part.) It was perfect for Skinhead Rob, and that song is still one of my favorites. I played live with Mickey a couple of times. He opened up for Blink, and he asked me to learn eight songs. He played for half an hour, and I played drums with him. I'm so proud of this song. It reminds me of Berlin's "Metro," and of surf rock and hip-hop. This is exactly what I like to do when I'm producing: mix genres and come up with something more interesting than what you hear on the radio.

I was thinking of Mickey the whole time when I came up with this track: he was living a faster life than any gangster rapper I knew around this time. There were times I'd walk in the studio, and I'd be thinking, *That don't smell like weed.* He'd be smoking heroin in the back.

PAUL WALL, *HEART OF A CHAMPION* (ALBUM, 2010)

I produced half that album. Texas hip-hop, especially Houston, has its own movement: a sound that's different from the sound in New York or LA. But on that album, Paul wanted to show that he could do more than that sound. He's so musical and so talented. He has a great cadence: he sits on beats right and has a good pocket. He's a professional, and one of my greatest friends.

EDDIE RAP LIFE, *PIECE OF MIND* (MIXTAPE, 2010)

He is an aspiring rapper/skateboarder from Rhode Island who I met through a couple of people on my skate team. He had a mixtape and was buzzing in LA. I wanted to see him succeed: I opened up my studio to him and I did a mixtape with him that had everything from Slayer samples to originals.

NOTTZ, "INTRO" (ON *YOU NEED THIS MUSIC*, 2010)

He's from Virginia, and his shit just bangs. People go to Nottz for those hard, ass-kicking beats. He's a great producer: when you hear one of his beats, it's almost not fair to the person who produced the track before or after a Nottz track. I did something for his solo album: I played drums on it, and then he asked me to film a video of me doing it. This was a blast to play on. I like catering to people and holding back where it's appropriate, but this was a blast: big, hard-hitting rock drums. Later we started working on a new project: Nottz producing, me drumming, and Asher Roth and Nottz rapping. He's the funniest dude—if he ever stops producing, he could be a comedian.

TECH N9NE, "HARD LIQUOR" (ON *BAD SEASON*, MIXTAPE, 2010)

Tech is the dopest independent rap artist out of the Midwest. He's got a cult following—I used to see pictures of him with his painted face and his theatrics. He can spit rhymes: he's part of that crew that can rap really fast. We did this track, and it appeared on his mixtape and my mixtape. I was able to put big drums on it but not change the swing of the record. He's dope; if he's in town, I'm always there to watch him play.

TRAVIS BARKER, *LET THE DRUMMER GET WICKED* (MIXTAPE, 2011)

This was a warm-up for my album *Give the Drummer Some.* I teamed up with DJ Whoo Kid, and he sent me verses, sometimes with tracks, and I would add my drums or freak the beat. I would get two or three e-mails a day from Whoo Kid and would be at the studio around the clock, putting drums on the beats that he was sending me. I had so many great guests—Tech N9ne, Wiz Khalifa, Royce da 5'9", Clipse, Big Sean—it almost could have been an album.

TRAVIS BARKER, *GIVE THE DRUMMER SOME* (2011)

This album was not only my dream, but Lil Chris's dream. While I would be in the studio making beats, he would be out partying and gathering rappers to bring back to me. I produced everything, except for one track that Pharrell coproduced with me. I had every MC I could have dreamed of on my album, from the ones I grew up on to the ones I love today. *Give the Drummer Some* was 120 percent me. It was challenging and rewarding, being able to give back to a genre I grew up on—but doing it in a new way, with live drums. I enjoyed it so much I'm working on part two right now.

BLINK-182, *NEIGHBORHOODS* (2011)

This was the first album we wrote after my plane crash. "Up All Night" was the first track we recorded at my studio in North Hollywood; I still had bandages and sores all over my hands and legs when we cut that, and my left hand was numb. I was nowhere near ready to be in the studio, but I was excited to record again. My favorite tracks on the album are "Up All Night," "After Midnight," and "Hearts All Gone." This album slowly came together via the Internet—we spent some time together in the studio, but we sent a lot of files back and forth. After being apart for so long, and having so many side projects, we had gotten used to working independently, so this was the beginning of us finding a way to be together, working as a band again.

BRITNEY SPEARS, "DON'T KEEP ME WAITING"
(ON *FEMME FATALE*, 2011)

I got a call from Rodney Jerkins, who is a great producer. He said, "Hey, man, I've got this Britney record I'm working on. Someone in her camp has requested that you play drums on it, and I'd love for you to do it." So two days later, I came over to the studio and played drums for a couple of hours. She wasn't there, and at the time, there was no singing on the track. I always get excited about opportunities like that, because they're so far from what I'm known for. And I like playing everything, so it's fun and different.

After that, we got a call from her management to my publicist saying that she was filming a new video and they wanted me to play her love interest. It was for a different song than the one I played on, so it seemed really random. I was up for it, but the timing didn't work out. When I finally saw the video, they had cast some super-dreamy model: the total opposite of me. He looked like what you would expect her love interest to be, whereas I would have looked like a criminal.

I've made cameos in some other videos where I didn't have anything to do with the track, like with Three 6 Mafia and other rap videos: "We just want you to walk in, vibe out to the song, and look over here." But normally I'm playing drums; I always feel like I have more energy if I play. I tell them I feel most comfortable behind my drum kit—you're not going to get me dancing in your video.

Britney's always been cool to me—when I was dating Paris, she was around a lot. And in Calabasas, she lived at the end of my street.

TINIE TEMPAH, "SIMPLY UNSTOPPABLE (YES REMIX)"
(SINGLE, 2011)

He's a really talented rapper from the UK. For a while, UK rap had a certain style: Dizzee Rascal and all that grime. Then it became a little more like American hip-hop. Tinie Tempah is cool, but there wasn't much to this: they sent over the tape and asked me to play drums. Then they used the track for a commercial for Lucozade, which is like European Gatorade, with me, Tinie, and Katie Taylor (a world-champion female boxer). When they asked me to appear in the ad, I said, "Hell, yeah, I'll do it." I won't do ads if I don't like the product, even when the money is right, but I actually liked Lucozade: when I'm touring in Europe, that's my go-to drink onstage.

SWIZZ BEATZ FEATURING LIL WAYNE AND LENNY KRAVITZ, "ROCK 'N' ROLL" (SINGLE, 2011)

We did this years ago, but I think the video is finally coming out. Swizz Beatz is like Yela: my brother from another mother. He always called me Twin. When I started doing remixes, he said, "Fuck that, we should do an album together and just blow it up." We ended up making our own solo albums instead, but he came up with the hook on "Can a Drummer Get Some."

He told me he was doing the Gumball Rally, which is a cross-country race in the priciest of pricy cars. It's the craziest group of people: fashion designers, photographers, rappers, fighters, sheiks from Dubai. And they're racing cars like Ferraris and Lamborghinis. I said, "Shit, we're supposed to do it."

"Let's do it together, Twin," he said. We took out his Rolls-Royce Phantom: it was basically me driving 140 miles per hour,* blunt in my mouth at all times, with Swizz riding shotgun and Lil Chris in the back. We were going as fast as the Phantom could go, driving it to the point where it was overheating. I would have my pedal to the metal and Lambos would still be zipping past us.

Once we drove past a cop giving a ticket to one of the Lambos: he had probably popped him for going 160 or 180. We floored it, going 140, past the cop—what's he going to do? Chris's job in our car was to look

---

* 150 miles per hour downhill.

out for cops—and we got away clean the whole race. There's all kinds of craziness—people have been pulled over and paid a cop two hundred grand to let them go, so they can get back in the race. And you can get bonus points if you take a picture of yourself holding a cop's gun.

The race lasted about two weeks, and every night we would all be partying in whatever city we were in. At the end of the tour, we got the Dirtiest Car award, because we never cleaned it—we figured that would just slow us down. It was a $500,000 Phantom, and we drove that thing into the ground like it was a Pinto.

ROYCE DA 5'9", "LEGENDARY" (ON *SUCCESS IS CERTAIN*, 2011)

One of the dopest MCs ever. He lives in Detroit, and he and Eminem grew up battling each other: I think the story is that they started off as friends, and then they went through times when they beefed. He had me play on this for one of his albums, and of course I was honored. Then he started the group Slaughterhouse with Joe Budden, Joell Ortiz, and Crooked I: there is no group in history with four MCs as nasty as those dudes.

They were the group that I was in the studio with the day I found out AM died. I left the studio, and they sent me verses later: it appeared on my album as "Devil's Got a Hold of Me." It's such a dark record: that news set the mood. It was heavy. We did this track shortly after; I got a call from Paul Rosenberg, who manages Eminem and Slaughterhouse, asking if I could turn it around right away. I was happy to: it was a high-energy song that called for live drums, and it's not painful listening to Royce rap while I drum. He's a beast. As a drummer, anytime you have the lyrics or the hook, it's easy to determine what to play and what not to play.

THE COOL KIDS, "SOUR APPLES" (ON *WHEN FISH RIDE BICYCLES*, 2011)

There was this whole movement of throwback rap, inspired by everything that was happening in the late eighties and early nineties. It sounded like old Beasties. The Cool Kids are Chuck Inglish and Mikey Rocks; I helped them out on one of their songs, they helped me out on one of mine, and we became really good friends. We went on tour together with Lil Wayne, the I Am Music tour. They said they wanted me to play on this track, so I set up my electronic kit at some hotel in Florida and recorded drums to this song at two in the morning.

YOUNG DRO, "CHECK OUT MY SWAG" (SINGLE, 2011)

He's part of T.I.'s crew. You'd see him in the back of T.I. videos, and he would have verses here and there. He's awesome: a really funny dude and a really smart MC. He has a crazy vocabulary, which is important for rappers: he'd be saying words rappers never thought of using in rhymes. He used to come out to LA: we'd hotbox in the car and he would beg us to throw on some Mickey Avalon. It was really funny, because he had this hard Atlanta twang from the woods, and he would be dressed head to toe in Polo: shirt, pants, shoes. You never would guess he'd want to hear Mickey Avalon talking about slamming some heroin and then fucking your bitch.

BURY THE HATCHET, "CYANIDE SERENADE" (SINGLE, 2011)

That was Skinhead Rob's band that he did for a little while. He said, "Hey man, will you play on this song?" I came in real quick and knocked it out. Anything S.R. needs, I'm always down.

SCROOBIUS PIP, "INTRODICTION"
(ON *DISTRACTION PIECES*, 2011)

Danny Lohner approached me—he was doing remixes of some Die Antwoord tracks and wanted me to play drums.* Then he hit me up a couple of months later and said, "I don't know, man, something happened with the remix, but I may end up using the music and the drums for this other dude, Scroobius Pip, are you down?" I said sure. When he sent it to me, I was amazed: not only had they moved everything around, turning it into a very different track, but it sounded like nothing I'd ever heard before. It's kind of rapping, it's kind of spoken word, it's kind of punk as fuck—it's just clever.

------

* Die Antwoord is an avant-garde South African hip-hop duo; Danny used to play guitar for Nine Inch Nails.

I'd love to get in a studio with Scroobius next time—I think he's something of a musical genius. To this day, he and I talk on Twitter: he's a huge MMA fan, and whenever there's a UFC event, we'll compare our picks.

YOUNG JEEZY, "TALK TO ME"
(ON *TM 103: HUSTLERZ AMBITION*, 2011)

The first time I met Jeezy was at the New York Rock Corps. His first single, "Soul Survivor," was buzzing hard in the streets at the time, and he was rolling seventy people deep. We've been good friends ever since.

TRAVIS BARKER AND YELAWOLF, *PSYCHO WHITE* (EP, 2012)

Paul Rosenberg (Eminem's manager) was managing me, and he sent me Yelawolf's mixtape and a picture. He warned me not to get mad, because Yelawolf looked like me. I looked at the picture and I was tripping: he looked like the Southern white-boy rapper version of me. But when I played the tape, I was floored. He was the truth.

Two weeks later, totally coincidentally, Rob Dydrek was hanging out with Yelawolf and said that Yelawolf wanted to meet up. "Shit, send him over," I said. He came over, and we got in the studio that very first day and recorded most of our *Psycho White* EP. We instantly clicked: he was like my long-lost brother. We had so much in common: skateboarding, Cadillacs, rap music, rock music, Johnny Cash, everything. We never had a plan to put anything out—we were just happy vibing and making cool shit. After a couple of years of doing that, we realized we had some great material and people should hear it. The record is full of songs and ideas that are unorthodox for rap, like the haunting whistles and marching drums on "Whistle Dixie." I produced this all myself, except for "Can't Push Us Around"—Tim Armstrong and I did that together and Yela instantly loved it. "Push 'Em" had a double-time punk-rock-meets-bluegrass feel—I came up with that track while I was on tour with Lil Wayne, at three A.M. in a hotel room in Florida.

I'll do anything for him, and likewise on his end.

XZIBIT, "NAPALM" (ON *NAPALM*, 2012)

I grew up listening to Xzibit—he was part of that whole clique with Snoop Dogg and Dr. Dre. I lost touch with him after my plane crash, but he texted me, came over, played me the record, and I played on it right there. When I heard it, I thought, "Damn, Xzibit is *pissed*." I love that—I'm a fan of hip-hop and punk rock because they have a definite feeling behind them: anger. When you're putting live drums on hip-hop albums, you can only wish for beats like this to play on top of.

CHESTER FRENCH, "BLACK GIRLS" AND "FEMALE VERSION" (ON *MUSIC 4 TNGRS*, 2012)

When Blink first got back together, we played a T-Mobile gig, and AM and I turned out the after-party—it was the only time AM and I played the same gig as Blink. Afterward, we were walking through the crowd, and it was a who's-who of LA: actors, actresses, whoever's hot at the time. These two little skinny white kids, dressed very preppy in Polo shirts, came up to me and said, "Nice to meet you, Travis. We're in a band called Chester French and we were just signed by Pharrell Williams. We just want to give you our music and see if we can be friends."

I did my homework: Pharrell really had signed them. They were two young Harvard graduates, and they were working on an album. I thought, "Whoa, this is interesting." I took them on tour with us because they were such good kids—they opened for Blink. And they were so appreciative. These kids play every instrument and they were like geniuses. They became good friends of mine, and when they asked me to play on a couple of tracks on their second album, I was happy to do it. Their song structures are mapped and not boring, like the normal four-four run-of-the-mill pop songs. They're really creative songwriters and musicians.

JEROME FLOOD II, "SIXTEEN" (SINGLE, 2012)

He's an awesome drummer that won a Guitar Center drum-off; I think I was a judge that year. Anyone who wins that has disciplined themselves and practiced the way I believe people should practice. He got in touch with me and said, "I'm working on a drum album. I really appreciate what you did with your album, will you guest on my album, and play a twenty-four-bar solo?" I said yeah: it was cool to see another drummer aspiring to do an album, and I just wanted to show support.

I recorded it one evening at the studio. I listened to the groove, but I didn't rehearse anything: I just played it. When I said I was going to make a solo album, I think people envisioned me doing something like this, with lots of drum solos, but I wanted to reach a different group of people, which is why I did so many things with MCs and other musicians. But it was fun to do something just for drummers. Jerome is a good friend of mine to this day.

STEVE AOKI, "CUDI THE KID" (ON *WONDERLAND*, 2012)

Steve was really good friends with AM; I'd met him a couple of times. I was working on my solo album and he was working on his solo album, and I played drums on a song he was working on called "The Misfits." I was really hyped about it because it sounded very fresh and progressive: electro punk rock. Steve never really sings on tracks, but he was yelling on this one.

I had a song I did with Kid Cudi: he had come to my studio, and it was during a phase where he wanted to write songs, so we did something that was a very folky, Beatlesque song. I played it for Steve, and he was more hyped about it than "The Misfits" song he had showed me. And I was more hyped about "The Misfits," so we traded. It made sense: he had so much luck with his remix of "Pursuit of Happiness" with Cudi, so he flipped my track into what became "Cudi the Kid," and it became this electronic dance anthem. I was in love with his interpretation of the song and how he added dynamics: the verses are small and then it gets really big. We ended up filming a video for "Cudi the Kid," with kids playing Cudi, Aoki, and me—my son Landon played me. I put "The Misfits" on my album, and Aoki and I have had a really cool relationship since then.

He's a workaholic like me. He will not waste a minute of a day. He does three hundred shows a year—although he flies. One day he's in Spain, the next he's in Russia, the next he's in Philly. When I'm not using my tour bus, sometimes I rent it out to him. Steve and I play together all the time—recently we did a show at the Shrine and appeared on *Jimmy Kimmel* together with Waka Flocka Flame to play "Rage the Night Away."

STEVE AOKI (COLLABORATOR)

I've been on a million tour buses—Travis's bus is the best bus in the world. He made it into a proper apartment. I've produced a lot of music on that bus, just because it's so comfortable. It shows you just how important environment is. Sometimes when I'm on the bus, I'll find Landon and Alabama's old coloring books—it's not a bachelor pad, because he's a family man. He doesn't have to give me that bus—he's renting out his most prized possession. When I'm on that bus, I respect it like it's Travis's home. We keep it spic and span, we even take our shoes off. I rarely let anyone else onto that bus.

THE TRANSPLANTS, *IN A WARZONE* (2013)

This was basically the Transplants reunion album: we worked on records once a week, calling it "Transplants Tuesday," only taking breaks when one of us had to go on tour. We went back and forth from my OPRA studio to the Boat, which is Flea's studio. We'd go in and jam and then listen back, easily writing two or three songs a day. Rob and I were smoking about twenty blunts a day each. We had guests like Bun B, Equipto, and Paul Wall. The opening track, "In a Warzone," is a good indication of what the album sounds like: we come out with fists swinging. For the most part, the album is hardcore punk—we weren't experimenting with so many styles of music. That wasn't a strategy. It was just what came out of us at that time.

RUN THE JEWELS, "ALL DUE RESPECT" (ON *RUN THE JEWELS 2, 2014*)

El-P and Killer Mike have been big influences on me, and I've always admired both of their work. Killer Mike's cadence on any beat made you want to play drums. We became friends, and when they were in LA, they were recording with Zach de la Rocha from Rage Against the Machine and invited me down to the studio. They asked me to play on their album, and I was stoked. El-P is one of the best producers my ears have ever heard—he's a mad scientist of sound, as if Jesus Christ himself came down and produced the beat. They sent me this file, and it was a crazy beat with congas and shakers and bongos. I opened up the file at the studio, and after I heard it once, I immediately played it again and pressed record. I was so excited, I didn't bother learning the drum pattern—I just started playing. After four takes, I couldn't pick a favorite, so I sent El-P everything.

DJ DEORRO, "KILL IT WITH A KICKDRUM" (TRACK, 2015)

DJ Deorro came to me and said, "I want to create something with you that really showcases your drumming." And he wasn't lying: within the first sixteen bars, there was a drum solo. I played with him at Coachella in the Sahara Tent, one hour after I did a set with Run the Jewels. Deorro's whole movement is called "PandaFunk," so he had people onstage in panda suits playing violin. He's a really talented artist; I think that song is a masterpiece.

RIFF RAFF, "SPAZZ OUT" (SINGLE, 2015)

Riff Raff came to me—he had a genre and a sound he was aiming for. Instead of the normal rap he was known for, he wanted heavy 80s synths and driving drums. For reference, he sent me some videos of him singing over random chord progressions: when I was in the studio, everyone who heard those videos immediately fell in love with what he was doing.

AFROJACK, "WORK" (SINGLE, 2015)

I got a phone call: Afrojack wanted to get into the studio with me. It turned out he had rented out the entire Record Plant complex, which meant he was working in four or five rooms at once. Usher was in one of them; Chris Brown was in another. He gave me a high-energy track to listen to, and then he came back an hour later and asked if I was ready to record. I said, "I already did." He listened back, and he loved what I added. Then he said, "Shit, you're already here. Can you play on nine other songs?" They were all different: he's so innovative and progressive. And filming the video was fun: I got to destroy a white drum kit.

TRAVIS BARKER FEATURING KID INK, TY DOLLA $IGN, IAMSU!, AND TYGA, "100" (SINGLE, 2015)

I got back from tour and I felt like I needed to get into the studio. I almost had anxiety from having too many ideas. Kevin Bivona and I made this beat, and immediately I thought it sounded like something on the radio. I played it for Ink, and then he laid a chorus down—I could hear the potential immediately. Tyga lives next door to me; when I saw him, I told him, "I got this song—I think it might be a radio smash." He recorded his verse, then Ty Dolla $ign rerecorded the chorus and Iamsu! added his verse. It has so many people you're used to hearing on it, the song immediately sounds like it belongs on the radio. That it's a huge summer song is a big deal for me. This is a great warmup for the rest of my album.

ANTEMASQUE, SECOND ALBUM
(TITLE AND RELEASE DATE TO BE DETERMINED)

I've loved Cedric and Otis from the early days of At the Drive-In—we almost crossed paths so many times. But then I got a phone call from Cedric saying, "I heard you really like Dag Nasty and Husker Du—is that true?" When I said I loved both those bands, he said, "We're working on a second album—would you be down?" I said absolutely, and he sent over music—I didn't listen to anything else for two weeks straight. The songs were amazing: technically challenging but great singalongs, halfway between progressive rock and punk rock. They flew out to record with me, and I told them they were more than welcome to stay at my house. We knocked out eight or nine songs in three or four hours one day—they didn't think that we would go that fast, so they had booked three days. They said, "Well, let's make some more songs." We did another four tracks the next day, including a cover of Joe Jackson's "One More Time." They're amazing guys—why didn't we hang out ten years ago?